THE
TRUMP
WOMEN

THE
TRUMP
WOMEN

Part of the Deal

NINA BURLEIGH

Previously published as *Golden Handcuffs*

G

GALLERY BOOKS

New York　　London　　Toronto　　Sydney　　New Delhi

G

Gallery Books
An Imprint of Simon & Schuster, Inc.
1230 Avenue of the Americas
New York, NY 10020

First Gallery Books trade paperback edition September 2020

GALLERY BOOKS and colophon are registered trademarks of Simon & Schuster, Inc.

For information about special discounts for bulk purchases,
please contact Simon & Schuster Special Sales at
1-866-506-1949 or business@simonandschuster.com.

The Simon & Schuster Speakers Bureau can bring authors to your live event.
For more information or to book an event, contact the Simon & Schuster Speakers
Bureau at 1-866-248-3049 or visit our website at www.simonspeakers.com.

Interior design by Jaime Putorti

Manufactured in the United States of America

10 9 8 7 6 5 4 3 2 1

Library of Congress Cataloging-in-Publication Data

Names: Burleigh, Nina, author.
Title: The trump women : part of the deal / Nina Burleigh.
Other titles: Secrets of the women of Trump Tower
Description: New York : Gallery Books, [2018]
Identifiers: LCCN 2018032323 (print) | LCCN 2018039444 (ebook) | ISBN 9781501180224
    (ebook) | ISBN 9781501180200 (hardcover : alk. paper)
Subjects: LCSH: Trump, Donald, 1946– Relations with women. | Trump, Donald, 1946– Family.
    | Trump, Ivana. | Maples, Marla. | Trump, Melania, 1970– | Trump family. | Executives'
    spouses—United States—Biography. | Presidents spouses—United States—Biography.
Classification: LCC E914.T77 (ebook) | LCC E914.T77 B87 2018 (print) | DDC 973.933092—dc23
LC record available at https://urldefense.proofpoint.com/v2/url?u=https-3A__lccn.loc.gov_2
    018032323&d=DwIFAg&c=jGUuvAdBXp_VqQ6t0yah2g&r=7Powweyp97H7BrdRqAm
    -eJjycEUd2REgi140E_-eJsoFHotHpuSHVST6CEgk6PFC&m=DtGv38KLXqkUyiYjXpYgZfSR
    XniEp4p2ZQyy7ueAZJ4&s=nSYIgTw73oVYj9XYEC_2amaWoXpuzEAN2h0Tqt_zgPw&e=

ISBN 978-1-5011-8020-0
ISBN 978-1-5011-8021-7 (pbk)
ISBN 978-1-5011-8022-4 (ebook)

For my girlfriends

CONTENTS

◇◇◇◇◇◇

PART FOUR:
MELANIJA KNAVS, THE THIRD MRS. TRUMP

PART FIVE:
IVANKA TRUMP, FIRST DAUGHTER

THE
TRUMP
WOMEN

PROLOGUE

◇◇◇◇◇◇

The Trump Women

Election night 2016. New York Hilton. Two a.m. Outside on Sixth Avenue, hundreds of celebrants wave American flags in the dark and chant "Lock the bitch up!" and other profanities. American television will delete the expletives, but international television crews stationed every ten yards beam the scene back live and uncensored to daytime audiences in Tokyo and Istanbul and London and Paris. Inside the Hilton ballroom, lights are dim and the mood is expectant, as if for a surprise party. A chorus line of New York Fire Department officers in their dress whites stands at attention, present to honor their old friend, now the new president. The Star Wars theme erupts out of loudspeakers, eyes roll up, high, higher . . .

He has entered the room from above and is strolling a slow victory lap around the balcony. Trailing him, five human gazelles—leggy, youthful women, long hair perfectly straightened, so close in age and look as to seem like sisters. Eventually, the entourage descends to eye level, pushing through a velvet curtain and down some steps. Now the gazelles' party dresses and stiletto pumps are visible. None of them need look down while descending the staircase on these precarious shoes. Each one has perfected a rigorous self-consciousness of movement that mortal—that is, non–TV primed—women do not possess, but which Donald Trump requires of them all. Lined up on stage, the tableau sent an unmistakable message. Trump, a real man, is powerful enough to accessorize himself with silent beauties who dress and move like they stepped out of a luxury car ad.

I was inspired to write this book as I watched the Trump women on that stage. Like many journalists in New York, I had interviewed Donald Trump on occasion; he was always good for a quip. As a clan, the Trumps entered our consciousness during an era when newspapers still mattered and employed gossip columnists who were so powerful that powerful people would call them up personally and tip them off to what they were going to do next to this or that spouse. They belong to boomer tabloid wallpaper. Because he came of age during the era of the Rat Pack and Playboy bunnies, his ideal women wore diamond rings tabloid writers described as "dazzlers," along with their "sizzling" ensembles. I had watched that buffoonish persona morph into something quite different over the course of the campaign. But that night, for the first time, I really looked at and wondered about the gorgeous women attached to the president-elect with the most complicated public relationship to women in American political history.

From the witch-hunting, pussy-grabbing tone of his campaign to the dozens of women who have accused him of sexual abuse—before November 2016, Americans could not have dreamed that such a misogynist would occupy the Oval Office in the twenty-first century. As president, Trump has set women back decades politically and policy-wise. He has encouraged toxic masculinity in his supporters. He has promoted hundreds of anti-choice judges, mostly male and white, including two to the Supreme Court, putting legal abortion in jeopardy. One of those Supreme Court judges was credibly accused of sexual assault, and while such accusations were bringing down powerful men all over America, Trump pressed ahead with Brett Kavanaugh's nomination. Trump has instituted anti-woman policies at every level of government, from the Department of Education to the Department of Health and Human Services. He revoked protections for Planned Parenthood, a primary provider of health services to poor women. His administration rolled back requirements that companies disclose salaries by gender, hampering the fight for equal pay. Finally, his election convinced many politicos and donors that American women were unelectable to the highest office in the land— for at least another cycle.

What sort of women would participate in such an enterprise? Who are they?

This book is about all six of the Women of Trumpland: Donald's grandmother and mother, who shaped him, both immigrants; his three wives, two of whom are immigrants; and his favorite daughter. His homesick German paternal grandmother founded what became the Trump Organization during the Depression. His mother left a life in muck boots and a cramped peat-smelling cottage on a cold, impoverished Scottish island to live as a maid in New York, a transformation that occurred in the time it took a steamer to cross the Atlantic in 1929. All of Donald's wives embarked on an upward-mobile class journey—at a time when enormous wealth has shifted away from the bottom and middle and toward the top, enriching those lucky enough to be standing around when the wave crashed over them.

Trump has never acknowledged what I discovered about his mother during a cursory check of the U.S. Census records at the New York Public Library, but the find is the key to his desperate need to be seen as "classy." When the Trump family trooped into Buckingham Palace to meet the queen last year, the children of the American head of state shaking the monarch's hand were the grandchildren of a peasant from the British Isles. What politician would not celebrate this fact as evidence of the opportunities and class mobility the American nation offers to immigrants? Trump. And in this book, I explain why.

◇◇◇◇

The Trump women are commonly accused of being complicit. But before that, they must presumably be compliant. They must accept the extent to which their roles are transactional, archaic, and submissive, even while their connection to him is personally empowering, offering celebrity, money, promotions, and access. Theirs is a hobbled empowerment. They must be forever at their mirrors, camera ready, if they want to appear anywhere near him in public. Their fuck-me shoes require a rigor unfamiliar to most women. They exemplify the obeisance to patriarchy that the right demands of its "strong" women. They—like Melania—must purr congenially at leering innuendo from the likes of Howard Stern, or even from your own dad if you're Ivanka. It's just "boy talk."

In return, rich rewards: Melania Trump, daughter of a factory worker and a car mechanic, lives in splendor unimaginable back in her hometown of Sevnica, Slovenia. Similarly, his first wife, collectivist-educated, Russian speaking Ivana Trump—the ski champion who first introduced Trump to the Slavic world—could not have imagined, when she left her shoe-factory hometown in Czechoslovakia in the mid-1970s, that she would someday preside over a hotel and casino empire, albeit one careening into bankruptcy, and, even post-divorce, be rich enough to buy herself a yacht, a Manhattan mansion, and townhouses in Saint-Tropez. His second wife, even if banished from the realm, rode the wave of branded fame into a profession as a spiritual healer. His elder daughter is, of course, the chief beneficiary of all the riches available to women willing to put up with some very unusual and insulting behavior.

◇◇◇◇

Since this book was published in fall 2018, *Elle* columnist E. Jean Carroll even accused him of rape—a claim Trump has denied. For said denial, Carroll has filed a defamation case. A former Fox reporter, Courtney Friel, accused candidate Trump of inviting her to his office for a kiss—a pattern of behavior previously alleged by another reporter. And authors of another book on Trump and women uncovered 26 more allegations of "unwanted sexual misconduct" and another 43 claims of inappropriate behavior.

◇◇◇◇

The women's roles changed subtly after the 2018 midterm elections, as House Democrats opened inquiries into the array of constitutional challenges and scoff-law activities in which the Trump White House was engaged. It became clear that if Trump wasn't reelected in 2020, he could face a laundry list of lawsuits or even criminal charges from which the presidency was protecting him. That outcome—Donald in jail—would be devastating for Melania, a woman whose rise had so far required very little since her feat of harpooning a whale in the 1990s. Suddenly, she was stepping up. A month before the first publication of this book, Melania launched her own first media event—her first solo international trip. In Africa she dressed in costumes and posed for photo shoots that stylistically were a cross between Isak Dinesen and cover images for pulp fiction "romance on the Nile" novels. She gave her first-ever sit-down interview to ABC News, flashing a look of slit-eyed, icy rage when referring to "the left wing media who are criticizing me."

A month later, shortly after the disastrous midterm election, Melania emerged as her own power source. She demanded one of her husband's senior national security advisers be sacked, supposedly over disputes about airplane seating during her 2018 Africa trip. When Trump didn't jump to fire the woman, Mira Ricardel, Melania put out a statement through her spokeswoman, Stephanie Grisham. "It is the position of the Office of the First Lady that [Ricardel] no longer deserves the honor of serving in this White House," it read. A day later, Ricardel was out. The firing was Melania's first public act—beyond the "I DON'T CARE, DO U" jacket message and the slap-away of Donald's hand on an Israeli tarmac. It was relatively meaningless beyond the inner bureaucracy of the executive branch, but significant for what it presaged.

Her real power play came a few months later, when Trump installed Melania's spokeswoman Grisham, whose prior experience had been limited to state legislators in Arizona, as White House press secretary. Grisham had proven her loyalty to Trumpworld during Melania's mysterious 24-day disappearance after what was supposedly a simple outpatient kidney procedure. Under enormous pressure, Grisham maintained a shroud of secrecy. She built a moat for the castle and pulled up the drawbridge. (She was relieved of the duty during the coronavirus crisis and had not held a single press conference during her tenure.)

From the East Wing, with its new glam room and Pilates reformer studio, Melania has also maintained her public profile as the human clothes hanger. Many insist, absent any other verbal signals, that she sends intricate messages by her choice of attire. At the post-impeachment State of the Union 2020, for example, style writers decoded her black Dolce and Gabbana suit as a message of defiance aimed at the liberal female Democrats wearing white. Hanging a Presidential Medal of Freedom around Rush Limbaugh's neck was just an activity, an accoutrement to The Look. In early 2020, Melania traveled to Palm Beach Atlantic University—where some years before, one of Jeffrey Epstein's teen victims was tricked into becoming a sex slave—wearing a virginal white dress in front of a two-story American flag, to deliver a Hallmark card word salad of a speech: "It is my hope that by promoting Be Best values, we will give a voice to the concerns and struggles of our children, and help them overcome the challenges they face."

The speeches are banal, the clothing signals diverting, but since the election it has become clear that Melania's power over her husband is real. Gone are the days when he could whiff off a pretty young wife with a paltry million-dollar payoff and some threats, as he did with second wife Marla Maples. Donald is, in comparison to those carefree days, a slave to his hot "supermodel." As president, he is entirely dependent upon her continued willingness to accessorize him. He has grown accustomed to Melania's occult power, as old men with young wives tend to do. In his Tourette's syndrome style, Trump has even "joked" that Melania wouldn't care if he died. At a fundraiser for wounded Louisiana congressman Steve Scalise, Trump marveled at the way Scalise's wife had cried at the hospital. "I mean, not many wives would react that way to tragedy, I know mine wouldn't," he said.

◇◇◇◇

Melania's chief competition for power over and around Donald is and has always been her stepdaughter Ivanka. Since Trump's election, since her appointment as a "senior advisor to the President" Ivanka has wasted no time burrowing into the global power structure. The calling card doesn't always work. She is not always welcomed with open arms. A widely shared YouTube clip from a G20 meeting showed IMF chairman Christine LaGarde, French president Emmanuel Macron, and Canadian prime minister Justin Trudeau pointedly shunning her. It doesn't matter. Ivanka has written that she learned at her father's knee that "perception is more important than reality." She has played the media like a fiddle, carefully choosing outlets—the *Financial Times,* the *Washington Post*—for rare interviews, but mostly appearing on Fox or remaining silent. She possesses a quality crucial to all successful politicians: grit to a self-delusional degree. She can smile through levels of public humiliation that could destroy civilians. The rewards are worth it. Even if she doesn't run for president, in the last three years she collected the personal contacts of every powerful leader in business, government, and tech on the planet.

Her schedule during a single month span in 2020 includes a directory of the most powerful people on the planet. There she was at a Davos 2020 breakfast with Apple's Tim Cook, Microsoft CEO Satya Nadella, Salesforce CEO Marc Benioff, and the U.S. secretaries of labor, transportation, commerce, and the Treasury. There she is honored by the National Association of Manufacturers for creating American jobs, "like no one in government has ever done." There she is in Dubai at a women's empowerment conference (bad optics: a week later a British court accused the sheikh of Dubai of kidnapping and torturing his adult daughters in order to limit their empowerment). Then off to India with Dad and Melania, for a selfie in front of the Taj Mahal.

The best of them, Melania is capable of intense self-discipline and social isolation. She prefers the company of her family, a clan of Slovenian peasants who became rich beyond their wildest dreams, and have no earthly reason to relinquish it and go back to rolling *potica* in the Slavic heartland. She has never in her life needed parties or large groups, nor had any interest in wielding power.

Money, yes. Power, no. Her stepdaughter, on the other hand, is interested in power. She wants to be the first female president. She will perhaps realize an old family dream, becoming queen of the realm.

The future is female. Wink-wink.

PART ONE

Elisabeth and Mary, the Mother Figures

Elisabeth Ann Christ, Trump's paternal grandmother, was barely out of her teens when she left a German village with a husband eleven years older. Widowed as a mother of three children at home, an ocean away from her kin, she took her late husband's nest egg and started the Trump Organization, investing, building, borrowing, and building again, a cycle of debt and creation that became the hallmark of the company. Elisabeth was a stern, no-nonsense presence in her grandson's life until his late teens. The example of her strength and competence left him with an ability to trust a select few women—the ones he wasn't "banging," as one friend put it—to handle his schedule and other business matters. She also passed on an Old World propriety that emerged in Donald as germophobia, as well as a belief that German blood made a person cleaner and more efficient than others.

Mary Anne MacLeod, Trump's mother, emigrated to New York as a teenager and became a maid in an American castle, the home of Andrew Carnegie, one of America's richest men. From her, Donald inherited his craving for the royal and his enduring sense of being not "classy" enough.

CHAPTER 1

◇◇◇◇◇◇

Elisabeth Christ Trump

She so wanted to go home.

It was October 11, 1905, the day after her twenty-fifth birthday. Elisabeth Christ Trump lay on a bed in a Bronx apartment, wracked with labor pains. Her sister-in-law, Katherine Schuster, was in the apartment, helping her, along with other women from the German community in Morrisania, the German immigrant neighborhood in the Bronx, the borough of New York City where she and her husband now lived.

It was a modern metropolis, but horses still pulled carts outside the apartment building. Over a prairie six hundred miles west of New York, the Wright Brothers had just flown the first airplane that could stay in the air for half an hour, but Elisabeth would be a middle-aged woman before air travel became commonplace. The mirrored skyscrapers and palace apartments and black screens that her descendants would gaze into and inhabit were decades into the future. She would know almost none of it.

And yet she was bringing it, slowly and painfully, to life.

She could hear German being spoken, but the familiar sound did not make this place, 539 East 177th Street, home. Not at all. The passing Third Avenue elevated train outside reminded her of that fact with tedious regularity, a kind of screeching metronome to her labor pains.

Home, at this time of year, was a place where the grapevines had turned red and yellow, where in the afternoon on an October day like this one, the sun would turn the sloping fields that ended just at the back doors of the homes in the little village to shimmering gold. There were no screaming trains, no teeming muddy streets; there was no cement, no filth and plague and disease from the hordes of immigrants—like her, from Europe, but otherwise very different, not as clean—all of them jostling in the hot, loud streets and at the fruit and vegetable stalls.

She knew just how far away home was, having now crossed the ocean not once but several times, the first to accompany her new husband to this New World, New York, in 1902. She would cross the ocean twice more on steamers, trying to get the German government to let her husband stay, and failing, before finally surrendering to her fate as a German-American immigrant.

She'd had baby Elizabeth in her arms and was already pregnant again on the sad, last trip away from Europe and back to New York, a few months ago, on the steamer SS *Pennsylvania*. They left during high summer in Kallstadt, the season when everyone was so gay, grapes still green on the vines. They could walk through the vineyards downhill to Bad Dürkheim, the spa town where tourists came to take the healthy waters.

By the end of that day, she had delivered her second child, a boy. They named him Frederick, after his father, Friedrich, but with the new spelling. He would be, unlike them, an American. Unlike them, he would be able to hide his native origins. His mother's homesickness, her longing for the village in Germany, her preferences and dreams and fears, would pass into him as a desperate affinity for cleanliness

and efficiency, a disdain for frippery and nonsense, and a deep attach-
ment to order and self-control as a bulwark against chaos and urban
filth. And the boy, as a man, would pass those same qualities and
quirks, mutated and attenuated, but still recognizable, to his own son.

◇◇◇◇

In 1885, a fatherless but resourceful sixteen-year-old German boy
named Friedrich Trump, the second son in a family of two boys and
four girls, set off from a tidy little winemaking village near the border
with France, to seek his fortune in America. The boy had trained as a
barber, but haircuts and shaves didn't promise the great fortune that
he already knew beckoned in the far, far mountains of the American
West.

Millions of German immigrants were starting farms in the American Midwest. But young Trump's American dream was in the Far
West, where, legend had it, young men might make a fortune.

After a few years, he left New York and crossed the continent
to Seattle, where thousands of men—grizzled, beer-smelling, unwashed, and wearing the same set of clothes for months at a time—
were arriving on foot and by ship to prospect for silver and gold.
As his grandson would, Trump knew instinctively what those rough
men wanted and what they would pay for it. And he found a way to
sell it to them, from Seattle to the Yukon and to the very edge of the
Arctic Circle.

In Seattle, Trump bought a saloon and eatery called the Dairy
Restaurant, serving beer, food, and "private rooms for ladies"—code
for prostitutes. Long before jets and Microsoft, when it was still a
rough pioneer town, Seattle's chief industries were gambling and prostitution. Trump arrived in the city during the ascendancy of the latter
business, thriving with a ratio of men to women in town of around
a hundred to two. A few years prior, in 1888, legendary Madame
Lou Graham—also from Germany—had arrived and built a lavish,

genteel bordello opposite the city's chief Catholic establishment, the Church of Our Lady of Good Help. To drum up business, she and other "parlor house" proprietors paraded new girls around town by carriage.

Trump stayed in Seattle for two years, then spent the rest of the decade following gold and silver rushes, running, folding, and then re-creating saloon/restaurants to serve miners following word of newly discovered lodes and seams as far north as the Yukon. As prospectors moved to more promising territory, Trump simply packed his restaurant to follow the business—once by raft. Losing half of his equipment and furniture in a mishap on river rapids during that move slowed but did not cancel his business plan.

His last establishments were near the Klondike silver seam in Canada. In the spring of 1901, just as the North-West Mounted Police announced a plan to suppress gambling and liquor sales and to banish "the scarlet women" from the area, Trump sold off the furniture, pots, and pans, and left the Wild West behind for good. After ten years, the young man had saved up the equivalent of 80,000 deutschmarks, a tidy sum for a nest egg. He had enough to return to Kallstadt, deposit his money in the local treasury, and without delay, find himself a wife.

◇◇◇◇

It's unlikely that Friedrich Trump told his ten-years-younger bride the rude details of the origins of his nest egg—at least not in the beginning. Whatever rough habits he'd picked up in the outback (and according to his grandson, he was a "hard liver") he kept buttoned up while in Germany. But the porcelain-doll beauty who was destined to mold that small fortune into the roots of the Trump Organization was, despite her looks, no Bavarian cream puff.

In the photograph, in spite of the stern expression and the starched white, high-collar Edwardian dress, there's a delicacy to the pale, oval face. It's a very familiar face: Her genes are strong in her grandson Donald Trump, even more so in the faces of great-grandchildren she would not live to meet, especially the fairer ones: Eric, Ivanka, and Tiffany Trump.

Elisabeth Christ was born on October 10, 1880, the only daughter of Philip Christ and Ana Maria Christ. The family owned a little vineyard, but that didn't provide much income, and Philip Christ supported them as a tinker, repairing and polishing utensils and selling pots and pans out of the family home.

Elisabeth had three brothers. The eldest, Ludwig, fought for the Kaiser in World War I, survived, and became a mayor in a nearby town. The middle brother, Johannes, remained in Kallstadt and lost his own son Ernst in World War II. The larger Christ family, all distant relatives, lost a total of five men fighting in Hitler's army.

When Elisabeth was a girl, she lived in a small two-story traditional *fachwerk* house across the street from a slightly larger dwelling of the same type, which was the Trump family home. Both houses were simple wooden-and-plaster structures, but the Trump home had a walled-in garden, whereas the walls of the Christ house were planted in the edge of the road.

The couple married on August 26, 1902, then sailed to New York to set up their first house in an apartment in Morrisania, the Bronx. Trump went to work as a restaurant and hotel manager, barbering on the side.

◇◇◇◇

In the first decade of the twentieth century, New York City, with its electric streetlights, skyscrapers, soaring bridges, streetcars, and ferries, was a hive of human life thrumming with noise, people rushing hither and yon, and it surely overwhelmed the young village girl who was Trump's bride. But she wasn't entirely alone either. The city was packed with German transplants like her and her husband, as well as second-generation Germans whose parents had arrived in the city during earlier migration waves.

For fifty years, New York City had boasted the third-largest population of Germans in the world—only Berlin and Vienna had more—and by 1900, one in four New Yorkers was of German descent. Their ranks included engineers like John Roebling, a German immigrant who built the Brooklyn Bridge (and died on it), and millionaires like John Jacob Astor, born near Heidelberg, who turned his fur trade fortune into a real estate empire.

But for every Roebling and Astor there were hundreds of anonymous Germans who would live and die in relative poverty and obscurity in the smoky, seedy neighborhoods of early twentieth-century Gotham. They belonged to a city buzzing with change and growth. Old, low buildings were being razed for steel-frame skyscrapers and office towers of more than twenty stories. The vast majority of German immigrants in New York were working as laborers, maids, or servants of other kinds. Trump's sister worked as a cook for a member of the prominent New York Cooper family.

Fred and Elisabeth Trump were a small cut above the unwashed immigrant herd, living in one of the first Bronx apartment buildings with running hot water, private bathrooms, and electricity.

In April 1904, Elisabeth gave birth to her first child, a daughter they called Elizabeth—her name, but with the American spelling. Almost immediately, the young mother—overwhelmed by the anonymity of the big city, alone with the duties of child care so far from her family—was stricken with homesickness. The new home wasn't idyllic either. Frederick (he'd Americanized his name) was ambitious and energetic, but a hard drinker, possibly even alcoholic, a man roughened by a decade in the mountainous West.

A few months later, as the steamy New York City summer was ripening the horse dung, sewage, and food rubbish, the Trumps were on an ocean liner again, headed to Germany. Back in Kallstadt they enjoyed the summer wine festivals, and reconnected with loved ones. Elisabeth wanted badly to stay in Germany, and so did her husband. But the government of Germany would not repatriate Trump because he was technically a draft dodger (a family trait—neither his son nor his grandson would serve in the wars of their generations either), for having left the country before he was eligible and then returning when he was too old to serve.

During one blissful year in Kallstadt, while her husband wrangled with the authorities, Elisabeth raised her baby girl, cozily tucked away in the *fachwerk* home where she grew up, tending window boxes and walking among the vines.

Then, it was over.

A last letter from the German government exiled Friedrich. The Trumps—with Elisabeth now pregnant again—sailed back to New York. Trump set up shop as a barber at 60 Wall Street. The same building a century later housed the American offices of the German giant Deutsche Bank, implicated in Russian money laundering and the bank that loaned Frederick's grandson Donald Trump hundreds of millions of dollars when American bankers would no longer touch him.

Elisabeth was no happier in New York in 1905 than she had been before the trip home to Kallstadt. Even after moving to a newer apartment in a building with iceboxes and hot water, she longed for Germany. Frederick Trump tried to get back to Germany again, sending off another pleading letter in December 1906. In it, he explicitly stated that his wife was "unable to adjust to life in the New World."

Eventually, Trump gave up and refocused his efforts on making his way in the New World. He took a job managing one of Manhattan's new hotels, one with a new liquor license. That job—which put him back in a more refined version of the saloon lifestyle he'd left behind in the West—kept him away from home for long hours, leaving

Elisabeth alone in an apartment with two children under the age of five, and very soon, a third on the way.

◇◇◇◇

Elisabeth gave birth to Frederick Christ Trump, her second child and first son and the father of the future President of the United States, on October 11, 1905—a day after her twenty-fifth birthday. As with the first child, she delivered her second at home. The witness who signed the birth certificate was a Dr. Haas, the same doctor who would witness the birth of her third and last child, John, also at home, two years later.

Despite the doctor's signature, American childbirth in 1905 was a social, domestic event, and even more so for the German immigrant women, who clanned with one another in the alien city. Friends and family came together during the labor, taking turns encouraging the mother and bringing fresh water and linens to the midwife. At the time, home childbirth was the norm for most American women—not just German immigrants. More than 90 percent of American women—urban and rural—had their babies in their own beds, with women around them and a midwife attending. Families with money—and the Trumps were middle class—also had a doctor on call, usually a male, with forceps and the latest medical birthing knowledge and technology at the ready. Except for the doctor, if one was invited, men were not in the birthing room. It was the ultimate precinct of women.

◇◇◇◇

In 1910, Frederick bought a house and an adjacent vacant lot on First Street, a quieter street in Queens. It wasn't Kallstadt, but it was heavily German, and at least here the children could play outside in summer, and ice-skate and sled in nearby parks in winter. The neighborhood was so Teutonic that the Kallstadt wine was on sale at a German market nearby.

In the decade before World War I, "German-American" was a hyphenated label that bothered no one. Among his own people, Frederick Trump did business in the German language. He and Elisabeth spoke German inside the home and publicly with shopkeepers and other neighbors. And their three children didn't speak much English until they went to school. They felt no shame to being German. Even as the Great Powers chafed against each other in Europe, the thought of an armed conflict between the US and Germany struck most German-Americans as "absurd."

But, in 1914, war broke out in Europe, and it soon directly affected the German-American community. The United States entered the war on April 6, 1917, instantly erasing all pride in the label "German-American." Now Elisabeth, Fred, and every other German in America could hear themselves called by a new epithet—Huns. Walking down the streets of New York, they might also hear a number of other muttered wartime slurs—Jerry, Kraut, and Fritz. Overnight, the designation "German" disappeared from businesses, and the names of practically all higher institutions. Rampant Germanophobia cost countless men their jobs, and made them and their families pariahs in non-German communities. The bands at the beer and social clubs went quiet.

And, most important for Elisabeth Trump, German speakers took their language indoors.

◇◇◇◇

While war raged abroad, at home Elisabeth settled into the life of a suburban wife, toiling at domestic chores that were still not easy in the era before dishwashers and machine laundry. She had enough to do at home and did not need to join the women taking the jobs that millions of male soldiers had left behind. For American women, the war years and just after were significant. The first woman was elected to the US Congress. Women marched for the right to vote (granted in 1920) and risked jail to teach others about safe birth control methods.

None of this meant very much to Elisabeth Trump, a foreign-born woman far more comfortable in her native tongue than in English, living in a German enclave as a housewife, and financially cared for by a husband who went off to work and handled their finances. But she was forced out of domestic tranquility and isolation on a sunny May afternoon in 1918 when Frederick Trump died in a matter of days of the Spanish flu. He was forty-nine. He did not live to see the end of World War I in November 1918, or to enjoy the short-lived rehabilitation of the German identity in his new country.

In an interview late in life, his eldest son, Fred Trump, recalled the day his father died. Fred was twelve, and he and his father were walking on Jamaica Avenue, where preparations were under way for the next day's Memorial Day Parade. Frederick Trump suddenly turned to his son and said he felt sick. At home, Fred's father went to bed and never got up again.

The death was so sudden—the Spanish flu killed young people with a rapid-onset pneumonia—that the boy felt nothing at first. "It didn't seem real," he recalled in an interview years later with family historian Gwenda Blair. "I wasn't that upset. You know how kids are. But I got upset watching my mother crying and being so sad. It was seeing her that made me feel bad, not my own feelings about what had happened."

Widowed and with three children under the age of fourteen to care for, a German immigrant after four years in a wartime country that had stripped German names off foods like hamburger and sauerkraut and outlawed the teaching of German, Elisabeth was suddenly very much on her own.

She faced all the social and legal restrictions that women of that era had been fighting against, plus being regarded as a Hun.

She could legally be denied an application to open her own bank account, and she could not vote. Nor—given both her circumstances as a mother and the legal restrictions on women working—could she easily find work outside the home.

She took in sewing, and applied her husband's nest egg, worth $31,359, the equivalent today of $508,360, to the first Trump building investment. Elisabeth's business model was an embryonic form of the debt-leveraging, borrow-build-borrow style that remains a hallmark of the Trump Organization today. With "extraordinary determination," a local Queens newspaper reported, she had hired a contractor to build a house on the vacant lot her husband had left her along with their house, then sold it, and used the money to buy land and build another, banking the mortgage money. When she had $50,000 in capital, she incorporated. On April 16, 1927, the newspaper announced the incorporation of a business called E. Trump & Son.

The story of Elisabeth has been written out of the official Trump saga. Her grandson, just shy of twenty when she died, gives all glory to his father, and credits Fred with the idea that became the seed of the Trump Organization. According to Donald, Fred only needed his mother around to sign the checks, because he was too young. That story would require that young Fred, at the age of fourteen or fifteen, had the financial understanding, business acumen, and wherewithal to conceive how to apply his father's nest egg to a small piece of property and develop it using a fairly sophisticated (for a fifteen-year-old boy) scheme of development, debt, and mortgages.

As a man, Fred Trump could look back on his mother's role in the family business and easily write it off, and write himself into the business history, because every law and custom in America in the 1920s conspired to build a wall of challenges against any woman—immigrant or American-born—who wanted or needed to run her own life. Under state laws, husbands were designated as "head and master" of the household, with unilateral power over jointly held property. Laws kept women out of the workplace. The minimum wage did not apply to them. Private employers could legally refuse to employ women with preschool children, pregnant women were legally refused employment, and at the same time women had little choice in the question of whether or not to bear children. Politically and legally women were barely citizens. In the matter of inherited money, men were granted automatic preference over women as administrators of wills.

But Elisabeth Christ Trump's central but almost invisible role in what became a real estate empire coincided with a moment of change too. In the 1920s, a "New Woman" appeared on the scene. She was younger than Elisabeth, part of a generation that came of age with the Jazz Age and the right to vote, and who believed females could have careers and families simultaneously. These women were also beneficiaries of nascent Freudian psychology, the gateway to sexual liberation.

The Austrian Jewish doctor who had revealed the sexual underpinnings to all human behavior hailed from her neck of the woods, but Elisabeth was definitely not a New Woman. Widowed mother Elisabeth was just a little too old, and much too Old World and too formal and too busy with survival to belong to the flapper generation, the wild young things who discarded corsets and heavy, stiff dresses, aiming for a gamine, thin, flat-chested, and long-limbed look, who publicly smoked, drank gin, and swore.

The once homesick china-doll beauty would never relinquish her Victorian formality in dress or manner. In one of the few pictures of her that survive in the public domain, she is wearing the high lace collar and corseted, stiff shirtfront of the turn of the century, when she came of age. Fred inherited his mother's stern, joyless fortitude in facing the challenges of being a single mother in Depression-era New York. Her other legacy to him was her yearning for a mythic—to him—homeland, and an Aryan sense of racial superiority.

At age twenty-one, on Memorial Day in 1927, Fred was among those arrested at a Ku Klux Klan rally that turned into a melee involving a thousand white-robed men marching through Queens. Three months later, across the Atlantic and deep in Middle Europe, in August 1927, Hitler's Nazi Party held its third congress, called the Day of Awakening, in what is now remembered as the first Nuremberg Rally.

Elisabeth's homeland, Germany, was about to lose most of its sons—including at least one of her nephews—to Hitler's war.

CHAPTER 2

◇◇◇◇◇◇

Mary Anne MacLeod Trump

Mary Anne MacLeod was the tenth and last child born to a fisherman and his wife, on May 10, 1912, in the tiny town of Tong on the Isle of Lewis in the Outer Hebrides. She was just a wee thing, as the islanders would say, only seven years old, when catastrophe struck that would mark her people and her generation. Two hundred of the island's finest young men drowned in a shipwreck within sight of the village. The tragedy was probably one of her earliest memories. In the way that history shapes individuals, who then unwittingly shape history themselves, the disaster was a catalyst that ultimately sent the girl who would birth a president far from her home.

The Isle of Lewis, a windblown speck of rock and peat at the northerly edge of the Hebrides, had been controlled by local clan chiefs, the MacLeods, MacDonalds, Mackenzies, and MacNeils. In the nineteenth century, the English and their allies the landed Scottish lords instituted a brutal policy called the Highland Clearances, expelling peasants from farms and communities all over northern Scotland in order to empty the land for sport hunting and sheep grazing. Crofters, who had lived for centuries on the land, eking out a bare subsistence from the rocky soil by constructing "lazy beds" on which to grow potatoes and other crops that could withstand the fierce and ever-changing weather, lost everything.

Genealogists believe that Mary Anne MacLeod's ancestors were among the poor farmers kicked off their plots by the landowners, and forced to live for generations in destitution in the small towns to which they had migrated seeking food, shelter, and work. Her branch of the MacLeod family had remained on Lewis through the hard years of the 1800s, while tens of thousands of mainland Scots and Hebrideans, facing starvation, emigrated to Canada—some under threat of force.

When Mary Anne was born, the remaining islanders maintained ancient traditions, crofting as tenants, fishing on all but the stormiest of days, and speaking Gaelic at church and school even as the English overlords discouraged it. Mary Anne was born in a croft house, which her father had owned since 1895. The two-bedroom house had recently been converted from an ancient and indigenous island "blackhouse"—constructed of stone and with a thatched roof, which let smoke from the open peat fire seep out without need of a chimney. Ten siblings, the two MacLeod parents, and probably some grandparents, all shared the cottage.

Mary Anne learned speech, songs, and psalms in a Gaelic-speaking household. When she was old enough, she studied English, her second language, along with other fishing and crofting children at the little Tong school. On an American immigration form, Mary Anne reported that she was educated to the equivalent of America's eighth grade, meaning she left school at around age thirteen or fourteen, presumably to work on the croft or in some other job to help boost the family income.

The Isle of Lewis was and still is deeply religious, and at the time it was experiencing a series of hard-core revivals with a tinge of popular rebellion against the establishment. Church was serious business. Women and men both wore black to services, and four Sunday services made the Sabbath a daylong affair.

The MacLeod family belonged to the Scottish Free Church, a relatively more conservative congregation, in the nearby town of Stornoway. The dignified gray stone structure was planted on the gentry's street, Matheson Road, lined with handsome brick mansions built by and for the families of the local merchants and wealthier landowners. To distinguish the residents of Matheson Road from the rest of sheep- and fish-smelling islanders, in their muck boots and oilers, the town forbade the poor from walking on the street.

The ban would have included the fishing MacLeods.

The MacLeods lived on the edge of what the locals called "the saltings," a several-miles-square tidal flat between the hamlet of Tong and the larger town, that at certain times of the day turned into quicksand as the tide rose. To get to church, the family would pick its way across the flat in muck boots—a perilous journey that only the fishing families who lived on its edges would attempt. Even with their knowledge of the safest route, people were regularly lost.

As a girl growing up in Tong, Mary Anne had a single example of a more opulent way of life, in the gray, three-story Tudoresque Lews Castle, perched on a hill across a tidal inlet from the main harbor. Built in the mid-1800s by the same Matheson after whom the high road was named, the turreted and perfectly intact castle was surrounded by sprawling manicured woods and a great green lawn, all of it long since scraped free of peat-smelling crofters and their sheep. From any point along the harbor, the little girl could look across the muddy inlet and up at the crenellated turrets and beveled, jewel-like windows, portholes into a life of elegance, wealth, and ease.

After the clearances, the First World War devastated the community's population. The Isle of Lewis and the fishing town of Tong were a long way from the trenches of the Great War, but they gave a higher percentage of young men to the effort than most places, having been promised they would get land in return for men. (When the owners did not keep that promise, Lewis men rebelled, and won back their crofts.) The island's surviving soldiers were further decimated by the shipwreck in which more than two hundred of them returning from the war drowned on New Year's night 1919, during a storm and within sight of Stornoway. The captain and the soldiers had been celebrating and drinking, and failed to notice the harbor rocks until it was too late.

Because of war and that disaster, by the time Mary Anne was old enough to notice boys, the women of Tong dramatically outnumbered the men. Without available husbands, Tong offered the MacLeod girls no future. They left for the United States, one by one. Mary Anne's older sister Catherine left first, fleeing the scandal of having become pregnant out of wedlock. She gave birth and left her newborn daughter at home before setting sail for New York in 1921. Within a few years, two more sisters, Christina and Mary Joan, emigrated.

Mary Anne arrived in New York on May 11, 1930 (some reports suggest November 29, 1929), after nine days on the steamship *Transylvania*. In paperwork, she declared her intention to file for US citizenship. Although her son Donald would later claim she came to New York on a holiday, papers show that she listed her occupation as "domestic" and had no intention of going back. On one passenger list for all aliens—anyone not a US citizen—she declared that she intended to seek American citizenship, and in answer to "whether alien intends to return to country whence he [*sic*] came," she wrote, "no."

For girls from the fishing hamlet of Tong, the swells under the steamship churning westward would have been familiar. But the first sight of New York City from the harbor was not. Smokestacks poured black coal pollution. The air was hazed with it and with wood smoke from fires. Horses and carriages were still in use, but so were cars and trucks, so the noise of braying and horns and engines added to the cacophony of men shouting in multiple languages.

The magnitude of the metropolis overwhelmed all newcomers, but it also offered a chance to remake oneself. Mainland Scots and those already in the US considered Mary Anne MacLeod a bit of a hick, raised so far from cosmopolitan people and attitudes, under-educated and speaking the Gaelic language. But she had an advantage. Immigrant country girls rendered anonymous in a city so vast and so full of dark alleys might go astray. But the MacLeod girls did not, thanks to a network of recently arrived British, Irish, and Scottish butlers, maids, and footmen all employed in the homes of some of the wealthiest New Yorkers. When Mary Anne arrived, her sister Catherine was married to a butler named George A. Reid. Her sister Mary Joan also worked as a domestic and was married to an English footman named Victor Pauley.

Upon arrival at New York, Mary Anne informed immigration officials that she would be staying with the butler's wife, Mrs. Catherine Reid of Astoria, Long Island. But Mary Anne was soon residing as far from Astoria as it was possible to get—at least in terms of the American class hierarchy. She settled in at 2 East 91st Street in Manhattan, a maid in the service of the widow of the richest Scotsman in the world, Andrew Carnegie.

◇◇◇◇

By 1930, Andrew Carnegie had been dead almost a dozen years, but he was a legend in his native Scotland and the United States. Born in Dunfermline, Scotland, to a politically radical mother and a weaver father in 1835, he emigrated to the United States as a boy in 1848 with his parents. Thanks to a combination of resourcefulness, audacity, and fortuitous timing, he manifested the notion that America could turn any man into a king.

Carnegie's first job was as a bobbin boy in a Pittsburgh textile mill. He went on to build a vast empire of coal, steel, and real estate. In 1901, he sold his company, Carnegie Steel, for $480 million, the equivalent of about $13 billion today. Among the Gilded Age robber barons who accumulated wealth on a scale comparable to the global oligarchs, Wall Street tycoons, and tech billionaires of today, Carnegie stood out for his community spirit, having vowed to give away as much of his fortune as possible before he died. By the time of his death in 1919, he had donated $350 million—about 90 percent of his fortune. "The parent who leaves his son enormous wealth generally deadens the talents and energies of the son," he said.

While Mary Anne MacLeod was growing up in Scotland, Andrew Carnegie was already famous and had been handing out millions to libraries, auditoriums, educational institutions, and teachers. Still, he had more of it left over, and in 1901, he built himself an American palace on Manhattan's Upper East Side, where his widow, Louise Whitfield Carnegie, lived when the teenaged Mary Anne arrived at her doorstep.

Like a character out of Charles Dickens, crofter child Mary Anne landed with the Carnegies, almost magically transported from gazing across the water to the Lews Castle in Stornoway, straight through its windows and into the interior of an even larger castle, this one all-American. Her live-in maid's position meant she spent her days— and presumably nights (she is listed in the census as a household member)—in an American palace, rubbing shoulders with the closest thing Americans had to royalty, during the depths of the Great Depression.

The Carnegie Mansion was a sixty-four-room gray stone and brick Georgian Revival building, four stories high, covering more than an acre of land on Manhattan's Upper East Side. Among its Trumpian excesses: a hand-carved staircase leading to a massive foyer, a dining room that could accommodate three hundred, multiple fireplaces of Carrara marble, Persian rugs, an art gallery, and a library. Carnegie's personal favorite after-dinner room was paneled entirely in hand-carved teakwood.

A massive Aeolian pipe organ, its pipes extending three floors, held pride of place on the first floor. During Carnegie's final years at the house, he hired an organist to play it every morning as his wake-up call. A renowned church organist arrived before the house-hold was up, and, "the music drifted to the second floor bedrooms of the Carnegies where they were gently wakened by their favorite tunes," wrote one historian. Then the mansion's twenty servants—of whom Mr. Carnegie wrote, "No man is a true gentleman who does not inspire the affection and devotion of his servants"—went to work organizing the day.

The house was large enough to host massive dinners, and guests from Carnegie's vast and eclectic group of colleagues, friends, and as-sociates were always in and out, from American writer Samuel Clem-ens (aka Mark Twain) to international heads of state.

After Carnegie died in 1919, his widow, Louise, remained in the great house, and when Mary Anne arrived to work as a maid, her mistress was in her seventies but still a very vigorous, civically en-gaged woman, passionate about church, music, dogs, travel, and her grandchildren. The mansion was always filled with music, from organ recitals every Sunday afternoon; to Toscanini, a favorite of the widow, who kept the radio tuned to broadcasts of his recorded concerts; to the Boston Symphony, often on the phonograph. Louise maintained an active social schedule, and Mary Anne watched her bustle in and out, decked in furs and finery, with footmen at her side, headed to operas at the Metropolitan, to dinners with foreign dignitaries, and to lunches with ladies with marquee names like Edison, Colgate, and Rockefeller.

Louise and her retinue also annually voyaged to the Carnegies'

Skibo Castle in Scotland in summer. It's not certain Mary Anne traveled with them, but ship manifests indicate she did go back to Scotland more than once between 1930 and 1934—a frequency of travel that would have exceeded the budget of a domestic, unless in service of someone paying for passage.

CHAPTER 3

◇◇◇◇◇◇

The Queen of Queens

Ensconced in the Scottish-American community, polishing banisters and silver in a New York castle, one thing remained for Mary Anne MacLeod to do: find a husband.

She met the ambitious, mustachioed Frederick Christ Trump at a dance in Queens. He was six years older, and spoke, like her, with an accent. He owned a burgeoning New York–area building concern. "He was the most eligible bachelor in New York," Mary Anne would recall, years later, in an interview with the BBC. The two fell in love. Fred Trump was, like Mary Anne, no stranger to hard work. He'd been laboring since his high school years, one winter even substituting his own back for the mules that hauled construction materials to icy job sites. Once out of high school, he went straight into business with his mother. Fred built his first home the year after he got out of high school, for $5,000, and sold it for $7,500. He turned that cash into more houses, and built as fast as he could, selling them before they were completed in order to get the cash to buy materials for the next. "Borrow, build, borrow, buy" became the Trump creed.

In January 1936, Mary Anne married Fred Trump at the Madison

Avenue Presbyterian Church in Manhattan, followed by a wedding reception for twenty-five guests at the Carlyle, a posh Upper East Side hotel now best known as the venue where Woody Allen liked to play the clarinet. The *Stornoway Gazette*, Mary Anne's hometown newspaper, published notice of the event. The bride wore a "princess gown of white satin with a long train and a tulle cap and veil," and her bouquet was of "white orchids and lilies of the valley." The matron of honor was Mary Anne's elder sister Mary Joan Pauley, and the best man was the groom's brother John Trump (who had by then earned a PhD in physics at MIT).

The couple honeymooned in Atlantic City, but only for two days, as workaholic Fred had deals to get back to in New York City. When the honeymoon was over, Mary Anne MacLeod was no longer living at the Carnegie Mansion, but was listed as a resident of the modest Trump family home at 175/24 Devonshire Road in Jamaica, Queens, the middle-class neighborhood where she was destined to spend the rest of her life. The household was still headed by Elisabeth. Fifteen months after the wedding, on April 5, 1937, Mary Anne gave birth to a daughter, Maryanne, the first of five children, to be followed by Frederick, Elizabeth, Donald, and Robert.

The home life of a Queens builder's wife was hardly high society, but it had its privileges. As Fred prospered, he moved his family into a larger house. By 1940, his wife, the former housemaid, had her own domestic from the British Isles, a naturalized Irish lass named Janie Cassidy. It was a houseful of immigrants. Besides Elisabeth flitting in and out and, eventually, an Irish nanny, there was Mary (she dropped the Anne after marriage), who remained a foreign national until 1942, when the US District Court in Brooklyn made her a naturalized citizen.

Fred's alien heritage was a problem, though. As Hitler rolled over Europe, a second wave of anti-German sentiment infused America. When America went to war against Germany again, Fred Trump declared himself to be Swedish, and he passed himself off as a Swede for the rest of his life, a lie that his son would double down on later, and which would even show up in Fred Trump's *Daily News* obituary in 1999. "He had thought, 'Gee whiz, I'm not going to be able to sell these homes if there are all these Jewish people,'" Trump cousin John Walter, the self-appointed Trump family historian, told the *Times* later. And once they started lying, they couldn't turn back. "After the war, he's still Swedish," Mr. Walter said. "It was just going, going, gone."

◇◇◇

At home, and in his business attire, Fred maintained what his son Donald would come to think of as a particularly German attention to cleanliness. He always appeared in both public and private in suit and tie, immaculately shaved, the mustache trimmed. He was so formal that he wore a tie and jacket at the dinner table with his children and so fastidious that he would come home after work, shower, and change into a fresh shirt.

Fred Trump never dispensed with his mother Elisabeth's Old World thrift. He exemplified and amplified the work ethic and habits of resourcefulness that Elisabeth Trump had passed down to her children by example. He worked like an ant as soon as he was a teen, and by his early twenties was building small suburban houses at a prodigious rate. He wasn't just throwing up tin-and-plywood shacks. The snug, well-built brick Trump home was known at the time as the perfect starter home for a family on the way to a solid middle-class life in the New York suburbs.

He and Mary were an effective, if odd, couple. In their life together, Mary gladly relinquished the style and habits of her homespun childhood, reveling in what her husband's growing fortune could buy. But his frugality was legendary. No expense was so small it couldn't be reduced further. Instead of buying a commercial product for the thousands of gallons of disinfectant it took to clean out his apartments, Fred bought samples of all the available floor cleaners, sent them out to a lab, found out what was in them, and had some mixed himself. "What had cost $2 a bottle, he got mixed for 50 cents," his son Donald later recalled.

The growing Trump clan lived in one of the first gated communities, a development that was a grander version of the Trump homes, on Midland Parkway in Queens. Visitors had to check in at the gatehouse before entering the enclave. The Midland Parkway area is now teeming with immigrants from the browner nations, but then it was all-white, a leafy suburban Norman Rockwell diorama where neighbors attended dinner dances and Christmas-caroled at the clubhouse.

The Trumps' house was a Carnegie mansion manqué, a suburban builder's vision of grand, an early McMansion. Fred Trump built several of the houses in Jamaica Estates, but he saved the finest and largest for his own family. The twenty-three-room, nine-bath, red-brick colonial had six two-story columns flanking the door and a large basement garage. No Aeolian pipe organ, but there was a curving staircase, the super-modern additions of an intercom and a television inside a library with "more shelves than books," according to family historian Gwenda Blair. Outside, little black lawn jockeys guarded the entrance, instead of Scottish footmen. But Fred Trump had a chauffeur to drive him around in his Cadillac, in addition to a maid.

Inside the home, Mr. and Mrs. Trump maintained order, respect for elders, and most of all, reverence for and faith in family. Mary churched the kids on Sunday. As the boy who would become president remembered it later, Mary Trump was "the perfect housewife," who didn't "sit around playing bridge and talking on the phone." She took care of her brood of five, with help, and according to her son, "cooked and cleaned and darned socks." She also did charity work at the local hospital. Meanwhile Fred was "the power and the breadwinner."

As a young wife and mother, Mary Trump also served as a hostess for Fred's business parties. To grease the deals, the Trumps hosted gatherings at New York area hotels for politicians and prospective lenders and partners. At these events, Mary's flair and sparkly personality kept things gay while Fred did business. The parties were not grand gatherings of international literary, commercial, and diplomatic figures, like the ones at East 91st Street, but they sufficed as backdrops for financing and building baby boom suburbia.

As a wide-eyed young woman in the Carnegie household, the backwoods Scot immigrant had been taught some social niceties such as how to arrange the silverware and which fork went for what. But by watching Louise Carnegie's personal style, she absorbed much, much more than most other immigrant women arriving ignorant of the customs and mores of upper-class American society.

She loved pomp and money, was obsessed with social status, and loved being chauffeured through suburbia in a Rolls-Royce, and her fourth child inherited that trait. In that way, Mary was the opposite of her husband, who would use the Rolls to drive Donald to the subway station, but never drive him all the way to school, as a sort of lesson in hard living. Mary's airs were the antithesis of her mother-in-law Elisabeth Trump's—and Fred's—way of life.

For Fred, all aesthetics were a waste of money. His Queens properties were solid but purposefully devoid of luxuries. "Design was beside the point because every building had to be pretty much the same: four walls, common brick facades, and straight up," Donald later wrote. "You used red brick, not necessarily because you liked it but because it was a penny cheaper than tan brick."

When Donald built his own Trump Tower, he chose to sheath it in the most expensive type of glass, called bronze solar. His father was mystified and scornful. "Why don't you forget about that damn glass?" Fred opined when Donald showed him the plans. "Give them four or five stories of it and then use common brick for the rest."

Donald recalled, "It was classic Fred Trump, standing there on 57th Street and Fifth Avenue, trying to save a few bucks. I had loftier dreams and visions." Fred rolled his eyes at the petite Versailles his son planned to construct on the top floors for himself.

That was pure Mary.

◇◇◇◇

Mary Trump delivered five children over eleven years between 1937 and 1948—half the number her mother had borne over twenty years at the cottage on Lewis. Unlike her own mother, or her mother-in-law, Elisabeth, who gave birth in their homes, mid-twentieth-century American women went to hospitals and labored in large maternity wards where they were told to keep quiet until it was time, then gave birth in sterile delivery rooms. Women were kept in the hospital for ten days after birth and separated from their babies in the early days to prevent infection, which was still killing American women at a greater rate than most Western Europeans.

Mary Trump would not escape the hospital maternity ward unscathed herself.

While pregnancy in the 1940s was no longer a reason for a woman to cloister herself, and maternity clothes were the norm, in the Trump household an Old World squeamishness about expecting prevailed. Mary's eldest daughter, Maryanne, recalled: "Years later, when I was pregnant, I said something about my state, and my father said, 'Your mother had five children and never used that word.'"

Mary Trump was no rebel, certainly not one of the American flappers of her generation who had won the right to vote, drink and smoke in public, and dance until dawn, and who were now settling down as mothers. Mary's concept of home and American motherhood was rooted in the experience of being the youngest of ten in a cramped, spartan, and God-fearing Scots fishing cottage, raised by older sisters as much as her mother, and then in her stint in the

Carnegie household, where Margaret Carnegie raised the late Andrew Carnegie's lucky little grandchildren in a palace full of servants.

Fred's curfews, rules, and regulations were all Grandma Trump. She remained a constant presence in Fred and Mary's lives, and in the children's until her death in the 1960s. A graying blonde, dressed formally like her son, Elisabeth minded the children at Trump parties for business and political contacts. The kids' neighbors recalled that she was the antithesis of a cuddly, hugging grandmother. The children both feared and respected her. And so did Mary, who suffered her mother-in-laws judgment daily.

"She was very hard on Mary," one Trump family member recalled.

Between Elisabeth—his father's lifelong advisor—and yearning, class-obsessed Mary, whose airs were ridiculous to both Fred and Elisabeth, little Donald grew up listening to two women speaking heavily accented English, fearing one and half pitying the other.

Fred Trump's treatment of women fixed his son's attitudes toward females for life. Fred listened to and respected one female—his own mother. She was close to him until her death when Fred was sixty. But his own wife was another story. By all accounts, Fred was a philanderer, a man who viewed women through two lenses—what they could do for him in private, and, on a much less dramatic scale than his son would use the same lens, how they might be employed as props to advance his career and sell his properties. He had a long-standing affair with his personal secretary, and was such a man of habit that he took her to lunch at the same Italian place near his office in Brooklyn for years.

While her workaholic husband cut a swaggering swath through the Brooklyn business community, Mary Trump was becoming an increasingly frail woman, and in her forties and fifties, somewhat lonely. She was social, and loved hosting parties for seventy-five or a hundred people at clubs in Jamaica or Manhattan hotels. She belonged to a few charity boards, and she drove around Queens in her rose-colored

Rolls-Royce, but Fred wasn't faithful. He was known for his numerous affairs in that city, according to biographer Harry Hurt, who
wrote that his "alleged extramarital dalliances along the Florida Gold
Coast had earned him a reputation as the 'King of Miami Beach,' a
place the Trumps visited on holidays. He continued the affair with his
secretary, taking her to lunch almost daily on Coney Island, near his
modest office, with its plastic plants and cheap furniture, on Avenue
Z. Fred's five children knew about the mistress, and, as adults, "treated
her like one of the family," one family member recalled. But Mary
Trump never accepted the woman, excluding her from business and
family events. Donald observed and imitated this, but he didn't learn
every lesson early enough. Years later, when Fred's son was making
the daily tabloids for an affair, Donald's secretary Norma Foerderer
overheard Trump Sr. lecturing his son: "You can have a thousand mis-
tresses if you want, but you don't have just one. And whatever you do,
you never, ever let yourself get caught." Foerderer later recalled that
Donald didn't take too kindly to that advice, telling his father, "You
don't know what you're talking about." At which point the old man
stormed out of his son's office.

In spite of Fred Trump's professional and personal transgressions
outside the home, he ran the Trump household strictly. His own
children were punished for cursing, calling each other nicknames,
and the girls for wearing lipstick. In an interview years later, eldest
daughter Maryanne Trump Barry described a completely patriarchal
household where order was maintained via Fear of Dad. Mother
Mary and the nanny cataloged the children's misbehavior during
the day, and reported it to Fred at night. He alone would decide
what punishment to mete out—often including paddling with a
wooden spoon. His capacity for violence over minor transgressions
was such that even neighbors were cowed. One friend recalled that
"you didn't utter a curse word in that house or you got your neck
broken."

Inside the Trump manse, Mary and Fred passed down the tics and traditions of their deeply deprived childhoods. They lived in a large house and were, by income level at least, members of the upper middle class. But the children had to eat their plates clean, take summer jobs, collect empty bottles for pennies, and understand the value of a dollar. They were not raised rich, even though they were, and Maryanne Trump later told Trump family historian Gwenda Blair that she was a teen before she first realized her family was wealthy, when a friend said to her, "Your father is rich." Maryanne "was stunned. We were privileged but I didn't know it."

That privilege was obvious to her mother, though. The Scots fisherman's daughter, who arrived in America with a small suitcase and few dresses on an immigrant steamship, was now a New York mother who could afford furs, domestic help, and regular hairdressing. She eventually came to sport a signature yellow cotton-candy bouffant that rivaled the one her son would craft for himself years later, a mother-son link that speaks volumes about her role in his life as a kind of style arbiter, a measure of what was truly *classy*. By early middle age, she was taking cruises and flights with her family to the Bahamas, Puerto Rico, and Cuba, besides regular summer trips back to the Isle of Lewis. Eventually, like Louise Carnegie, but on a much lower rung of the New York social ladder, she supported philanthropies, especially one dedicated to cerebral palsy and intellectually disabled adults.

Her children don't seem to have known that she once worked as a servant to the widow of the richest man in America. But they did notice her reverence for the grander life, a taste that her son inherited along with her magnificent hairdo. In his 1987 book, *The Art of the Deal*, Trump wrote that his mother loved "splendor and magnificence," a characteristic that irritated his hardworking father, a man who valued work above the trappings of its rewards, and who abhorred leisure.

"I still remember my mother . . . sitting in front of the television set to watch Queen Elizabeth's coronation and not budging for an entire day. She was just enthralled by the pomp and circumstance, the whole idea of royalty and glamour. I also remember my father that day, pacing around impatiently. 'For Christ's sake, Mary,' he'd say. 'Enough is enough, turn it off. They're all a bunch of con artists.' My mother didn't even look up. They were total opposites in that sense. My mother loves splendor and magnificence, while my father, who is very down-to-earth, gets excited only by competence and efficiency."

Mary loved attention, and could be the life of the party at social gatherings. "She always had a flair for the dramatic and grand," Trump wrote of his mother. "She was a very traditional housewife, but she also had a sense of the world beyond her." He thinks, "I got some of my sense of showmanship from my mother."

Mary retained her Scottish brogue, but hid evidence of childhood impoverishment under her furs. Her dramatic, regal style, learned as a teenaged maid serving rich lunching ladies in one of the finest palaces in Manhattan, and her intelligence so impressed him that, Trump wrote, no future women in his life could live up to her.

"Part of the problem I've had with women has been in having to compare them to my incredible mother, Mary Trump," he wrote. "My mother is smart as hell."

CHAPTER 4

◇◇◇◇◇◇◇

Child Donald

The most important influence on me was my father
Fred Trump.

—DONALD TRUMP

That may well be true.

But it's a good bet the first pair of eyes he ever looked into were Mary's, and the job of actually raising little Donald—whether he was aware of it or not—fell to his mother, and to a lesser extent, his grandmother. Mary changed his diapers, Mary carried him around when he couldn't walk, dressed and fed him. And Mary, when he was two, left him for a long, long time.

Mary gave birth to her fourth child, a son, at a hospital in Queens, on a Friday, June 14, 1946. It was, as she would say at home, a bonny day, and he was a bonny little blue-eyed boy. There was nothing unusual about the labor or the baby. Mother and boy left the hospital after the requisite ten days. Mary and Fred named the blond baby boy Donald John, after one of her relatives, and Fred's brother.

The boy was born in optimistic, thriving postwar America, the first great atomic superpower, while the rest of the world was still in shambles. Social attitudes were slowly changing: The US Supreme Court struck down a Virginia law requiring segregation of white and black bus passengers. Harry Truman signed the National School Lunch Act committing the federal government to feeding poor children—one of the many federal "entitlement" programs that would be created during Donald Trump's younger years and ultimately provoke a backlash and a new conservative movement.

At New York's Hunter College, a few miles away from the hospital where Mary was delivering Donald to the world, the United States representative to the nascent United Nations Atomic Energy Commission was proposing that the UN take control over the world's nuclear weapons. That proposal didn't pass, and nuclear weapons development soon proliferated, beginning with the Soviet Union. An American historian would later write that the proposal was the closest the planet would ever come to one world government—another great modern conservative bogeyman.

Back in the big house on Midland Parkway, the infant grew up into a towheaded hellion. A problem child. From the time he was a toddler, his behavior was a nightmare for caretakers, from the Irish nanny to his own mother. At the age of two, little Donald suffered a severe emotional shock when his mother disappeared for a long time. And when she returned, she couldn't take care of him as she had before.

At thirty-six, Mary suffered a hemorrhage following the birth of her fifth and final child, Robert. Doctors performed an emergency hysterectomy that went awry, and she developed peritonitis, a dangerous abdominal infection, requiring more surgeries and long hospitalization. Penicillin had been available for two decades, and the historic dangers of childbirth for mother and infant in hospital wards were greatly reduced. The drug probably saved Mary's life. But she nearly died and never recovered her full strength.

While Mary's life hung in the balance at the hospital, Fred Trump told the children to carry on. At one point, he even told his eldest daughter that her mother "wasn't expected to live, but I should go to school and he'd call me if anything changed. That's right—go to school as usual!" Maryanne Trump Barry told Gwenda Blair.

Mary survived, and came home to nurse and care for her fifth and last child, while little Donald was in his terrible twos. Exhausted and confronted with a demanding child who posed a daily trial for the household, she didn't have the energy to fully bond with the boy. Psychoanalysts say that a disruption of this sort at that age is crucial to human development. By all accounts, including his own, little Donald became an aggressive, impulsive, and sometimes downright sadistic little boy.

In the 1950s, when Donald was lashing out at teachers and schoolmates, school counselors, doctors, and parents were not on the lookout for aggression and impulsivity as a sign of emotional or developmental problems. On the contrary, they worried over the mental health of the introverted, shy misfits. In the postwar years, American boys were expected to be boisterous—it was a sign of robustness that matched the postwar national mood. The children that the psychiatric community identified as problematic were the opposite; shy, nervous, withdrawn, introverted children were the ones to look out for.

Donald learned to be proud of his belligerence, as a boyish/manly and even patriotic attribute. "Even in elementary school I was a very assertive, aggressive kid," he wrote in *The Art of the Deal*. He recounted an incident that's become part of the Donald legend: "In the second grade I actually gave a teacher a black eye—I punched my music teacher because I didn't think he knew anything about music and I almost got expelled. I had a tendency to stand up and make my opinions known in a very forceful way."

As Trump recalled it, his behavior made him "always something of a leader in my neighborhood." Never the most introspective man, Trump identified the cause of his acting out as "aggression." He was "most interested in creating mischief" and "I'd throw water balloons,

shoot spitballs, and make a ruckus in the school and at birthday parties. It wasn't malicious so much as it was aggressive."

Today, pediatricians and teachers are on the lookout for that set
of behaviors. Since Donald's childhood, the constellation has been
deemed a syndrome, and it has a name. Today, he would have been
diagnosed with a well-known childhood learning disability called attention deficit/hyperactivity disorder.

"He has the attention span of a nine-year-old with ADHD!"

That is the conclusion of Trump's *Art of the Deal* ghostwriter, Tony
Schwartz, who has probably plumbed the depths of Donald almost
as deeply as his interviewer/psychotherapist Howard Stern. Schwartz
issued his amateur diagnosis during a desperate publicity blitz he
mounted to try to stop the Trump Train during the 2016 presidential
campaign. Schwartz, filled with remorse for his role in creating the
Donald legend, had concluded that he wasn't sure whether anything
Trump ever told him about his childhood was true.

Nevertheless Donald's childhood behavior has been corroborated
by his own siblings, neighbors, and schoolmates over the years, and
Schwartz is not alone in his analysis.

"I think he's definitely got attention deficit disorder," said Trump
biographer Michael D'Antonio, who interviewed Trump five times
for a total of eight hours in the years before he ran for president,
and who found himself frustrated trying to get him to concentrate
on answers to questions about his parents, his childhood, just about
anything. "That doesn't mean he isn't really smart—it just means he's
not at his best when he's asked to dwell on a topic."

Trump looks back on himself as a little "wise guy." He bragged
to biographers about it—he was the kid who would toss an eraser in
class, and give the teacher a black eye, and throw cake around at a
birthday party. "When I look at myself in the first grade and I look at
myself now, I'm basically the same," Trump said to his *Art of the Deal*
ghostwriter. "The temperament is not that different."

"Who could forget him?" said Ann Trees, who taught at Kew-Forest School, where Trump was a student through seventh grade. "He was headstrong and determined. He would sit with his arms folded with this look on his face—I use the word *surly*—almost daring you to say one thing or another that wouldn't settle with him."

Based on his behavior, and reports that he can't or won't read, ADHD experts speculate that Trump has one or two common, undiagnosed, and untreated childhood learning disabilities related to impulse control, reading, and attention. The most likely and benign diagnosis would today probably be ADHD. ADHD is a common neurodevelopmental behavioral disorder usually diagnosed in boys. According to the Centers for Disease Control and Prevention, the average age at diagnosis is seven, and boys are more than twice as likely to be diagnosed with it as girls. Adults can also demonstrate symptoms and be diagnosed as well.

ADHD was first mentioned in medical literature in 1902. British pediatrician Sir George Frederic Still described "an abnormal defect of moral control in children." He found that some affected children could not control their behavior the way a typical child would, but they were still intelligent. Throughout the 1940s, the medical community was blaming the symptoms of what we now call ADHD on "minimal brain damage" and implicating the mother or caretaker. Six years after Donald Trump was born, the American Psychiatric Association (APA) published the first *Diagnostic and Statistical Manual of Mental Disorders* (DSM), in 1952, listing all recognized mental disorders. In 1955—as unruly Donald was being sent off to military school—the FDA approved Ritalin, a stimulant and now the drug of choice, for treating ADHD. But the APA did not recognize ADHD until 1968, when it included what it called "hyperkinetic impulse disorder" in the DSM for the first time. By then, Donald was twenty and beyond the reach of schools and pediatricians.

It would be 1980 before the DSM mentioned Attention Deficit

Disorder by name, combining three symptoms (inattentiveness, impulsivity, and hyperactivity) into a single disorder called ADHD. In the 1990s, the number of diagnoses skyrocketed, and it has continued to climb. A meta-analysis of diagnoses in 2013 found that more than 13 percent of American boys under age eighteen were diagnosed.

Today's helicopter parents, pediatricians, and teachers are hypervigilant to the smallest first signs of any unusual behavior in children. ADHD is now one of the most common childhood disorders being diagnosed and treated in the United States.

Dr. George Sachs is the founder and director of the Sachs Center in Manhattan, specializing in the testing and treatment of ADHD in adults and children. He has declined to diagnose Trump at a distance, but he has laid out the myriad symptoms of adult ADHD that Trump displays: "Whether he wins or loses, Donald Trump could very well benefit by having an ADHD specialist at his side."

Donald's wild childhood was hard on Mary Trump's frail health, and the family had no doctors to tell them that perhaps his behavior was a learning disability. With four other children to mind, she couldn't rely on the nanny's help alone to keep the family home in order and ride herd on the children's meals, homework, and deportment, while also focusing on the problem kid. Finally, Donald's behavior exploded into a family crisis as he reached puberty. And, as with all serious matters regarding the children, Fred would decide what exactly to do.

Trump has claimed that "I was never intimidated by my father." But everything about Donald Trump's adulthood suggests a boy forever marked by a rigid, demanding, pathologically fastidious, and even possibly physically abusive father.

As the boy hit adolescence, the bad school reports kept rolling in. The last straw was when Fred Trump learned that Donald was emulating the gangs in *West Side Story* and, with a friend, sneaking into Manhattan on the subway to purchase weapons for a growing collection of switchblades.

At that point, Mary despaired and Fred acted.

"When I turned thirteen my father decided to send me to a military school, assuming that a little military training would be good for me," Trump later recalled. "I wasn't thrilled about the idea, but it turned out he was right."

Instead of Ritalin, hyperactive, aggressive little Donald was treated with hazings and beatings at the New York Military Academy in up-state New York. By all accounts, including his own, while it didn't turn him into a great student, he took to the regimen like a fish to water, reveling in the maintenance of his uniform, the polishing of his saber, and the pomp of the campus musters with martial music.

He emerged about the same as when he entered, untreated and un-cured of whatever made him a non-reader and at the mercy of whatever psychological demons made him a bully. He retained a strong sense of intellectual insecurity, manifested in scorn for book-learned experts in anything, probably related to his own substandard reading skills. Later he would make of this disability a virtue for a crowd of Americans who decided that democracy meant that ignorance was as good as knowledge. "The most important thing I learned at Wharton was not to be overly impressed by academic credentials," Trump wrote in *The Art of the Deal*. "It didn't take me long to realize that there was nothing particularly awesome or exceptional about my classmates, and that I could compete with them just fine."

His lack of literacy amused his family. "The family joke was, well, maybe now he's read one book—after the *Art of the Deal*." His staff joked about it too. When writer Dave Shiflett was writing Trump's book on politics in 2000, *The America We Deserve*, a reporter called to ask Shiflett what author had most influenced Trump. Shiflett called Trump's office to find out, and he was told to pick any writer he wanted to. "So I told them he likes Dostoevsky," Shiflett said. "It was all just good times; the spirit around him was kind of mirthful. Everybody understood that and nobody took any of it very seriously."

The laughter was only dampened when the reading material involved national security briefings, but by then it was too late.

◇◇◇◇

Donald Trump does not think of himself and his family as immigrants. Both he and his father were the sons of immigrant mothers, but he has never embraced the aspirational immigrant story like some sons of new arrivals. On the contrary, he's spent most of his life trying to deny and escape outsider status. That denial is the essence of Trump's loneliness and mental instability, and might well have a pathological cause. Psychiatrists have studied the effects of immigration on the mental and emotional health of the second generation and have found increased depression, PTSD, and other psychological problems compared to the settled population. The sons of culturally conservative Muslim women raised in gender-permissive Western cities tend to be more vulnerable to calls for jihad. Both Donald and his father, Fred, as sons of white newcomers to America—scorned for their German-ness and their lower-class origins—might have been all the more vulnerable to the appeal of an extremely ruthless form of capitalism, its own kind of social terrorism.

By the 1950s, Elisabeth Christ Trump was spelling her name with a Z instead of an S: one small accommodation to her son's self-Americanization, perhaps, or a response to lingering anti-Hitler sentiment in her adopted country. In the last twenty years of her life, the daughter of a German tinker who sold pots and pans out of their house lived in relative luxury across the street from her wealthy son's growing family. She participated in the upbringing of little hellion Donald with a severe, if ultimately ineffective, hand.

Elizabeth had reason to be satisfied with most of her accomplishments. Against the odds, she had launched not only Fred, but all three children into successful American lives. Besides Fred the builder, her daughter Elizabeth had married a banker. The youngest Trump, John, was successful in a different way—thanks to Fred's money, he had been able to afford a university education, earning a doctorate in electrical engineering and eventually becoming a professor of nuclear physics at MIT. John's family became the "Boston Trumps," a quiet, reserved clan light-years different from the New York Trumps in their reverence for academic education and intellectual, as opposed to financial, success.

In her seventies, when grandson Donald was old enough to be going around to job sites with his dad, Elizabeth, as frugal as ever, helped collect coins from the Laundromats in hundreds of Trump buildings.

Her German heritage remained a big part of her private life, even through the years of the Second World War, when her son was pretending to be Swedish. She returned to Kallstadt twice after her husband died, once in 1929 with her children, now adults, and again in the 1960s. Genealogists I consulted are uncertain about what happened to the greater Christ family, offspring of the brothers she left behind. It's possible the war years blasted the family apart. Christs don't own the old house anymore, and have not in living memory. The Kallstadt Church does not have records. A plaque in the center of town commemorating the townsmen who gave their lives in World War II lists no Trumps, but five Christs. Only one of them, Ernst, can be traced to Elizabeth directly—he was her nephew.

What, if any, of the Nazi theories of Aryan superiority did her relatives and then the blond Elizabeth Christ, or her son, share with their supporters of Hitler back home? One sign is that in 1927, two years before Elizabeth took her three grown children back to Kallstadt for a visit, and the same year that she incorporated E. Trump & Son, a Fred Trump, still living at Elizabeth's address, was arrested at a KKK rally in Queens. He was not charged. But anti-black racism—and anti-Semitism—was also endemic among American whites in that generation who did not ascribe to Hitler's theories.

Fifty years later, Fred Trump and his son Donald fought federal charges that the Trump Organization was red-lining blacks out of its apartment buildings. The charges so incensed Donald that he hooked up with one of the most cartoonishly evil lawyers in the history of New York City, Roy Cohn, commencing a mentorship and alliance that would shape his personal and business style forever.

Kallstadters remember that Elizabeth came home one final time, to celebrate her seventieth birthday in 1950, among old friends. She died sixteen years later, at the age of eighty-five, in a hospital in Manhasset, Long Island, on June 6, 1966, eight days before her grandson Donald turned twenty. By that time, Donald had finished two years at Fordham University and was getting ready to transfer to Wharton in the fall. She was buried in Queens shortly before his birthday.

The *New York Times* did not note the death, as it would her son Frederick's decades later. The family put a small paid notice in the *Long Island News*, buried in the alphabetized death notices, naming her children and noting that she had ten grandchildren and eight great-grandchildren. The two-line notice informed readers that the viewing would be at a Queens funeral home, and to "omit flowers." The burial service, it read, would be private. On the same page, one larger article eulogized a New York City train operator.

The life story of Elizabeth Christ Trump ends humbly and quietly on Long Island. For all intents and purposes, she was then written out of the family legend, despite her enduring involvement in the life of her first son, Fred, who spent the first sixty years of his life in close proximity to his mother, despite the fact that he had shared his family life and business with her on a daily basis.

In *The Art of the Deal*, and in subsequent Trump Organization promotional material, grandson Donald minimized her history—erasing Kallstadt altogether—and her role in the founding and development of the family company. He wrote that his grandfather Frederick "came here from Sweden as a child, owned a moderately successful restaurant," and "died when my father was 11 years old."

Of his German grandmother, Donald only wrote that she went to work as "a seamstress" to support her three children. In his version, Fred gets all the credit for the Trump Organization, as a business prodigy from the age of sixteen. Donald relegated his grandmother to a passive, secondary role. "*He* [italics added] called his company Elizabeth Trump & Son because at the time he wasn't of age, and his mother had to sign all his legal documents and checks." When a German filmmaker interviewed him in his office about his German roots, Donald repeatedly pled ignorance about the details of his grandmother's life. And it's quite possible he was telling the truth. There were parts of her life that might never have been passed on to him. Her legacy as a German was, at least for a while, a family secret maintained for Fred's business purposes. By the time Donald came of age, the Second World War was not even a memory among his generation, whether hip, square, or flower children. Grandson Donald would have had no reason to hide his German roots. If his first wife is to be believed, he even kept a copy of Hitler's speeches around (although given his reputation as a non-reader, it's difficult to imagine him studying them closely). In a 2014 documentary called *Kings of Kallstadt*, about Friedrich Trump and John Henry Heinz, another Kallstadter who came to America, and whose son started a ketchup empire in the United States, Trump said: "They're strong people and they're smart people. They grow them well in Kallstadt. They get things done. That's the German culture. I'm proud to have that German blood. Great stuff." The filmmakers also got him to record, in a surprisingly good German accent, the statement "*Ich bin ein Kallstadter.*"

Although he professed not to know the story of how she started the Trump Organization, Donald did emphatically recall Elizabeth's power in the family. "She was a great woman but she was really really strong, right? She didn't play games!"

Elizabeth bequeathed Donald the notion of clean German blood. It's easy to imagine his grandmother insisting on his hand washing as a boy, while Mary was sick or busy with other children, her measured affection dependent upon his being neat and squared away, and instilling in him his clean-hands compulsion. Hygiene was in the blood, he thought. When the German documentary filmmaker showed him a photo of the Kallstadt house where his grandfather was born, the first thing he noticed was its cleanliness. "See how well maintained it is? Everything perfectly maintained." Later in the same interview he told of how he had been grand marshal of New York's Steuben Parade, a celebration of German heritage. "They say it's the only place where the streets are cleaner after it's finished. Every other parade it's a mess at the end. Well. That's a German trait."

That sensibility would shape his authoritarian political tendencies—order over chaos—and his lifestyle preference for home and habit over travel and experience. And it was key in his choices in and behavior with his own women—who had to be both publicly submissive and always hygienic and spotless. Elizabeth's example of competence and strength, however, had much to do with why, over the years, he was known to rely in a different way on certain women— schedulers, secretaries, an engineer, a high-level Trump Tower saleswoman. His unlikely ability to trust a small group of women—as opposed to the women he married and had sex with—has as much to do with the example of his grandmother as it does with his fear of his father—who had taught him that every other human was a natural predator and every engagement a zero-sum competition.

◇◇◇◇

When his grandmother died, Donald Trump was turning twenty and was already a tall, rich young bully, with a face like a Swedish architect crossed with Elvis Presley. He was a budding playboy, and his sleepy eyes and rosebud lips allowed him to present himself as irresistible to women. Trump was quite young when he intuited that having some hot female arm candy wasn't just cause for personal pleasure: in his estimation, it increased a man's status. Even as a teen he seemed to understand the competitive value of showing off a pretty date, and his all-male high school classmates voted him "Ladies' Man" in their senior yearbook.

He didn't lack confidence. In college, he asked the actress Candice Bergen out on a date. Bergen was already a blond celebrity, having starred in the 1966 film adaptation of Mary McCarthy's *The Group*, which touched on the then-verboten topic of lesbianism. They went to dinner once, according to her, although he has suggested they dated more frequently. She recalled that he was very fond of wearing the color burgundy at the time.

By the early 1970s, Donald was apprenticed to his father, learning lessons at the side of an utterly ruthless businessman whose primal motivation had always been keeping at bay the wolf of inefficiency and poverty that had terrified his mother. By the 1970s, Fred had built some ten thousand middle-income apartment units. His deals were mostly done in and for the New York area, but he became adept at taking advantage of federal government–backed mortgage housing programs that were juicing the postwar building boom.

A conservative, eventually a Goldwater Republican, Fred Trump understood power and how to use it to make money, cultivating connections to New York Democrats, including Abraham Beame, eventually New York's mayor; the powerful City Planning chief Robert Moses; and even an aspiring younger lawyer named Cuomo, future governor of New York whose son would be governor when Fred's own son Donald got elected president.

As his career progressed, Fred Trump made profitable use of these and many other lesser known New York politicos and fixers who could grease the regulatory wheels for him and fix him up with lucrative contracts. The connections paid off especially in the form of government financing for new home and apartment building. Fred Trump, with political cronies, turned several federal programs aimed at housing in Brooklyn into windfalls for himself. For this cleverness, in 1955, he got hauled to Washington to testify before a congressional committee about why he overcharged the government on a Federal Housing Authority project. In a hearing that made national news, Fred protested that what he had done was not illegal, and that he overcharged simply because he could, just like any smart businessman. He was called up again for overcharging the state of New York, on a similar scam. His answers before that committee in 1966 were so supercilious that the State Investigations Commission Chairman, Jacob Grumet, called Fred and his partner "grasping and greedy individuals" and asked state housing officials, in public, "Is there any way to prevent a man who does business like that from getting another contract with the state?"

The officials answered Grumet in the negative. "I don't think so under our present laws," one state auditor replied.

"Beyond the specific scams, the stench of criminal abuse hung over the entire insider network around the FHA, including those closest to Fred," Trump biographer Wayne Barrett wrote in his book *Trump: The Greatest Show on Earth: The Deals, The Downfall, The Reinvention*.

Fred's unscrupulous but not exactly illegal method of doing business became Donald's professional hallmark too. But he wasn't all Fred. From the beginning of his career, Donald was aiming at something more luxurious, something more Mary.

Donald would later say his version of the Vietnam War was dodging herpes in the disco years. Donald's running buddy was a legendary New York lawyer and evil genius named Roy Cohn, who built a career working for the dark side: the New York mafia, red-hunting Senator Joe McCarthy, and eventually Donald Trump. Cohn became the Trump family lawyer when Donald hired him to fight the Department of Justice case against his company for racially discriminatory practices at the Trump apartment complexes. Cohn fought the DOJ to a draw (the Trumps settled without admitting guilt), and Trump decided that the lawyer was "a total genius" who "would kill for somebody that he liked." And Cohn liked Trump. A lot. He (reluctantly, as he didn't want his studly friend to get married) wrote several draconian pre- and postnuptial marriage contracts for his protégé's first marriage, to a Czech immigrant named Ivana Zelníčková Winklmayr.

Like Trump's dad, Fred, Cohn was a dandy, always dressed impeccably in fine suits, silk ties, and matching pocket square. Unlike Fred, Cohn was gay. Like Fred, who was chauffeured around in a Cadillac with his initials on the plates, Cohn had a Rolls-Royce with ROY C on the vanity license plate. Unlike Fred, he trawled the clubs and bars of New York for young men, and it's quite possible that he took a more than paternalistic shine to the tall blond with the rosebud lips and the Queens rough edge. For his part, Donald Trump, fresh from Queens, not gay, regarded Cohn's look and style as the epitome of Manhattan sophistication. Donald soon made a uniform of the three-piece suit, sometimes in colors like maroon and light blue, always wore matching patent leather shoes, and got himself a Cadillac with DJT plates.

In some ways, Cohn might be considered the seventh woman in Trump's life. He loved to surround himself with straight men like young Donald, and Cohn's cousin once told a reporter that Cohn was in love with Trump. "Thwarted loves obsessed Roy Cohn's life," a lawyer who first met Cohn in the 1960s told *Vanity Fair* journalist Marie Brenner. "He would become sexually obsessed with cock-tease guys who would sense his need and not shun him. These were unrequited relationships. The way he would expiate the sexual energy was possessive mentoring. Introducing them to everyone in town and taking them places."

Together the two men cruised the city's hot spots, albeit seeking hookups with different genders. Their haunts included the 21 Club, Studio 54, the Four Seasons, and especially Le Club, a members-only restaurant-bar-discotheque packed with New York movers and slinky sylphs in Halston. At Le Club, Trump lived up to his high school "ladies' man" moniker and met older, powerful men who could help him move the outer-borough Trump Organization into Manhattan, where he had his eye on making his mark. At Le Club, he learned how to act around celebrities and royals too. Regulars at Le Club included Diana Ross, Al Pacino, and various Kennedys, including Jackie Onassis. Thirteen princes and four barons were on its membership rolls. The Maharaja of Jaipur and the Duke of Bedford were on the board of directors.

At Studio 54, Trump avoided the drugs, but not the debauchery. It's easy to imagine the sweaty outer-borough boy clad in his polyester maroon three pieces, observing with quivering awe. He would later say of the club: "I would watch supermodels getting screwed, well-known supermodels getting screwed, on a bench in the middle of the room. There were seven of them and each one was getting screwed by a different guy. This was in the middle of the room."

According to their oft-told love story, Trump first laid eyes on Ivana, and picked up a vibration in her energy that matched his, at another New York singles venue, where there was no public screwing— Maxwell's Plum. The establishment had opened in April 1966. It was decorated in the then-hip, and hippie, Victorian Art Nouveau style— leaded stained-glass ceilings, wall sconces, Tiffany lamps, ceramic and bronze animals. In its heyday it served more than twelve hundred customers a day, including celebrities like Cary Grant, Bill Blass, Barbra Streisand, and Warren Beatty. But its real claim to fame was as one of the first and most famous "singles bars" of the late sixties and seventies, and it was there that destiny found Donald.

In Ivana's memory, the night might not have happened at all, since she was exhausted from a day of walking around New York City in the July heat, falling in love not with a man, but the city. She was, she wrote in her memoir, "ready for air conditioning, room service and bed." But her fellow models "really wanted to go out and see the swinging seventies singles scene." And so they went out, hoping to catch a glimpse of a movie star like Warren Beatty, but nothing more. "I was living with George [her then-boyfriend], happy with my life, and not on the hunt for true love or a fling. Really I wasn't interested in anything but dinner."

The problem was, the young women didn't have a reservation, and as out-of-towners, they had no juice with the maître d', who took one look at them and decided to show the young women in miniskirts and heels to a central location at the bar—but not to a table. Ivana was hungry and annoyed. Then she felt a hand on her arm. "I spun around, ready to give the hand's owner the commie death stare, and found a tall, smiling, blue-eyed and handsome blond man."

With the disco beat of the Bee Gees and Diana Ross crooning "Love Hangover" as backdrop, she realized she was going to get a lot more than a bowl of chili and a hot dog at Maxwell's that night.

Ivana would later recall: "He said, 'I'm Donald Trump and I see you're looking for a table. I can help you.' I looked at my friends and said, 'The good news is, we're going to get a table real fast. The bad news is, this guy is going to be sitting with us.'"

After the meal, Donald paid the bill on the sly and disappeared.

"I said, 'There's something strange because I've never met a man who didn't want anything from a woman and paid for it,' " Ivana recalled. But when she walked outside, there was Donald, in the driver's seat of his own limousine. And he drove her home.

This athletic, foreign-born beauty would be different from the New York girls, who were, yes, beautiful but, as Donald would later remember, vain, crazy, or "phonies." They judged him and found him wanting. "I quickly found out that I couldn't take these girls back to my apartment because by their standards what I had was a disaster."

Fresh out of the Wharton School of Economics, where he had earned a degree that he later sneered at, he was still in his maroon three-piece suit and matching Cadillac phase. Women he found most desirable, especially the sophisticated chicks whom he had quickly identified as most desirable—the cool and connected Candice Bergen, for example—wouldn't give him the time of day. They recognized this sweaty, insecure real estate developer from Queens for what he was—a Cro-Magnon, not to the manor born.

But. For a woman from a gray slab of a Communist country, who had grown up around factory workers who rode public buses to and from work, and whose English was so bad that even her best friends in New York wouldn't be able to fully understand her for many years, the man in the three-piece suit who got her and her friends a table at Maxwell's Plum and then took them home in a shiny boat of a car was about as "all-American man" and sophisticated as it got.

For Donald, with this one, there would be no judgment. When she talked, her accent was vaguely familiar and deeply comforting; the same purring absence of the interdental fricative and the same Ws transformed into Vs echoed that of a primary caretaker, his German-born grandmother, blue-eyed Elizabeth. But best of all, this one appreciated what he had. From Communist Middle Europe and Canada, she didn't have the faintest notion of whatever it was that the New York sophisticates thought he lacked. In her eyes, he could be everything he thought he was, and was meant to be, not an unread, rich blowhard with a sweaty upper lip in patent leather shoes from the outer boroughs, forever looking in at the window of New York City's aristocracy of consciousness, but a *smooth operator, coast to coast.* This one didn't know Manhattan from Queens.

With this one, he could be king.

PART TWO

Ivana Marie Zelníčková, the First Wife

Donald's first wife was a leggy, blonde beauty born and raised in a closed Communist country during the Cold War, who grew up yearning for the branded luxuries she glimpsed on the other side of the Iron Curtain. An adored only child in a working-class family, fluent in Russian, speaking English with a purring Slavic accent, she was pretty enough to have been a real-life James Bond girl-villain. Queens boy Donald would probably never have visited Moscow the first time without her.

She was the first and only true partner in his life, the mother of his first three children. The failure of their marriage taught him that he couldn't partner with a woman unless he molded her himself.

CHAPTER 5

◇◇◇◇◇◇

A Girl in Gottwaldov

The land around Zlin is monochromatic, all fields and flat. There's the occasional farm, a knot of a village with a church spire. The farms end at shopping strips and then a glowing row of familiar logos—BMW, Audi, Mercedes—plus a billboard of a woman in black lingerie advertising a fat reduction procedure. None of these bear Ivana Trump's name, just her style, her ethos, her penchant for excess.

In Abraham Maslow's theory of human motivation, what he called the hierarchy of needs, the physiological needs come first. Food, shelter, and clothing are the foundation of the pyramid. Then, going up the triangle, the needs are safety, friendship and love, self-esteem, and at the peak, self-actualization, the ability to be your best self.

Zlin is a no-nonsense kind of town. It looks like any Midwestern town in America, populated with bored, practical people who toil sunless under a perma-cloud during long winters, people who don't try to outdo one another in style and don't put on fancy airs, a place where the egalitarian effect of Communist rule on society is still palpable. It was for a long, long time a town focused on providing the lowest rung of primary human needs. And for the decades when Ivana

Zelníčková was born and lived there, it produced the most foundational need of all—shoes.

Ivana left Zlin, then called Gottwaldov, decades before the luxury car dealerships popped up, long before she met Donald and gave birth to the children: Don Jr., Eric, and Ivanka. She left long before she metamorphosed into what her nine grandchildren call "Glam-ma," a self-described businesswoman and brand juggernaut who divides her time between Saint-Tropez and Manhattan, sometimes in clothing so beaded with crystal that she can't even walk.

Ivana Zelníčková was born eight weeks premature on a Sunday, February 20, 1949, into a country still struggling to get its bearings after German occupation in World War II, locked behind the Iron Curtain of Soviet influence, cut off from the West. Geopolitics had shifted into two superpower poles, and her birthplace was very close to the dividing line between them. When she was three months old, the Soviets detonated their first nuclear bomb, kicking off an arms race that would last decades, to the end of her first marriage. In her first years of life, tensions between East and West were acute. The Soviet blockade of Berlin had been in place since the prior summer, and allied planes were dropping tons of food and supplies into West Berlin. And when baby Ivana was still a frail preemie, inside the hospital, George Orwell published *1984*, the classic Western critique of totalitarian Communism, the political system into which the little girl had been born and would live into adulthood.

Ivana's mother, Marie, was a telephone operator and her father, Milos, was an electrical engineer, sometimes employed by Gottwaldov's signature industry at the great Bata shoe factory. She spent her formative years in a collectivist city in the grips of international socialist ideals. Education and medicine were free, and workers were paid more than managers. Everyone was legally required to have a job. In exchange for those amenities, Czechs accepted (some more willingly than others) an anti-materialistic lifestyle, the flattening of the social hierarchy, and the fact that no matter how hard one worked, it was impossible to climb financially, because the ladder no longer existed. Some—but not all—got used to the spartan creed, and did not crave the chocolates, fashions, and fancy cars available across the borders in Vienna and Italy. But many, Ivana included, were riveted by what they could sometimes glimpse—in smuggled magazines, or in the clothes and other luxuries flaunted by wealthy families of high Party officials.

In those days, Zlin was about as far away from power and luxury as was possible in Europe. It wasn't even called Zlin—after World War II, the Communists had renamed it Gottwaldov, honoring Klement Gottwald, the first Communist president of Czechoslovakia, a despised man who presided over a series of purges and show trials in the 1940s to cement power. He died in 1951, suffering from heart disease, syphilis, and alcoholism. But his name remained on Zlin until 1990, after the Soviet Union collapsed.

The Czech Communist government's ties to Russia were strong. The nation was key to Soviet geopolitical power in Europe. College was free and those who qualified—like Ivana—would have studied eleven years of compulsory Russian by the time they graduated.

There was no point to haute couture in Gottwaldov, rare was the fashion magazine. Coca-Cola was as much a luxury product as reserve Armagnac. For baby boomers like Ivana, there were no blue jeans and no rock and roll. Parents lined up for rationed meat, sewed clothes for their children, and made special treats of oranges, only available briefly, around Christmastime.

Still, people who grew up in Gottwaldov around the same time as Ivana don't recall childhoods of deprivation. They were happy—they knew nothing else. Without TV or radio, as one resident put it: "We were in our own world."

The collectivist ethos prevailed in schools and at work. In high school, Ivana Trump participated in annual work *brigadas* for teens, two-week trips to harvest crops or build playgrounds for the state for no pay, exercises to enhance communal spirit while learning in class about how the West was corrupted by capitalism. Authorities let students read a few Western writers with perceived socialist leanings, like Mark Twain, Zane Grey, and John Steinbeck, whose books were available in libraries. The local movie theater showed preapproved Western films, like *The Magnificent Seven*, to workers during their lunch hours.

The residents of Gottwaldov weren't entirely isolated, just cloistered from capitalism. Located in the middle of the former Czechoslovakia, the town became a key city to the larger Soviet Union. It was home to the international Bata shoe company and factory complex, an industrial giant founded in 1894 by a visionary entrepreneur who introduced the American conveyor-belt factory to Europe.

Tomáš Bat'a was a ninth-generation cobbler's son, and before Ivana Trump, he was Zlin's most famous resident. Bat'a founded what would become the world's largest shoe manufacturer, a global concern, first all over Europe and then in Asia. He also transformed the shoe factory town into an industrial utopia. He hired Le Corbusier's modernist architects from Paris to come to Zlin and build his notion of a "factory in a garden"—a planned town in which happy workers would be born, educated, work together in a decentralized management system, play together, and then retire, having raised families in the cube-shaped buildings made of brick and with open-structure design elements that matched the factory buildings themselves.

Ivana Trump grew up with her parents in one of the city's distinctive, cube-shaped "Bata houses," designed in the 1920s as futuristic Corbusier school experiments in family housing. Hundreds of these cubes still dot the hillsides around the town. Identical, divided vertically into four two-story duplexes with separate entrances, they were meant to house happy, healthy, and collective-minded workers. And they were built in the decades before Communism, by a man who remains a local hero.

Ivana's working-class parents' lives were shaped by Bat'a's philosophy and the changes he brought to the community. Bat'a dreamed of turning Zlin into a model factory city, where workers and managers socialized together. He built "Halls of Residence" for young men and women. The Bata School of Work and the Bata School of Work for Young Women aimed to produce factory workers "steered toward responsibility, economy, cooperation, obedience and healthy self confidence." The School of Work educated ten thousand people, and Ivana Zelníčková's father, an electrical engineer, was among them. Her parents met at one of the residence halls.

In 1932, Bat'a died in a plane crash taking off from a nearby town. When the Germans invaded Czechosolovakia, they requisitioned the company, and Zlin workers turned out millions of clogs for the Nazis—leather and other materials for more traditional shoes being in short supply. In 1945—four years before Ivana was born—Czech Communists nationalized Bata, and top managers were dismissed or their power reduced. But the pro-labor, collectivist traditions Bata had instituted provided fertile ground for Communist ideals.

Gottwaldov, with its huge factory, large population of workers, and central location, was an important hub in the larger Soviet world. The Hotel Moskva, a concrete Soviet-style behemoth with eerie, mint-green hallways, held pride of place on a hill overlooking the city, the headquarters of the local Communist Party. When Ivana lived there, Gottwaldov hosted conferences at the Moskva, and on the shoe factory grounds, every few months. Communist Party members and local shoe suppliers from far-flung regions of the Soviet Union would often attend. Throughout the 1950s, when Ivana was a Gottwaldov schoolgirl, citizens of the vast Soviet empire, from as far away as the Eurasian steppe, made pilgrimages to the city to trade rubles or barter local wares for bushels of shoes to take back to their remote towns. Some of the traders came from regions so desperate, size didn't even matter.

Today, books of Bat'a's sayings can still be picked up at the Bata Shoe Museum. "Work is a better friend to me than to many other less lucky people" is one of them. "Through my work I mostly put into practice my own ideas. Many other people carry out somebody else's instructions through their work. . . . My work is a service to life."

The men and women of Ivana's generation who grew up in Zlin and stayed there remember those Bat'a principles and the Soviet teachings, including the idea of dignity in labor. The sayings and lessons of their childhood years stuck, even as the system that taught them crumbled.

She has returned often to her home country over the years. But Ivana has had little use for paeans to the worker.

◇◇◇◇

It is possible today to meet people in Zlin, and even among the sophisticates of Prague, who are quite sure that Ivana Zelníčková escaped from Communist Czechoslovakia dramatically and illegally, skiing, like Matt Damon in *The Bourne Identity*, down an Alpine slope during a slalom race, and then, rather than stopping at the finish line, gliding over the Austrian border to freedom, evading a hail of Eastern Bloc bullets.

Ivana Trump came of age during the 1960s, when the desire to leave Czechoslovakia was overwhelming for young people who had started to see—thanks to increasing government laxity—what existed beyond the country's borders. As the decade wore on, Czechs became more aware of what was available in the West—a mere four-hour drive away, yet out of reach for people without hard currency. Only those favored by the regime got to travel abroad.

Sports was one way to gain that favor.

Czech Communists were proud of their sports stars and film stars, but those who defected disappeared from national news. Czech media reported on tennis star Martina Navratilova's every move until she left for the West in 1975, after which they didn't even cover Wimbledon. It was a little harder to erase film stars, but when director Milos Forman defected, he was persona non grata until he cut a deal to shoot the movie *Amadeus* in Prague in the 1980s, bringing millions in hard currency back to his home country.

Encouraged by her father and propelled by her own ambition, Ivana became a good skier as a child. Uphill from the Zelníčkovás' apartment, there was a little bunny hill with a jump, where local kids could practice. Her father and other parents formed a small ski club and gave the kids rudimentary training on the little hill and, on weekends, in the foothills of the Carpathian mountains to the east. A small band of parents and about a dozen kids, whose parents usually couldn't clock out of work until Saturday afternoon, took a bus two hours east that would drop them at the base of a mountain. From there, they hiked up in their homemade ski clothes, carrying the food and other supplies they needed for a weekend. The slopes were ungroomed, and the lift was a simple rope on a pulley that skiers attached themselves to by rudimentary hooks. "If you could ski there, you could ski anywhere," recalled one of the club members in Ivana's generation.

From those rude beginnings, Ivana distinguished herself enough—and her father used his connections—to get into a ski camp in Italy. The combined effect of that camp and the skiing weekends propelled her onto the Czech national ski team. In the late 1960s, the Czechs were not known for skiing. On the contrary, the Czech ski team was small and relatively poorly trained. No Eastern bloc steroid infusions, no hard-driving coaches, barely enough money for any gear, although they did get sponsorship from an Austrian brand at one point.

But by the time she got to college in Prague, her involvement in the little ski team had taken Ivana Zelníčková to Italy and Austria many times. She had grown intoxicated by the moneyed scent of the West, of the perfume, the varieties of chocolate, the luxury cars and clothes and hard currency. And although she only studied physical education, the lean, leggy beauty was cosmopolitan enough that she was soon embraced by Prague's hip, young, and mobile crowd.

Cold War historian Oldrich Tuma, roughly the same age as Ivana, was at Charles University during the same years. Sport, he recalled, was one of the ways to the West for young Czechs—even if it was only the lowly and underfunded national ski team. "In the 1960s, you needed an invitation to leave the country, because we had no hard currency. People in sports could get those invitations. But I still don't know why Ivana chose skiing, because it was rare for people here to make any successful career with it."

The slopes did lead to Ivana'a escape, although her dramatic Alpine defection is a piece of fiction she wrote years later in 1992, a novel called *For Love Alone*, which was made into an American television movie, and dubbed in Czech. The truth is that—just like countless immigrants to America—she pulled off a sham marriage to get herself an Austrian passport, by wedding Austrian skier Alfred Winklmayr. Winklmayr was a friend of her then-boyfriend, a fellow Czech ski-racer name George Syrovatka. Of Winklmayr, Ivana would later write: "Why did he go along with it? He was a friend and he wanted to make a noble gesture to help someone flee an oppressive regime." Fred, as Ivana calls him, came to Prague and married her in a government building, then went back to Austria. Her boyfriend George was at the wedding. On her wedding night, she even slept with him. He had gotten himself a passport through his well-connected family and was soon to leave for Canada. When he left shortly thereafter for Canada, the couple did not cry, because, Ivana wrote, "he was getting out! Instead, we celebrated his freedom."

Freedom, for young Ivana, meant *things*. "I was in awe of the beautiful things in Vienna," she wrote later. "The stylish clothes on the women walking down the street, stores selling books, furniture, art, musical instruments, hats, beautiful shoes, candy, chocolate, pretzels, beer. . . . For me, luxury was salt."

Like Mary MacLeod getting her first taste of posh inside the Carnegie mansion, Ivana Zelníčková was forever transfixed and transformed by her youthful brushes with the brands and lifestyle that had seemed out of reach to her as a child and young woman. Soon there would be no more need to choose sturdy Batas for her feet. Raised by utilitarians to be a model anti-materialistic girl, she would be forever helpless against the the lure of big shiny cars, jewels, fancy clothes, and champagne.

Luxury, for her, would never get old.

CHAPTER 6

◇◇◇◇◇◇

The Loves of Ivana's Life

Prague was and still is a fairy tale city of spires, crystal, marionettes, alchemy, and baroque architecture. In the late 1960s, when Ivana Zelníčková arrived as a lissome seventeen-year-old college student, the city was also a brewing revolt. And the center of resistance was Charles University. To have gotten there from Zlin was a further sign of her access and special situation. "If not for my grades and skiing I would never have been permitted to go there to study German and English," she wrote in her 2017 book, *Raising Trump*. Ivana, however, was not intellectual, and lots of brainier students were not accepted, suggesting that perhaps her connections were paying off in other ways besides border crossings to the West.

The months leading up to the 1968 revolt, the Prague Spring, were edgy and exciting. Ivana and friends listened to Western music and played and sang banned Czech nationalist songs. They gathered in cafes and at each other's apartments on the cobbled streets of the old city around the university, blaming the Communists for things like lack of toilet paper, sharing rumors and rare goodies like branded chocolates and blue jeans. Ivana even had enough money to buy herself a navy Fiat Cinquecento, the first of many snazzy little sports cars in her life. In her book she says the money came from Austrian ski company sponsors.

"Lots of things were in short supply if you were not a ranking member of the Communist Party," Cold War historian Tuma recalled of those years in Prague. "There were queues and shortages, but always the special cut of meat under the counter at the butcher's—for Party members. There were always two levels: If you knew someone in the Party, you could get anything. If not, you couldn't. Ivana might not have known she was privileged when she got sent outside, she might have thought she was simply 'better,' but her father probably had contacts."

The Prague Spring resistance was shut down brutally when the Soviets rolled in with tanks, arrests, and a show of force from armed forces all over the Warsaw Pact region. A pall fell on the city. In November 1971, Ivana got her Austrian passport, planning to get out. But then she met and fell in love with a dark-haired, dark-eyed, soulful, slightly chubby songwriter named Jiri Staidl. Staidl wrote tunes and lyrics for Karel Gott, a popular music star with fans not just in Czechoslovakia, but all over Europe. Staidl had founded his own musical theater, the Apollo, in 1965, and when Ivana met him, he was twenty-eight and a young star on the Prague arts scene. Besides songwriting, he was collaborating with other young Czech actors and composers in an ensemble called Karlins Cultural Cabaret. He wrote short stories to be performed at the cabaret, and left, when he died in 1973, two hundred original song lyrics performed by a number of pop singers. He also transformed Western songs into Czech tunes, like his version of "What's New Pussycat?" called "Zofie." He has racked up thirty-four soundtrack credits on films—posthumously.

Staidl was a ladies' man, and had a thing for sporty young women. Before Ivana, one of his great romances had been with a figure skater named Hana Moskova. Besides his soulful, artistic appeal, Staidl was more famous than any of his girlfriends, a real star. The combination of his celebrity and romantic style made him irresistible. Ivana was smitten. "He was talented and sweet and he made me laugh," she wrote in her memoir. "We were deeply in love, and I became his muse. While I studied, he'd be at the typewriter. From the other room, I'd hear tap, tap, tap, and I knew he'd found the words for a new song, probably about me."

Ivana was in her prime, tall, confident, and already more well traveled than the average Czech girl. As Staidl's girlfriend, the girl from the provinces gained added cachet and entrée to Prague's cool crowd. Like her, many of the young men and women in that fashionable and Bohemian set had some limited access to the West. And like her, because of that access and because of their politics, they were watched and infiltrated by members of the Czech Secret Police.

From that point on, if not before, Ivana was on the Czech—and therefore the larger Soviet spy network's—radar. She would remain of interest until the USSR crumbled, possibly even longer.

In August 1973, she dissolved her sham marriage to the Austrian, partly because she wanted to marry the love of her life. The marriage had served its purpose: she had the Austrian passport. And nobody got his feelings hurt, except maybe George, the boyfriend waiting in Canada. Now Ivana was in no hurry to leave.

In October, Staidl died in a car accident. "I was devastated, just destroyed," she wrote, more than forty years later. "The man who had made my life a song, who had made life living under communism bearable, was now gone. I'd lost my love in a moment."

The tragedy was a turning point. After going home to grieve with her parents, she returned to Prague to finish her degree, then packed up and left Czechoslovakia for Canada, where loyal ex-boyfriend George was waiting. But she never forgot Jiri. Forty-four years later, after three kids, four marriages, and divorced from the President of the United States, she grieves him. "Even after all these years, recalling that time is deeply upsetting," she wrote in 2017. She has sent flowers to his grave on the anniversary of his death every single year since.

◇◇◇◇

In Montreal, Ivana moved in with George Syrovatka, the skiing boyfriend who had set her up with the Austrian passport marriage. But now, with her freshly grieving over the soulful Jiri, her relationship with George was more friendly than passionate. He helped her make contacts, and get jobs, first as a ski instructor. She cut a striking figure on the Green Mountains, shivering in what she called "a skimpy ski suit, with a sleek jacket and tights underneath the pants," an ensemble she habitually chose over warmer options because "I don't participate in sport if I don't look elegant."

In Montreal she also learned the basics of modeling, in a designer's showroom. The training left her with a lifetime habit of posing with one leg forward, toe pointed out, for photographs, but she was never the "top model" in Montreal that her future husband would claim she was. Strutting her stuff as a showroom model for department store buyers and in ads for a local furrier, she did make decent money, though, enough to buy herself one of the Italian sports cars she liked, this time a Fiat X1/9. She and George, whose ambitions ran no higher than running a ski and bike shop, lived together without great passion, no marriage on the horizon, just passing the time.

And that was her situation in the summer of 1976, when she was sent, along with a group of models, to New York City, for an advertising shoot related to the Olympic Summer Games, which were to be held in Quebec that year.

After their encounter at Maxwell's Plum, Donald pursued Ivana with the same confidence and single-minded determination that he applied to New York real estate. He called every other day after she got home, even though she was still living with George. He jetted up to Montreal and arrived unannounced at one of her fashion shows. He sent roses and notes and clippings from newspapers—about himself. "During my years as a model, I'd had my pick of wealthy men, and they'd all left me cold with their entitlement and superior attitudes." But Trump, to her way of thinking, was more of a regular guy. "Donald liked simple food and simple pleasures."

Back in New York, Donald was busy rewriting his new love's already somewhat altered history to fit his own purposes. "She moved to Montreal and very quickly became one of the top models in Canada," he would insist. Before long, he had moved her up to Olympic-level skier too. He enveloped the pretty Czech immigrant in a warm nest of all-American advertising hyperbole. It felt pretty great.

Donald's endearments reached a pitch when he called Ivana, still living with her boyfriend, just before Christmas and suggested a vacation together. "Beach or mountains?" She chose snow at altitude, and he made arrangements for a week in Aspen, at "a very sexy chalet" with mirrored ceilings, a fireplace, and "a chinchilla throw on the bed," she recalled.

A scene worthy of a 1970s Riunite commercial ensued, a couple locking eyes before a fireplace, seen through a Vaselined lens. On New Year's Eve, in the sexy chalet, after knowing her for six months, Donald proposed, with a relatively meager—for him—two-carat diamond ring.

He explained the deal. "If you don't marry me, you'll ruin your life."

Ivana thought about how she was about to turn twenty-eight, and how much she wanted children, and replied, according to her, "My life is saved. I'll marry you."

Later she would say it was all about their shared "energy"— a chemistry fantasy of mutual specialness that each of his three wives would eventually lay claim to, and in almost the same language. "We had the same kind of energy and drive," Ivana said. "Not a lot of people are like us, and we recognize those qualities in each other."

Back in New York, Trump's request for a prenup dampened the romantic heat and almost derailed the wedding. Roy Cohn didn't think marriage was a great idea for his young protégé, but couldn't step in to stop it. He could, however, insist that Donald protect himself and make the bride sign a prenuptial agreement. Cohn then wrote one with such draconian terms, including the demand that she give back any gifts in the event of a divorce, that Ivana was furious, and stormed off. Donald soon relented, agreeing to let her keep his gifts, plus throwing in what she called a "rainy day" fund of $100,000, basically mad money.

Ivana was more put off by the contract than by her first experience of the Trump family. Fred Trump took the newly betrothed out to brunch with the rest of the family at Tavern on the Green in Central Park. The waiter took orders and one after another of the Trumps ordered steak.

Ivana decided on the fish.

That didn't sit well with Fred, who corrected her and told the waiter, "No, she'll have the steak." She ignored him, and ordered the sole. The table was "dead silent"—apparently no one in the family disagreed with Fred.

She stood her ground, to Fred's evident disapproval, but afterward Donald harangued her over it.

As time went on, she and Fred Trump came to a kind of grudging truce, but he never got over his new daughter-in-law's "cleavage-baring, sleeveless" dresses that she said "showed off my décolleté and a lot of leg."

Mary, on the other hand, was "kind and patient," Ivana recalled. She and her mother-in-law hit it off. "Mary . . . was a doll. She had a charming Scottish accent and the biggest heart in the world. She raised her five children by herself in their Queens home without the help of nannies, housekeepers or cooks." In fact, the Trumps had had an Irish nanny. "I have no idea," Ivana continued, "how she did it. . . .

Like my mother, Mary was sustained and supported by the obvious love and affection of her husband and the devotion of her children."

Ivana and Donald were married on April 7, 1977, at the Marble Collegiate Church on Fifth Avenue, where the Trump family had been parishioners, listening to the self-help and prosperity gospel of best-selling author Norman Vincent Peale, who presided over the wedding. The Trump women—mother Mary and Donald's sisters, Maryanne and Elizabeth—had planned it, without much input from the bride, whose English was still not sufficiently understandable. The church was filled with the scent of Easter lilies, and six hundred Trump family friends, dignitaries, and business associates, people like New York mayor Abraham Beame, filled the pews.

Ivana's parents couldn't afford two tickets to fly over to New York from Gottwaldov, and Ivana was too embarrassed to ask Donald to pay for them, so her mother, Marie, didn't see her only daughter, a shy bride in calf-length white chiffon and a veil, or sense the loneliness and fear that two of Ivana's Canadian friends—among the bride's few wedding guests besides her father, Milos—noticed.

After the ceremony, the party retired to a sit-down dinner around the corner at the 21 Club. The wedding, by Trump standards, was relatively spartan. Before a year was out, Ivana's new New York friends would tease her about the size of the tiny engagement diamond. She didn't care. She was in love. They honeymooned in Acapulco, but it lasted only two days because Donald had to get back to a pending deal in New York, converting a derelict hotel at Grand Central into the Grand Hyatt.

Nine months later, Donald Junior arrived, on New Year's Eve 1978. The family joke is that he was birthed early, for tax purposes.

◇◇◇◇

When Donald first brought Ivana to New York, she could barely speak English. One of the first friends she made was a gal about town named Nikki Haskell, who went on to become a celebrity interviewer, diet pill entrepreneur, and all-around fabulous, bicoastal character. They met while Ivana and Donald were having dinner at Elaine's, and Haskell soon set about introducing Ivana to the customs of the city.

Ivana now calls her "ladies who lunch period" very brief. But in fact, those ladies and those lunches taught the newcomer how Manhattan women of a certain age and income level lived as the eighties dawned. "I was part of the socialite circle of women who met for grilled radicchio and shaved fennel salads to gossip and drink all day. Problem: I was never much of a drinker [this statement is something of a stretch]. A glass or two of wine with dinner is fine, but martinis in the afternoon? Not for me."

The lunching ladies became her tutors. They introduced her to the philanthropic circuit, where she developed a look—big blond hair, big puffy ball gowns by Arnold Scaasi—that came to epitomize the Reagan years. Donald stood aloof, outside this charmed circle, but her access to it was added brand value for him, and she worked to alter his look to better fit in. She got him to wear ties that matched her dresses, and took him shopping once or twice a year to replace his maroon polyester with Italian suits.

They were, for a while, an effective team. He got richer, and her Barbie-doll big hair became a New York City eighties icon as she grabbed seats on charity boards. She thought of herself as primarily a wife and mother, and called herself a traditional "European wife. . . . I don't mind that Donald is the boss. I like it that way. I have to have a strong man. . . . This is why most feminists aren't married and have no children. I like to have both."

But the core of Ivana's lunching ladies was a quartet of connected, wealthy working women who had a regular table at Le Cirque, an Upper East Side institution that made *pasta primavera* famous, but where the cuisine came second to the scene. At the table, Ivana was quite unlike the three working women, whose husbands came second, or who were on their second husbands.

"She wasn't trying to do it all," recalled one friend. "She was a sweet lady. There was nothing tough about her at all, a soft lady. The most important thing to Ivana was raising her children correctly. All she did was talk about children."

Soon enough, though, Ivana's competitive streak kicked in. She decided that she wanted to be more like her three friends, women who worked. "She wanted to be a businesswoman in the Trump Tower and she got her dream, which was to decorate the Plaza Hotel across the street," which she did after first running a Trump hotel in Atlantic City, the friend said. "Now she had a staff and we would come up and meet her. Now she was equal to us, she's a businesswoman. I think she probably wanted to be like her girlfriends."

CHAPTER 7

◇◇◇◇◇◇

A European Wife

You can bring home the bacon. Fry it up in a pan. And
never let him forget he's a man! Because you're a woman!
—ENJOLI PERFUME AD, 1978

The second wave of feminism, like the revolution, would be branded
too. When Ivana came to New York, the Enjoli television jingle was becoming iconic: a woman came home and metamorphosed from office
drone to hotness. Soon, that would give way to the era of shoulder pads.
Man suits. Big hair. Newly empowered women could have it all: motherhood, sex, fashion, and even—if they beat out the other woman—
corporate power, like whispery Melanie Griffith as the working-class
stockbroker's secretary who sweetly slays the bitchy career woman and
ends up with a corner office in *Working Girl.* As Ivana came of age as
a professional woman in New York, Hollywood was starting to weave
a certain working woman trope into stories. By the late 1980s, Americans were lining up to see *Working Girl*, Glenn Close's psycho single
woman in *Fatal Attraction*, and Julia Roberts as Richard Gere's favorite
hooker in *Pretty Woman*, all navigating a new version of the Madonna/
whore paradigm, except that they were also expected to—and expected
themselves to—work like men.

Donald Trump responded to the post-feminist era through his own sexist lens: he saw a new and eager sector of the labor market to exploit. He did hire women. He put a female engineer—extremely rare in those days—in charge of construction at Trump Tower.

But Donald Trump was no feminist.

"He hired me for a specific reason: Because I was really good," Trump Organization engineer Barbara Res would later say. "And he told me, and he believed this, that women had to be smarter and more willing to work harder than men."

Donald Trump would say to Res: "Men are better than women, but a good woman is better than ten men." Res thought he meant it as a compliment, and that's how she took it.

Ivana started out doing little things inside their house. She dove into decorating their apartment. She had experimented with decorating up in Canada, while living with her bicycle-and-ski-shop boyfriend, and produced some results in dubious taste, like covering one wall at his family's retreat with fake bricks (which they removed as soon as she left). In New York, she favored décor that was expensive but slightly bizarre, including a set of hardened goatskin-covered coffee tables, another table made of bone. She also had a comfy-cozy zone: she strung a hammock in front of the large window overlooking Central Park.

Her small duties might have stayed that way had hers been a regular, bite-sized woman's life in a regular town in America. But married to The Donald, as she had taken to calling him to the delight of the New York media now sniffing around behind this dashing duo, and associating with high-powered women in shoulder pads, her interior design duties grew big, bigger, biggest.

After she had decorated their apartment at Olympic Tower, Donald decided (after getting jealous of gunrunner Adnan Khashoggi's palatial pad in a nearby building) that he wanted something much less cozy. He hired a decorator who designed lobbies and high-roller suites in Vegas and Atlantic City, who kitted out the Trump family apartment in a look that Donald found *classy*—gilt, mirrors, canopies—the faux-royal style that became the Trump signature look. Ivana was an eager participant. "If something could be leafed in gold or upholstered with damask, it was. Italian marble? I bought a mountain's worth," she wrote in her memoir.

"That gold look is all her," a lunching pal recalled. "That European look, like a palace. That European gold." It was only partly true. Ivana didn't exactly mind the royal trappings, the gold moldings, Czechoslovakian crystal chandeliers, the canopy bed with cherubs painted on the roof, and the twelve-foot waterfall in the living room. But she hadn't brought them all in. Not yet.

Ivana's best-known Trump job is the interior of Trump Tower. Donald bought the Fifth Avenue site next to Tiffany & Co. two years after they married, and by 1983, the lobby and atrium shops were open for business. Before they opened, Donald dispatched his wife to Italy, where she selected slabs of distinctive *breccia pernice* pink-brown marble for the atrium, initially suggested by their architect for its quality of being "conducive to shopping."

She soon discovered she had a knack for the exacting standard and a native talent for managing minions—especially the many who wouldn't talk back to the boss's wife. What she didn't know, she learned on the job. Engineer Barbara Res, who went with her to Italy, recalled that Ivana would walk up to the wall of marble in the quarry and put her hands around a small piece and say, "I want this." The contractors and marble experts would have to explain to her that it was impossible to get tons of just that, that marble changed and looked different every few inches. Later, she took credit for picking the best bits and returned to New York with a wall of marble that Donald fell in love with at first sight. In her account, she found the bits while picking her way around the quarry in stiletto heels, like a rare blond mountain goat.

She distinguished herself as a manager early on, showing up at jobsites, ordering contractors to redo jobs to her specifications. A story she and Ivanka both tell is about how, while she was pregnant with Donald Jr., she went daily to the worksite of Trump's first big Manhattan project, the Grand Hyatt, running the crews ragged with her requests. The hardhats waited eagerly for her delivery date, assuming that she would retreat into the nursery for good. Instead, she was back on the site a few days after giving birth.

The glass skin and sawtooth silhouette of Trump Tower was incongruent with the nineteenth-century limestone-and-granite buildings on Fifth Avenue when Trump and his architects designed it. It was, Trump boasted in his book *The Art of the Deal*, "a building the critics were skeptical about . . . but which the public obviously liked. It pleases the public. I'm not talking about the sort of person who inherited money 175 years ago and lives on 84th Street and Park Avenue. I'm talking about the wealthy Italian with the beautiful wife and the red Ferrari. Those people—the audience I was after—came to Trump Tower in droves."

She didn't know it then, but Donald's description of his ideal "audience"—Italian men with hot babes and red Ferraris—would become a leitmotif in Ivana's future life.

By the mid-eighties, Donald Trump had expanded from Manhattan development into the casino business in Atlantic City. In 1985, he bought a Hilton hotel for $320 million, renamed it Trump Castle Hotel and Casino, and put Ivana in charge of running it. By 1986, with three children under age ten at home, she was spending the entire workweek in Atlantic City, putting in fourteen-hour days. She commuted to Atlantic City in a helicopter Trump had named the *Ivana* (and which was sometimes piloted by a drug-dealer named Joey Weichselbaum, who allegedly supplied the casino high rollers with whatever they needed).

She supervised both the casino hotel's reconstruction and the interior design and eventually comanaged the project. During her three years as CEO of Trump Castle she made a name for herself as a serious, capable businesswoman, winning awards and overseeing a staff of thousands.

In 1988, Trump bought the Plaza Hotel, a National Landmark and storied French Renaissance building anchoring the southeastern base of Central Park, for $400 million. He named Ivana president of the Plaza Hotel and vice president of interior design for the Trump Organization, and put her in charge of the hotel's $50 million renovation. She took that job so seriously that she would spy on the Plaza front steps through binoculars from her perch in the Trump triplex a kitty-corner block away, to make sure doormen were always on high alert and no trash was blowing around. Under her leadership, the Plaza was recognized as "The Best Luxury Hotel in the USA."

Even as he promoted his wife, Donald undermined her. "I pay her a salary of one dollar a year and all the dresses she can buy," Donald famously joked to a reporter shortly after he named her president of the Plaza Hotel.

By the late 1980s, Ivana had been responsible for the interior design of all of Trump's major real estate: the Grand Hyatt Hotel at Grand Central in Manhattan, Trump Tower, the Trump Plaza Hotel and Casino in Atlantic City. In 1988, a *New York Post* writer suggested Ivana was "the woman beside and not behind the man."

In a January 1989 interview for a *Time* cover story on Trump (a real *Time* cover, not the ones he used to decorate his golf clubs) Ivana seemed to believe in the hype. She could have it all—loving rich husband, kids, and a powerful job. "If Donald were married to a lady who didn't work and make certain contributions, he would be gone."

The lunching ladies quartet were bemused and delighted by their friend's transformation. Ivana was now the complete executive, a feminine Donald. "She had a team and an office and assistants and these outfits—daywear Chanel, stunning—and she would wear major jewelry with her outfits." No longer was Ivana just a professional woman who, at the beginning, would wear the same business suit three days in a row, like a no-nonsense working woman from Czechoslovakia. She was bigger than that.

◇◇◇◇

At that moment, Ivana, the Icarus of yuppie mother-wives, was at the apex of her orbit, and failing to notice the warmth on her wax wings. She thought she and The Donald were soaring together, on their dual, force-multiplied, fabulous mutual energy. "I think what attracts us so much together is not only the love and all that stuff, it's the energy," she would say later in an interview. "That fabulous energy. You see people who are doers, they have this energy, this life, this spark. It's a part of Donald that that energy gets from one person to another. He's just a great leader the way he motivates people."

Ivana believed she was on her way to becoming an equal partner to Donald in leadership and motivation, and in terms of energy. For a decade she had helped build him, and bore him three of the five children he said he wanted (to ensure that one "turned out like me"). And she was not wrong. "Ivana really was a partner and really helped build up Trump," one of their friends recalled. "She was a working mother, a working partner, she wasn't just a trophy wife who did nothing. She was on that helicopter to Atlantic City, she was in those buildings, she was building and decorating the Plaza, no matter what you think of it—how she did it. She was part of creating that empire, and I'm not sure she got all the money she deserved, all the deals she deserved."

Meanwhile, Donald saw it differently. In 1988, he told Oprah, "There's not a lot of disagreement because, ultimately, Ivana does exactly as I tell her to do."

By 1989, there were ominous signs. Ivana was no longer acting like a "European wife." Obviously, Trump had never thought to investigate whether such a creature actually existed in the egalitarian society where she was raised. At home, the stressed-out and multitasking yuppie mother was losing the "softness" that Donald would later say had attracted him to her in the first place. Instead, Donald would come home from his office and find her on the phone "screaming" at employees, at the very hour when all he wanted was meat and potatoes and a soft wife.

When Ivana teased him for being a "male chauvinist," everybody laughed. But behind the scenes, she was not laughing. Trump's female engineer, Barbara Res, came to Ivana's office at the Plaza to discuss a problem she was having with Donald in the late 1980s. To her surprise, Ivana burst into tears.

"She tells me that I don't know what it's like. 'I have to be with him twenty-four hours a day,'" Res recalled Ivana saying, through tears. "I felt so sorry for her."

Trump would later write, in his second best-seller, *The Art of the Comeback*, long after his marriage was over: "My big mistake with Ivana was taking her out of the role of wife and allowing her to run one of my casinos in Atlantic City, then the Plaza Hotel." He would repeat versions of that many times over the years, advising men that putting their wives to work was a bad idea, earning the loathing of feminist America, itself a badge of honor among his political base.

"Behind every successful woman, there is a man in shock," Ivana Trump wrote about her fifteen-year marriage in her 2017 book.

That perspective, needless to say, Trump did not and does not now share.

◇◇◇◇

In the 1980s, the rich were trying to be even more different from you and me than they were when F. Scott Fitzgerald first remarked on the difference. Old money traditionally tried to blend in, and, if possible, disappear behind the great hedges. It adhered to the goal of having one's name in the newspapers exactly three times: birth, marriage, and death. The Trumps of Fifth Avenue threw out that rulebook. To go a week without appearing in the news was dispiriting.

They came of age socially and professionally during the Reagan years, when bank deregulation unleashed the first great wave of Wall Street barbarians, rough sons of builders, merchants, and quants who had studied engineering and economics and had gotten unimaginably rich thanks to the new rules, men for whom money was not just the coin of the realm, but the ultimate raison d'être. These Midases amassed piles of money, sums previously unimaginable, sums that dwarfed the trust funds. And they flaunted it. Cash and what it could buy were not about pleasure and enjoyment but about winning, about who had more. They took seriously the adage "the difference between the men and the boys is the price of their toys."

The old guard sniffed, looked aghast, and then tried to figure out how to rope these new beasts into service at their favorite charities. The new generation of rich redefined "classy," and if old money was horrified, it didn't have the street smarts to do anything about it.

At this point in his life, Trump was well on his way to becoming Oscar Wilde's definition of a cynic, the man who knew the price of everything and the value of nothing. Trump understood the value of many things—mansions, boats, people—but only in terms of how much they could impress other people and bolster his sense of self-worth.

When he bought the Plaza in 1988 for about $400 million (equivalent to about $800 million today), he placed a full-page open letter in the *New York Times* to boast about it, stating, "I haven't purchased a building, I have purchased a masterpiece—the *Mona Lisa*. For the first time in my life, I have knowingly made a deal that was not economic—for I can never justify the price I paid, no matter how successful the Plaza becomes."

Rather than own things for pleasure, Trump acquired things—and women too—for effect. Economist Thorsten Veblen during the Gilded Age—1870 to 1900—gave the name "conspicuous consumption" to the habits of the American business titans before Trump, who displayed social status with money like dogs leaving their gilded mark on expensive fire hydrants.

The traditional ultimate status symbol was the yacht. The Andrew Carnegies had been Yacht People, a century before Trump, sailing in Florida and off the coast of Scotland at the turn of the century. The lower classes admired their lifestyles; the way in which these people enjoyed and took pleasure from the world was an ideal to which to aspire.

The new Yacht People were different. Donald Trump took no pleasure in his yacht, or any of his gorgeous homes, or perhaps even in the gorgeous women he took out. They were just settings and props and extras. He was competing with a small group of other men, similarly immune to finding enjoyment in the fruits of success, over whose toys were bigger.

While he was married to Ivana, Trump's toys were among the biggest. He had a huge black French-made military helicopter with red lettering on the side—"TRUMP"—that could travel 180 miles per hour and for which Donald had paid $2 million. He had a private Boeing 727, also kitted out with the Trump name, and finally, he had a yacht he renamed from its Arab name to *Trump Princess*. "A certain level of quality" was how Trump described Adnan Khashoggi's 281-foot yacht *Nabila*, the one he bought in 1987 for $29 million and renamed.

But he never sampled that quality. He avoids sun, and doesn't do ocean swimming (according to porn star Stormy Daniels, he's terrified

of sharks). He really had no use for the yacht. He admitted as much
when he bought it. "I'm not exactly into them. I've been on friends'
boats before and couldn't get off fast enough."

In pictures with Ivana on the *Princess*, Donald looks posed and
like he can't wait to get back to his desk. He called the boat "the ultimate toy." It fell to Ivana to actually enjoy it, which she did, inviting
her girlfriends on floats to Miami and hosting parties on the yacht.
She designed a nifty crest for it, two griffons bearing her initials, to
emboss on invitations to parties on the boat.

Besides the yacht, Trump bought himself another upper-crust
badge, a Florida mansion built in the 1920s by cereal heiress Marjorie
Merriweather Post. Mar-a-Lago was a tropical Kubla Khan on seventeen acres, bounded by the ocean on one side and the Intracoastal
Waterway on the other, prime Palm Beach real estate. It boasted 118
rooms, crystal chandeliers, gold leaf, tons of marble, and tens of thousands of square feet of carved stone. When Post died in 1973, she
deeded the mansion and grounds to the federal government, imagin-
ing it as a winter White House. But the federal government couldn't
afford to keep it up, and the family had put it on the market. Trump
snapped it up for less than $10 million.

Mar-a-Lago is worth $200 to $300 million today.

Trump set about turning it into a private club, a moneymaking
proposition, infuriating the old moneyed WASPs who lived nearby
and who already had their own private playground, the Palm Beach
Bath and Tennis Club (or B&T as the initiates called it), to which the
Trumps were not invited. Asked about it, Trump hissed, "They kiss
my ass in Palm Beach," according to biographer Wayne Barrett.

When Trump turned the Mar-a-Lago grounds into a golf course,
and transformed part of the residence into a club and spa with initia-
tion fees of $100,000 and annual dues of $14,000, the Palm Beach
Town Council tried to limit membership, party attendance, and photography. Trump fought back against most of the restrictions, and

won, partly by shaming his neighbors and their club with accusations that they refused membership to blacks and Jews (true).

The Trump family assault on high society, from Palm Beach to New York, along with the rise of unprecedented stashes of new money, changed everything. Before Donald came along, New York society consisted of people whose status was defined by blood, philanthropy, aristocracy of consciousness, refined sensibility, and then, of course, money. The Trumps ushered in a new age, in which absolutely nothing but money mattered. In just one decade, the old guard went down.

They were already on the way out, but didn't know it, in 1987, when Ivana Trump answered the door for a *Town & Country* photo shoot at Mar-a-Lago in head-to-toe sequins. Her decorating and sartorial style, she would later write, "was how Louis XVI would have lived if he had had money." Trump's more traditionally Waspy and reclusive younger brother, Robert, once left a Manhattan dinner party early during the 1980s as his older brother and his sister-in-law were ascendant, joking that he "had to go home and watch *Dynasty* to learn how to act."

What was happening was that old money was growing thin, and its accounts couldn't match what the corporate raiders of the Reagan era were piling up. Out went the noblesse oblige, out the seclusion of wealth behind the hedge. And in came a new marker of status, one that the old guard considered grubby.

"I mistakenly viewed the Trumps when they came to my attention in the early '80s as a joke," the late columnist Liz Smith recalled. "I liked them okay. He used sports to impress people, introducing them to real celebrities like Muhammad Ali or Don King. And I assumed they wanted to break into what tattered remnants were left of what we call *quiet society*, people like Mrs. Astor and the Rockefellers, people who not only had money but prestige. I think I was mistaken about that. The Trumps were just all out for what they could get."

What they could, and did, get was not the respect of old money. They got a brand. A brand that could be leveraged to sell more and more things, until finally, it sold a flawed man to the American public.

And Ivana Trump was very much part of building that brand.

"The jet set, cafe society, loved her," said R. Couri Hay, another longtime New York Trump-watcher. "She was an outsider in Palm Beach because she's too flashy. She was and is Ivana—international, flashy, and it's new money. And she chose to work, she didn't just decide to be a gala member of the grand ballroom set. She wasn't Annette de la Renta, she wasn't Anne Bass, she wasn't Nan Kempner, she wasn't Mrs. Buckley, she certainly wasn't Mrs. Onassis or Bunny Mellon. She was in a flashier jet set group."

As for Donald, he always professed that he didn't care about old money, but he said it so often, and used the word "classy" so frequently, that it was a case of him protesting too much. Whether he was at his tropical estate or on his own yacht, there was Mary Anne MacLeod, fisherman's daughter, looking in at the castle window. The yearning was, of course, unresolved, not even with gold fixtures on his personal jet, not even with the finest marble, not even with the European artisans painting cherubs above his canopied, kingly bed. The girl in muck boots was still outside the window. And he was with her.

"Marrying Ivana didn't suddenly put him in society," said Hay. "I think in Palm Beach she probably had a hard time because Trump had a hard time. There's a certain group that likes Donald and there's a certain Waspy group that doesn't like Donald. He's flashy, he's pushy, he wants to get things done, he breaks rules, he upsets people. He's not trying to get on the Social Register."

After the Trumps bought Mar-a-Lago, snickering grandees who deigned to accept their invitations recoiled at a table garishly decorated with a giant silver bowl spilling plastic fruit. Donald sat at the head, clad in a New York City business suit, rather than the pale linens and espadrilles of the B&T set. Guests ate the meat and potatoes that Donald liked, and were forced to get up and give little speeches about themselves, Ivana's experiments in hostessing that participants likened to being in a boardroom or at a marketing convention.

Mar-a-Lago also gave Donald access to a bit of regal paraphernalia that his mother, Mary had forever admired—a family coat of arms. In 1939, British authorities granted a family crest to Marjorie Merriweather Post's third husband, Joseph Edward Davies. The crest is decorated with three rampant lions and two chevrons on a shield, a hand holding an arrow, and the word "Integritas." Without consulting heraldic authorities, the Trump Organization took possession of the crest, switching in the word "Trump" for integritas, while retaining the rampant lions and chevrons. The British, for whom these insignia actually signify, declined Trump's trademark request. The Scottish coat of arms authorities were even more strict and refused to allow it to be displayed on Trump's Scottish golf courses. Nonetheless, Trump trademarked the emblem in the United States, and it can now be found on golf courses and other Trump products (including, for a while, Trump University) across the land.

Ivana knew the Trump clan were laughed at, but she maintained her dignity, smiling on outdoor receiving lines, using every ounce of her athletic training to balance on her tiptoes so that stilettos didn't get stuck in the Florida muck.

"In 50 years . . . Donald and I will be considered old money, like the Vanderbilts," Ivana once told one of her guests at Mar-a-Lago, the writer Dominick Dunne.

Another time, she said to a reporter, "In 50 years, we will be the Rockefellers."

And so it would come to pass, and before fifty years had gone by.

◇◇◇◇

On October 30, 1981, Ivana Trump gave birth to her second child and only daughter, and she named the girl after herself. It was a Friday, the day before Halloween. The trees in Central Park were gold and red in the customary glorious, autumn in New York. The moon was in a waxing crescent phase and radio listeners were hearing a lot of the super-schmaltzy hit song "Arthur's Theme (Best That You Can Do)" with its catchy line, "If you get caught between the moon and New York City/The best that you can do/Is fall in love." Two days prior to the baby's delivery, the LA Dodgers had snatched the World Series championship from the Yankees at the sixth game in New York.

The baby's eyes opened into a world where her parents were already a pair of New York media fixtures. Donald's antics were catnip to journalists, and Ivana was starting to believe her own PR. Some of it was good: the family was riding a wave that hadn't crested yet. Donald's $100 million renovation of the Grand Hyatt Hotel near Grand Central had opened a year prior, a massive success. He was building a new glass-and-steel tower that would plant the family name on Fifth Avenue, next to Tiffany's.

Some of the press was bad: behind the scenes, he was mounting a nasty war against hundreds of retired and elderly tenants in rent-controlled apartments in a building he'd purchased that summer on Central Park South, and which he was planning to demolish. Before the baby girl was ten, the family would be mired in bad press, their name a national joke.

Ivana brought the little girl she would call Ivanka—the Slavic baby derivative of her own name—back to a glitzy apartment kitted out to match the one owned by a Saudi billionaire gunrunner. There Ivanka joined her four-years-older brother, Donald Jr., and an Irish nanny named Bridget.

While Ivana climbed the ranks at the Trump Organization, multi-tasking on the charity circuit, overseeing thousands of casino employees, commuting to Atlantic City, and bearing one more child, Eric, Bridget served as little Ivanka's primary caregiver, second only to the Czech grandparents who spent half the year in New York and whose cooking filled the apartment with the smells of paprika and cabbage. Unlike her older brother, Ivanka would not learn to speak Czech, despite summers in the Carpathians. She was drawn to another foreign language, boarding-school English, a flawless, accent-free enunciation that was the opposite of the New Yorkese spoken by her father and his team of retainers.

In 1984, the Trumps moved into their Trump Tower triplex. Ivanka's first memories are of waking up in a room atop a soaring tower, with lilac walls, in a white canopied bed.

"In many ways, it was a lot like the bedrooms of other little girls my age," she wrote in her first book, *The Trump Card: Playing to Win in Work and Life*, ticking off the ways that it was normal. A Madonna clock next to the bed. The *90210* stickers and *Melrose Place* trading cards plus posters of Paula Abdul and Jon Bon Jovi. "I was a sucker for all those big-hair artists in the late 1980s and early 1990s," she wrote.

But one of the many ways the bedroom was not like those of other little Material Girls in the eighties was that Ivanka Trump would actually meet and talk to many of the big-haired stars they idolized. One of them, Michael Jackson, would even come to watch her perform in *The Nutcracker*.

Then there was the view: Central Park and the New York skyline, close enough, it seemed, to touch. And since her father was altering the skyline, touching it didn't seem out of the realm of possibility to the little girl. "As a future real estate developer I suppose it [the view] also reinforced the notion that even my wildest dreams were within reach," she recalled.

Unlike her grandmother, or her mother, Ivanka really was to the manor—if not the manner—born. She would love and grow up with the cooking of her peasant Czech grandparents, and she would come to recognize that most of New York society regarded her adored father as a boor. But she was two generations removed from the muck boots and the beer-smelling rough grandfather who'd scraped the Trump family nest egg off the floors of Western saloons. She was the grand-daughter of a multimillionaire. Not old money. Not by New York society standards, but not exactly a freshly minted fortune, either. She would be the vehicle that manifested her parents' and grandparents' aim at the pinnacle of American society—not just with money, which they now had, but with class and respect. In her, all that would be within the family's reach, at last.

Years later, in one of his rambling, stream-of-consciousness interview/therapy sessions with shock jock Howard Stern, Donald Trump confessed that he felt Ivanka "looks down on me." Stern had mentioned that Ivanka was dating an unnamed New York family scion.

"My daughter's becoming a blue blood," Trump said. "She's becoming very white shoe. That's true."

CHAPTER 8

◇◇◇◇◇◇

From Russia with Love

On May 25, 1988, Ivana Zelníčková Trump—mother of three, yuppie wife extraordinaire, internationally recognized as an American capitalist's wife, icon of big hair and big shoulder pads and big fluffy dresses—became a naturalized US citizen. She was thirty-nine. "This fulfills a dream I've had for about ten years," she said on the way out of the ceremony in downtown Manhattan, with Donald. "I was thinking about it for a long time." Trump beamed beside her: "It's a great country and that's where a great woman should be."

Ivana's new passport released her from fealty to a Warsaw Pact satellite of the dying Soviet Union, a nation that had molded her into the striving athlete and businesswoman she became. She already had an Austrian passport, but taking American citizenship canceled her Czech citizenship, a fact that made her rather sad, according to Czech police informants who kept a file on her and periodically interviewed her father and other Czechs she kept in touch with. Since marrying Trump, she had continued to visit her home regularly, bringing the children to the family cottage in the foothills of the Carpathians, organizing lavish parties at the Intercontinental in Prague, not only for her old crowd of singers and artists but also keeping close ties to scientists and other influential Czechs.

If Donald Trump's life story were a movie, this would be the point where the audience might hit pause and ask: Is there more to this home shopping channel entrepreneur, television and reality star, and jet-setting "first first lady" to the President of the United States?

There is no evidence that Ivana ever worked for the Czech or Russian secret police. But files indicate that they used her nonetheless.

It was Ivana who first revealed the appeal of Slavic women to Donald. It was a habit he couldn't break. It was Ivana who first took him behind the Iron Curtain, to look at business opportunities in Czechoslovakia that never panned out. And it was Ivana who took him on the first of at least five visits to Russia, visits that private investigator Glenn Simpson of Fusion GPS fame would later say were a bit mysterious since he concluded they didn't produce a single deal.

During the Cold War years, Czechs and the Russians had used gorgeous spies to entrap rich and influential men since the 1950s. Mod Ivana, with her Slavic accent, was so fluent in Russian that she even agreed to translate for Raisa Gorbachev, wife of the last Soviet leader of the USSR, who was planning to write a book in 1987. In beauty and accent, Ivana was out of Bond girl central casting.

Without Ivana, it's fair to say, there would be no Trump-Russia connection. Donald would likely never have visited Russia if Ivana hadn't been in his life. "He hates to travel," a source who has been close to the family for years said. "The whole family is like that. They are not sophisticated."

Ivana's relationship with the Czech Communist Party's secret police began in her adolescence. As a girl, her skiing trips across the border to the West—Italy and Austria—put her in a privileged class in the closed nation. The trips also made her subject to regular interrogations by the cops when she came home. "Every time I came back from a sporting event in the West, I had to report to the police station for a two-hour 'interview' (really an interrogation by the communists)," Ivana wrote in her book *Raising Trump*. Seated in "a metal chair in a room with white walls" she would answer questions from uniformed men about what Western people wore, what they ate, and what they talked about. Thinking back on it forty years later, Ivana wrote that she took away some useful tricks from those sessions. Besides learning that smiling and wearing miniskirts and boots helped cut the tension, she would bring her interrogators wine or chocolate, and act blasé and unbothered. "Pretending to be nonchalant was good training for dealing with the media later on in my life but it also conditioned me to block and hide my emotions," she wrote.

The *Státní bezpečnost* or StB—the then Communist state's intelligence agency, which dealt with any activity considered dangerous to the state or of Western influence—spied on Ivana throughout the 1970s and '80s when she made regular trips back. The police hoovered up information from a variety of informants, watchers in New York and in her hometown and in Prague who reported on everything they saw and heard. Some of their stories led down dark alleys of improbability.

One of the Czech informants told authorities a completely different story about how Ivana and Donald met. According to their records, Ivana met Donald in Innsbruck, where she had gone as a support coach for the Canadian ski team during the 1976 Olympics. The Czech shaggy dog tale has never been part of the official Donald-Ivana story, and is probably apocryphal, but it's fun to consider. Czech informants told the police that while Ivana was in Innsbruck, she took a taxi, and it broke down. The driver got out and flagged down the first car, which just happened to contain a handsome American tourist named Donald Trump. He offered her a ride, and sent her flowers the next day, and they left the Olympic Games together. The *Daily News* once published a third version of how they met, in which Donald and

Ivana first saw each other across a crowded room in Montreal in 1976, at a reception sponsored by a PR outfit for Olympic athletes.

If either of those accounts is true, it was never acknowledged by either of them.

After Ivana moved to New York and married Donald, the Cold War was still at its iciest, bristling with tens of thousands of weapons of mass destruction. The superpowers had thousands of megatons of nuclear power aimed at one another, enough to incinerate the planet many times over. The internet didn't exist yet, the full surveillance state of digital communications was decades off, and human spies were flooding the zones of both nations, working like ants to keep tabs on the enemy.

The KGB both used and did not trust local state securities like the Czech police. Cold War researchers believe the KGB opened a file on Donald Trump as early as 1977, the year he married the pretty Czech girl. The Russians would have been interested in Trump because in the 1980s they were trying to forge ties with American businessmen, especially those interested in going into politics. Whether the Russian spies did or did not open a file on him, the Czechs would have shared their intelligence product with their counterparts in Moscow. As a citizen of a Communist country, living in Manhattan and with access to countless powerful men and women, Ivana interested not just the KGB, but also the FBI and the CIA. She was watched from all sides every time she went back across the Iron Curtain, and probably in New York as well.

The surviving files that relate to her are stamped "Top Secret" and bear the code names "Slusovice" (the name of a small town where Ivana's father introduced Donald to some possible business contacts), "America," and "Capital." Some are surprisingly accurate. One of them details the Trump prenup. Another is focused on Trump's income, and predicts that he will be tax-free for thirty years. (Trump admitted during the 2016 election that he had taken advantage of this tax windfall due to real estate accounting.)

While her father, Milos, was never an agent or asset, he had a "functional relationship" with the Czech secret police, one that Cold War historian Oldrich Tuma in Prague told me might have dated all the way back to Ivana's childhood. While she believed—and believes to this day—that she was granted the privilege of traveling to the West as a teen because of her acumen on the ski slopes, someone in her family might have had some special connections with the regime in order for her to get such special treatment.

On the Fourth of July 1987 Ivana accompanied Donald on a trip to Russia, arranged by the KGB-controlled Intourist travel agency. The reason for the trip was ostensibly to introduce Donald to possible "deals" in Russia. He or his kids would make at least a dozen deal-hunting trips to Russia and its former satellites in the following decades. On Donald's maiden voyage, he and Ivana visited Moscow and St. Petersburg (then called Leningrad). The Trumps stayed in Lenin's suite at the National Hotel, near Red Square. The hotel was linked to the glass-and-concrete Intourist complex next door and was under KGB control. The Lenin suite would have been bugged.

Trump found Russia "extraordinary," and according to *The Art of the Deal*, he and Ivana toured "a half dozen potential sites for a hotel," including several near Red Square. "I was impressed with the ambition of Soviet officials to make a deal," he wrote later. But they never sealed it.

Ivana had a different perspective. She said that the Russian social gatherings arranged for the Trumps seemed less stiff than the ones she recalled from her years living in Communist Czechoslovakia.

Through Ivana's father, Milos, the Czech authorities confirmed that Trump intended to enter the 1996 US presidential race as an independent. "Even though it looks like a utopia, D. TRUMP is confident he will succeed," the police report said.

Trump has written that the idea for his first trip to Moscow came from then Soviet ambassador Yuri Dubinin, in the fall of 1986 at a luncheon hosted by New York cosmetics heir Leonard Lauder. "One thing led to another, and now I'm talking about building a large luxury hotel, across the street from the Kremlin, in partnership with the Soviet government."

In fact, the Soviet ambassador's invitation was not serendipity, but the result of long Soviet study and effort to make friends with powerful Americans. Manhattan during the Cold War was crawling with KGB: the Russian UN secretariat was packed with hundreds of spies, and more were operating undercover in academies and businesses. The Soviet UN delegation "had greater success in finding agents and gaining political intelligence than the KGB's New York residency," according to British journalist Luke Harding, who believes that Dubinin's invitation to Trump to visit Moscow "looks like a classic cultivation exercise, which would have had the KGB's full support and approval."

For Donald's business, the 1987 trip was a wash. But it juiced his political aspirations. Perhaps the provincial New Yorker's reception abroad convinced him that he could apply his dealmaking to American foreign policy too. Two months after he returned, he paid $94,801 for full-page advertisements in the *New York Times*, the *Washington Post*, and the *Boston Globe*—and not for his luxury Trump Tower condos (which were already hosting Russians with money to launder).

In an "open letter," Trump wrote: "The world is laughing at America's politicians" for protecting "ships we don't own, carrying oil we don't need, destined for allies who won't help." After the ad ran, in October, Trump went to New Hampshire, flying in on his French-made military helicopter. His speech at the Rotary Club in Portsmouth drew a bigger audience than the other Republican candidates, including Bob Dole, Pat Robertson, and Jack Kemp, hoping to succeed Reagan.

Two years later, the Berlin Wall fell, and shortly afterward, the

Communist Party's Czech secret police disbanded. Soon, researchers flooded in, preserving their files and combing through them, to try to make sense of the mysteries of the dark years under the regime. They found that the StB did keep a file on Ivana Zelníčková Trump. It had a registry number, but it wasn't available.

Cold War historians believe it was destroyed.

PART THREE

Marla Ann Maples, Wife Number Two

Donald's second wife was only in her early twenties when she first locked eyes with him. Unlike Ivana, she was American. Also unlike forty-something career-woman yuppie mother/wife Ivana, Marla was a woman who might be malleable. She presented Donald with an opportunity—he thought—to mold her, brand her, and make her a star. She turned out to be unmanageable, headstrong, tempestuous, and ultimately, not a good fit with the Trump female brand. In the tabloid Marla years, Donald made many mistakes, but the experience allowed him to practice and refine his act as a master media manipulator, including unprecedented feats of PR audacity, like becoming his own fake publicist. Marla also gave him his first taste of being Pygmalion to an unformed female.

He found that he liked it.

CHAPTER 9

◇◇◇◇◇◇

The Short-Fingered
Vulgarian and Georgia's
Most Famous Child

As the Berlin Wall fell in 1989, capitalism was finally fully triumphant. The Go-Go Eighties were ending on a high note for Americans, but there was still something missing in Donald's glittering,
glamorous life. And it wasn't the presidency.

The years after his 1987 Russia trip were heady ones for Donald.
He published *The Art of the Deal*, a best-selling bombshell of self-
promotion, to massive prole acclaim. Unlocking the secrets to his success was turning out to be a major success for him.

He had started believing his own PR.

At a lavish party he threw at the Tower for the book, he stood next
to Ivana in the receiving line, greeting celebrity guests, and locked eyes
with the baby blues of a twenty-four-year-old blonde from Georgia.

It was a moment that would ultimately upend his and Ivana's lives
forever.

In November 1988, Trump purchased the Taj Mahal in Atlantic
City from the Merv Griffin company for $273 million. His dream of
transforming it into the biggest and best casino any mogul ever imagined would end up helping drive his company nearly into the ground.

But that was in the future. For the moment, he had to knock his Glamazon yuppie wife down to size, and get her out of Atlantic City—the latter for reasons that would become apparent in due time. In 1988, with casino advisors joking that he should rename the highly successful Trump Castle "Ivana's Castle," he decided to fire her as president. In a famous scene, at her farewell ceremony in front of hundreds of her devoted staff, Ivana burst into tears.

"I don't need this, some woman crying," Trump sneered, in front of her and the assemblage. "I need somebody strong in here."

The trouble was, everything was getting old. Donald was in his forties and already running to fat. He was getting so self-conscious about hair loss that he would get scalp surgery less than a year later. Even Maxwell's Plum, part of the Trumps' love legend, the site of their meet-cute, had closed down. AIDS and *Looking for Mr. Goodbar*, the perils of zipless fucks, had put an end to their mutual era, the Disco-Sexy Seventies.

Worst of all, Donald was at the top of his game and getting no respect. *Spy* magazine had nicknamed him "the short-fingered vulgarian," an insult that pierced his soul and that would hurt for decades, as it related to his manhood. "Vulgarian" alone he probably could have lived with, but not the tiny hands.

Cruelly, the editors at *Spy* in May 1989 also went after Ivana, putting her, a delicately featured and "soft" wife, on its cover with the headline "Ivanarama! An Investigative Tribute to the Most Super-special Trump of All." The unflattering photo was a close-up of her face with a gummy and fiendish smile, crooked teeth, sticky with clown-red lipstick, and topped off with crow's-feet. The accompanying article depicted her as a shrieking harridan, a caricature of a bitchy boss, the worst example of a working woman the boomer boys at *Spy* could conjure up.

That image, beaming monstrously from newsstands and kiosks across New York City, was a gut blow to Donald, a man who barely read, who intuited the world based on pictures, and who judged women on their photo-genetics. He judged men on the hotness and desirability of their arm candy, and now he was tethered to this. Intolerable, especially when he had a fresh filly waiting on him in a suite at Atlantic City, a woman whose young face, perky breasts, and flaxen hair the *Spy* assholes would lust after.

The *Spy* cover image might have been more of a death knell for his relationship with Ivana than any affair. It decimated Ivana's self-confidence, according to her friends, so much that she decided to fly out to Los Angeles and get a face-lift from Michael Jackson's celebrity plastic surgeon. The procedure cost between $25,000 and $35,000, chump change for a billionaire, and bought her larger breasts, better cheekbones, fuller lips as well. "She looked fifteen years younger overnight," recalled Barbara Res, who worked for Trump and who was an admirer of Ivana's.

She had been pretty before, but she came home looking like Brigitte Bardot. She didn't even try to hide "the work." She told her tabloid consigliere, gossip columnist Liz Smith, "I never intend to look a day over twenty-eight, but it's going to cost Donald a lot of money."

The new look didn't have the desired effect. Donald hated the feel of her new plastic breasts and, she told friends, wouldn't sleep with her anymore. In any case, by 1989, Trump had been trysting with Marla Maples—a blonde he'd met sometime around 1985, maybe at a celebrity tennis tournament in Atlantic City, maybe a party in Manhattan. They'd locked eyes in the receiving line at his *Art of the Deal* book party, but Ivana hadn't noticed. Now they were hooking up all over a slice of the Eastern Seaboard, from Atlantic City, to the docked *Trump Princess*, and even in the pews of the Marble Collegiate Church on Fifth Avenue, right around the corner from the Trump family home.

Ivana was the last to know. Even as Trump was anxiously and aggressively trying to renegotiate their prenuptial agreement (a renegotiation to which she ultimately agreed), Ivana didn't sense anything amiss in the relationship. She had regarded the Plaza Hotel assignment as a plum, the deserved promotion after her successes managing Trump properties in Atlantic City. She had no clue that he just wanted her out of Atlantic City in order to clear the boardwalk for his special friend, a young woman who—like Ivana—was convinced that she shared a special energy vibration with the middle-aged tycoon.

Unbeknownst to Ivana, but known to countless Trump Organization lackeys, Donald had moved a new girlfriend onto the *Trump Princess* that summer of 1989. By fall of that year, rumors of the affair were rampant in New York. But no one had dared breathe a word about it to Ivana. In hindsight she had more clarity, and in her divorce deposition she said Trump had coaxed her into a revised prenup in 1987, and as early as 1986 had mentioned to her that he thought an open marriage might be interesting "but he knew I was too old-fashioned a girl to even tolerate any other sexual relationship or affair. He did not tell me that he was seeing another woman and having an affair with her," she said.

"She was madly in love with him," recalled Vicky Tiel, the designer, model, and staunch ladies' lunch friend of Ivana. "Why, I have no clue."

Years later, when it was all over and Ivana could talk about it again, or at least monetize the pain, she wrote an advice book for other divorcing women, called *The Best Is Yet to Come*, and there she claimed to know the signs.

"How do you know when a man is having an affair?" she said, plugging her book on a morning show in 1995. "You know when he goes and buys a new suit and he loses a thousand pounds and starts polishing his nails. There are usually signs that are out of character of the person. If he didn't do it for you before, who is he doing it for?"

As the 1980s, the decade of the two Trumps' glorious and unlikely triumph over New York City, came to an end, it wouldn't be long before Ivana found out.

◇◇◇◇

One could argue that, other than Princess Ivanka, the Queens of Trumplandia are all immigrants—including all-American Marla Maples. Besides the shared Native American roots of the town's name, Cohutta, Georgia, is so different from the island of *Manahatta* as to be actually another country. When it was sparsely populated with simple people in overalls except on Sunday, it was colloquially known as "Shakerag," after the grimy cloth would-be passengers would wave to alert the train to stop at the town. It was real Cherokee country too. For years, Native Americans held tribal council meetings at Red Clay State Historic Park nearby. Now it's white man's strip mall Dixie suburbia.

Viewers constitutionally able to consume large quantities of sugary platitudes without going into a diabetic coma would have learned from Lifetime's 1995 *Intimate Portrait: Marla Maples Trump* that theirs was "a love story ripped from the pages of a romantic novel—a leggy blonde, a master of the universe. . . . Theirs was a love they thought couldn't be, shouldn't be," and that Cohutta "is still a rich textured city with an easy pace where friendly neighbors call you by your first name."

Besides those notable facts, Cohutta's most famous child is Marla Maples. She was born on a hot Indian summer Sunday, October 27, 1963. By then, Cohuttans no longer shook rags at the oncoming train to get a ride into Dalton and stops down the line. The town still had a feed and seed store for the farmers, and a little grocery store, but farms were rapidly converting into tract housing, and Cohutta was on its way to becoming a bedroom community to Dalton, the "carpet capital of the world."

The pretty blond baby was an obedient child, and a tomboy—by

Southern girl standards. She was the adored only child of Ann Ogle-tree and Stan Maples, a small-time real estate developer and sometime Elvis impersonator, who divorced when Marla was in high school. The divorce was amicable. Stan (who was calling himself a real estate developer when the New York tabs came calling in 1990) remarried, to a girl younger than his daughter. Ann remarried too.

While Marla was selling Girl Scout cookies door to door in Co-hutta, Donald had already made a name for himself as a ladies' man. In Northwest Whitfield High School, Marla was known as "a very nice girl, decent and kind" according to her Lifetime biopic. She was so nice that her classmates elected her Homecoming Queen. "We thought she'd go far, but never anything like this," Cohutta post-master Peggy Henderson told *People* magazine.

She was athletic and tall enough to stand out on the basketball team, but Marla had an epiphany about the road to fame and riches while watching *Charlie's Angels* one day. She decided that Farrah Faw-cett was going to be her role model. "If she could do it, I thought, so could I. I thought I could do anything."

She attended the University of Georgia, but deviated from aca-demics and started entering beauty pageants and swimsuit competi-tions, doing modeling jobs at trade shows, taking gigs that showed off her toned and curvaceous body. In her biopic, she puts responsibility for that decision on others. "People were saying 'you should do it' and I was always a people pleaser," Marla explained, about choosing to compete in pageants.

The Southern beauty pageant was then and is now a cross be-tween Honey Boo Boo white trash fantasia and a real path to career success for Southern beauties. It is such a serious business that pag-eant coaches like Bill Alverson, "The Pageant King of Alabama," as the *New York Times* dubbed him, get paid big bucks to help train teen girls in makeup, deportment, and yes, life goals questions, and steer them to the "right" contests that will help them climb the ladder of pageant success, and not fall into a swamp of *Hooters* magazine covers.

Among the hundreds of beauties he has budded, Alverson has several Miss Americas to his credit. He steers his clients away from what he calls the "meat market" beauty contests—including the strictly bathing suit competitions that Marla Maples signed up for in the early 1980s. Alverson begs to differ with anyone who thinks beauty pageants are not a respectable way for a girl to get ahead in the world.

"Who decides what women should be?" he asked. If the judges want women walking around in a swimsuit and heels, that's merely a job hazard to be met as a challenge and overcome with grit and self-respect. "Some people are modest and uncomfortable doing that, but there are realities of life that are out there no matter what you do."

She won the first Miss Resaca Beach Poster Girl contest in 1983. The name is a joke. Resaca is a town near Dalton, and there is no beach except for the muddy banks of the Oostanaula River. It was best known for its Civil War reenactments until Victory Carpet Corp. president Dan Bowen of Dalton started the beauty contest as a promotional gimmick. Its winners have gone on to pose for *Playboy* and *Hooters* magazines.

A year later, Marla, a busty blonde with a cheerleader smile and blue-green eyes, was a runner-up for Miss Georgia. A year after that, she moseyed down to Daytona Beach and won the Miss Hawaiian Tropic International beauty pageant. Under "long term goal," Marla Maples wrote in well-curved, girlish scrawl, "I hope to become successful as a screen actress and someday do Broadway."

She dodged destiny and didn't meet Donald Trump there, although around the same time he was cruising pageants as a VIP guest of Hawaiian Tropic, a suntan lotion company that sponsored bikini competitions. "He'd come to our pageants because he enjoys being around the girls," recalled Ron Rice, the impresario who founded Hawaiian Tropic in 1969 and later launched the pageants. "He was kind of a regular with us."

◇◇◇◇

Trump women are all natural competitors. If they are not entering and winning beauty contests or stealing the photographic limelight with their poses, they are making money as "entrepreneurs" or "dealmakers." They "play to win" just like Donald, and they gravitate toward men who do the same.

That means they will never stand down from another woman's challenge. Just as the *Apprentice* reality show candidates and the Miss USA and Miss Teen USA pageant contestants have stepped into the ring in front of cameras and on stages to compete for Donald's approval, the Queens of Trumplandia have always been more than willing to get into the pit and fight to the finish, preferably without dislocating a strand of hair or breaking a polished nail.

The first and still the most famous female prizefight for Donald went down on a mountain in Aspen, Colorado, on December 30, 1989. By this time, Donald had been seeing—and hiding—Marla Maples in Atlantic City and New York for several years, tucked away on the *Trump Princess* at anchor, in Trump Tower, and in various hotels along the boardwalk in Atlantic City. She had ducked down in the limos and been driven to trysts by bodyguards in dark wraparound shades.

She was so very tired of life in the shadows.

And apparently, so was Donald.

After spending Christmas with Ivana and the kids at Mar-a-Lago, he sent his family on ahead to their annual Aspen ski holiday, claiming that pressing business would delay him.

He then directed the pilot of his jet to detour through Chattanooga, Tennessee, an hour outside Dalton, Georgia, where Marla's extended family clan spent their Christmas. He landed, and posed on the tarmac with Marla's mom, Ann, her stepfather, and other family members, including grandparents called Meemaw and Ding Daddy. Then he went on to Aspen, with Marla in tow, to be secreted yet again, in separate but, she hoped, equal lodgings.

What happened next on that triangular ski holiday occurred in full view of celeb and high-society vacationers and the tabloid reporters who had been sent to keep an eye on them. The venue was Bonnie's, a mountainside restaurant. Marla, in fluffy earmuffs, walked up to Ivana, who was standing in the food line, also in fluffy earmuffs, and asked her, "Do you love your husband? Because I do."

Ivana's *annus horribilis*, 1990, was only just beginning.

Most reporters later wrote that Ivana, in front of the resting skiers at Bonnie's, and her own kids, replied with some version of the following: "You bitch, leave my husband alone." Some would claim that she unleashed a stream of Czech profanity before reverting to her second language, English. She then took off after Donald down the slope, while some witnesses marveled at her skiing backwards in front of him and wagging her finger in his face.

Within a week, Donald was back in New York, instructing his staff to remove all the pictures of Ivana from his office. His wife and children were upstairs in the triplex, stunned and shocked.

Ivana's lunching New York friends were not shocked. "The reason they broke up was that she was a businesswoman now, which upset Donald," one recalled. "He tried to find a non-working woman and eventually, he did."

Ivana turned forty-one that February, and was feted by the loyal lunching ladies plus a pack of the social X-rays of New York society, dining on lamb chops at La Grenouille just days after Liz Smith reported on the Aspen incident. A well-wishing and curious crowd of civilians formed on the sidewalk outside the restaurant, while inside ladies comforted their friend—weeping into her Chardonnay, with heart-shaped chocolates.

◇◇◇◇

When Donald flew to Chattanooga after Christmas 1989, to pose
with the extended Maples family, scooping up Marla for a ski vacation
in Aspen, Marla believed that her lover and his wife had already split,
and that "boxes had been moved out."

She soon learned their timing was still off.

As Ivana was coming to terms with the fact that she probably
needed to get a divorce lawyer, Marla was in hiding. By February 11,
when the first Liz Smith scoop on the Trump breakup hit the *Daily
News*, she was holed up in Atlantic City, at the home of a Trump executive, jogging on the beach in a red wig to stay incognito. She moved
to the Hamptons, another borrowed house, and had a girlfriend along
who climbed trees to see if the coast was clear for grocery shopping.
In March, she borrowed a passport and escaped to Guatemala to hang
out with another friend, in the Peace Corps, touring impoverished
towns filled with smiling children ("the happiest month of my life,"
she later said).

Back in Gotham, reporters and paparazzi scraped and scoured for,
then begged, stalked, wheedled, and cajoled, everyone who had ever
crossed paths with the Dixie stunner. Day by day, the heat of the story
rose a notch.

Marla's hometown paper put a $1,000 bounty on her head, to
be paid to anyone who located her. Bookers and reporters filled the
information vacuum with surrogates. Marla's family and friends relented, flattered and seduced with promises of trips to New York City
and onto live morning shows and interviews. Out of the strip malls
and hollers they came: Meemaw and Ding Daddy. Stan and Ann. The
postmaster in Cohutta. High school cheerleading mates. Old boyfriends. *People* magazine put her on the cover, an old modeling shot
in a little black dress, with the headline TRUMP PRINCESS and the deck

"Sure it's a scandal, but the folks in hometown Dalton advise 'Go For It, Honey!'"

Liz Smith bagged a Stan Maples interview. "It is terrible for Marla to have to be in hiding," Stan said. "She detests seclusion. Marla is a very very stable individual and what Marla IS will show." And: "I don't tell Marla what to do. She may be influenced but she is not a puppet. . . . We are kind of soul mates, very close. Marla is what they call an old soul. My head has swelled with pride when Marla has given interviews saying 'My Dad is my best friend.' "

Smith took one long, sly, cosmopolitan glance at Stan and wrote: "Stan Maples is only forty-seven and quite good looking, with big blue eyes, all his hair and a natty appearance. I particularly liked his black loafers with tassels that the wags call 'Love Me Shoes' from down south. He was wearing two rings, one with diamonds, so I chalked him up as a bit of a sport."

Stan told Liz that he came from "generations of Georgian and Tennessean farming and timber families" and presented himself as a mini-Donald. "I am a real estate developer and a financial administrator. I've done many deals of loan structuring in New York with major banks."

Marla's mom, Ann, gave an interview to the supermarket tabloid the *Star*. Stan told Liz that Marla—from her undisclosed location— had been consulted on that decision too. "Marla and I both agreed that maybe it was the best thing for her to do rather than have a nervous breakdown."

Marla hid out in Guatemala for a month, adrenaline-fueled, living a lawyers, guns, and money fantasy, talking to her dad and Donald on the phone, in code, until finally she let them coax her back north of the border. She snuck through a series of airports in a wig and sunglasses, and emerged on *Primetime* with Diane Sawyer, making ABC the winner of that year's TV booker Olympiad. Marla believed a big TV interview would allow her to tell her story in one place, in her own way, shape her own story, and that it would satisfy the many media outlets hounding her and her family. "Do you love him?" Sawyer, a fellow Southern beauty pageant veteran, asked. With the television host nodding understandingly, Marla confessed, breathily, "You know, I, I can't lie about it. Oh, I do."

She framed the relationship on the astral plane. "I'm a strong believer in fate, in purpose, in a belief that there is a direction that we all have in life. I don't know what mine is, you know." One thing she did know: "I'm not the reason for that marriage having problems."

Then Diane dropped the big question: "Was it the best sex you ever had?" Marla declined to confirm or deny.

It was one of the most-watched television moments of the decade (until O.J. Simpson in the white Bronco).

By summer of 1990, Marla was on the public stage, in a spotlight that had glimmered, with a future somehow possible, during her teenaged epiphany watching Farrah Fawcett back in Georgia. She brought a *Vanity Fair* writer with her to the US Open that fall (tickets provided by Trump). She spent most of the time with her back to the action on the court, paying scant attention to the triumphant Pete Sampras, signing a big batch of eight-by-ten glossies of herself in cutoffs and a hard hat. The more sedate members of high society sneered and hissed at her. She ignored them. "Now he calls his beach house 'Marla Lago,'" she giggled.

Vanity Fair's Maureen Orth concluded: "Getting to know Marla Maples is akin to pressing your thumb on an aerosol can and watching mountains of Reddi Wip flow out."

For Ivana 1990 was an emotional abyss, but also a year of public love and public honor. She was named Hotelier of the Year, and she appeared on the cover of *Vogue*. But her kids were traumatized, and she had lost all of her "feminine confidence," as she put it, while her defeat in the game of love was covered minute by minute in the media. To make matters worse, Donald was viciously fighting back, comparing her to the notoriously bitchy hotelier Leona Helmsley and a dictator's wife, shoe-collecting Filipina Imelda Marcos.

A friend advised her to hire a criminal lawyer because a divorce lawyer wouldn't scare him enough. Trump responded by hiring his own criminal lawyer, Jay Goldberg, a man whose motto was "I'm a killer. I can rip skin off a body." And the two teams went at it, in the courts and in the court of public opinion.

On Christmas Eve 1987, Ivana had signed a third postnuptial agreement, giving her roughly $25 million—$14 million in cash plus properties. But in February 1990, after her run-in with Marla on the slopes of Aspen, Ivana challenged the contract, demanding more. A lot more, based on what Donald claimed about his wealth. Ivana's lawyer got Donald to agree to $50 million—twice the postnup—but decided to hold out for $125 million, about a quarter of the half billion dollars *Forbes* reported he was worth. Ivana's team had investigators gathering evidence from Trump employees on Ivana's central role in building the Trump empire, and they were using Donald's praise for her in his book *The Art of the Deal* as more leverage.

Team Ivana also tried to nullify the last postnuptial contract on the basis of their belief that Trump crafted it while he was already having the affair with Marla. Donald cruelly reminded Ivana that the third contract (she'd signed a second altered postnuptial agreement earlier in the decade) didn't explicitly include his "continuing love and affection," which the other two contracts had included.

Things bottomed out tragically. In the fall of 1990, Ivana's beloved father, Milos, died suddenly of a heart attack in Czechoslovakia. The vicarious stress of her ugly divorce killed him, Ivana believed. To make matters worse, Donald invited himself to the cemetery, trailing a horde of paparazzi, who snapped away at the grieving family by the gravesite.

That was the last straw. After months of very public back-and-forth over the status of her third postnup, and with Marla Maples now going at her on the covers of the tabloids, she was finished with Donald, and needed to put him in the rearview mirror.

Back in New York, Ivana instructed her lawyers to wrap it up. The lawyers were ready to fight on, but after her father's death, Ivana had reached the end of her tolerance for Donald's emotional double-dealing and the rigors of a long divorce battle. Having declined the $50 million, they were now stuck with the couple's last marital contract, plus a little more.

Her lawyers managed to wrest away the family's Greenwich mansion, a settlement of $10 million cash, $350,000 a year until she remarried, a $4 million housing allowance in New York, and $100,000 support per year per child, for a total of $650,000 a year, and in total around what she'd agreed to in the last postnup she'd signed. In the process, the lawyers had learned that the self-proclaimed billionaire and genius dealmaker might not have been worth more than $100 million. Not chump change, but not what he claimed. Ivana was pleased. According to Jay Goldberg, when the couple met with their lawyers a year later to iron out some latent matter, she took off a "very expensive piece of jewelry" and gave it to Goldberg's wife as a gift.

After the divorce settlement was reached in March 1991, Ivana went on *20/20* to tell her side of the whole story to Barbara Walters. Dressed angelically in white, her delicate features quivering, her accent as charming as ever, she let herself be soothed and seduced by Barbara's gentle talk therapy. Haltingly, she told her side.

WALTERS: And then came Christmas, Aspen, December 30— can you tell us what happened, what you felt, what you learned? It's still hard, isn't it?

MRS. TRUMP: It's tough.

The camera cut away to the mountains, to let her have a cry.

> WALTERS [voice-over]: At first, Ivana could not discuss what happened at Aspen Mountain that day, but later, she was able to talk about it. [interviewing] We know what Marla said about that day in Aspen—we have read about it in all of the papers—that she came up to you and said or you met her and she said, "I love Donald. Do you?" Is that pretty much the way it happened?
>
> MRS. TRUMP: It was pretty much the way it happened. Actually, I did find out first time on the telephone, when I did pick up the phone in the living room and Donald did take the phone in bedroom—
>
> WALTERS: In Aspen?
>
> MRS. TRUMP: —in Aspen and he spoke to the mutual friend of ours and he was talking about Marla. And I really didn't understand. I never heard a name like that in my life. And I came to Donald. I said, "Who is Moola?" And he said, "Well, that's a girl which is going after me for last two years." And I said, "Is that serious?" And he said, "Oh, she's just going after me."
>
> WALTERS [voice-over]: The next day, Ivana said, she was skiing on the slopes when she passed Donald with a dark-haired girl. She was told that girl was a friend of "Moola" or Marla, whom Donald said had been chasing him. Later, she saw that girl again.
>
> MRS. TRUMP: And I saw her in the line, in the food line and—
>
> WALTERS: You were at a restaurant—
>
> MRS. TRUMP: In the restaurant. And I said, "I understand from my husband that you have a friend which is after my husband for last two years." I says, "Will you give her the message that I love my husband very much." And that was

it and I walk outside. And I didn't know this Marla was standing behind this girl in line but because I never met her, I had no idea. And Marla just charged right behind me and she said—well, you said and in front of my children— they were about five feet away—and all were just looking up like nothing would happen, so—

WALTERS: She said, "I'm Marla and I love your husband. Do you?"

MRS. TRUMP: Yes.

WALTERS: What did you say?

MRS. TRUMP: I said—I really said—I said, "Get lost. I love my husband very much." It was very unladylike, but it was as much as I really could—that was as much as I—as harsh as maybe I could be.

WALTERS: And what did Donald say?

MRS. TRUMP: Not anything, nothing.

WALTERS: And that's how you found out?

Close-up of Ivana's face brimming with tears. Fade out.

In the months after the Aspen Incident, there was some aspect of the Trump breakup "being played out on the front pages of the tabloids almost every day," Ivanka Trump would recall.

The Trump children couldn't look away.

"One day the headline was THEY MET IN CHURCH!" Ivanka continued. "The next it was SEPARATE BEDS! The worst was a *New York Post* cover photo of Marla Maples, a woman I'd never met, who was being talked about as my father's new girlfriend, claiming that she had spent the night with my father beneath a headline that shouted THE BEST SEX I EVER HAD! Can you imagine?"

The third grader had no place to hide. Reporters waited outside the doors of her private school, The Chapin School, snapping pictures and hollering questions, including whether Marla Maples's claim about Donald's bedroom skills was true, she wrote.

"What type of person would ask a nine-year-old girl that kind of question? About her own father, no less?"

The school eventually noticed Ivanka's trauma and sent her home after she broke down in class one day. In February 1990, the *New York Post* reported an item about it: "One reason Donald and Ivana are 'making nice': Sources say little Ivanka, 8, had a very tough time of it last week with the teasing and questioning of classmates at the posh prep school she attends. One story, denied by Trump's office, was that Ivanka was hysterical one day and had to be sent home. Other sources say Ivanka's homeroom teacher gave a little lecture to the class asking for their understanding during this difficult period."

Added a *Post* source, said to be close to the family: "The children are all wrecks."

Watching all this, Donald's parents—dignified, traditional, family-centered, and in Mary's case, keen to mimic royalty and the upper classes—were horrified. Fred Trump had always rolled his eyes at Donald's champagne tastes and once supposedly said the world would be better off if both Donald and Ivana went down in a plane. But he took Ivana's side, as did mother Mary and Donald's sister Maryanne. The Trump women, plus Ivana's sister-in-law and socialite Blaine Trump, had all shown up for her forty-first birthday party at La Grenouille. Fred even tried to effectuate a reconciliation by hiring violinists to play for the couple when the family was together at Mar-a-Lago at Easter 1990. Donald was unmoved.

The First Great Trump Divorce was a tabloid sensation, a media event, and a private disaster for the children, and the Trump family. It certainly was not Donald's proudest moment. Friends of Ivana's believe he has genuinely regretted it for the rest of his life. The German part of him, Elizabeth's part of him, Fred's too, detested chaos, of course. But out of the batshit public craziness of that divorce, Donald Trump also broke free. He fashioned himself into a new man, one who believed that he could actually turn disaster to his advantage with good or bad PR while attracting ever more attention to himself. Arguably, it was during the years of his very showy divorce that he finally became the great showman, with the flamboyant confection of yellow hair that matched his flair for the dramatic, that his mother, Mary, had taught him to be by example.

CHAPTER 10

◇◇◇◇◇◇

The Rape Deposition

In March 1991, Donald and Ivana reached a divorce settlement (the divorce itself, granted on the grounds of "cruel and inhuman treatment," wouldn't be finalized until the following March) and Donald handed Ivana a $10 million certified check at the Park Avenue law offices of his lawyer. He agreed to pay her $4 million for housing after she vacated the Trump Tower triplex.

During his depositions in the divorce, Donald invoked the Fifth Amendment ninety-seven times, mostly in response to questions about other women. In her own divorce statements, Ivana—who had bragged about her role as a traditional European wife—now said she realized that Donald had needed to keep her subservient. "This was apparently what he wanted me to think because it was important to him (although damaging to the children and me) for me to appear submissive."

In the final hours, the last obstacle was whether Ivana would get to keep the 1987 Mercedes that Trump had bought for her. He churlishly had had it repossessed. She wanted it back. She got it.

The media had covered the divorce like a tennis match, zero-love, advantage Ivana, advantage Donald, set, match. The New York matrimonial bar, as is customary during any haute Manhattan divorce, reaped windfalls of free publicity, even though the couple had hired criminal lawyers to represent them in court.

But journalists didn't get their hands on everything in real time. The First Great Trump Divorce case revealed something darker about one of New York's richest families. Money, fear (and fear of loss of access to money attached to nondisclosure agreements), and a retinue of menacing lawyers together usually enable men in families of great fortune to get away with all manner of activities that, among men of lesser means, might result in police reports and restraining orders. Donald Trump was always a ladies' man. And he was also always a brawler. He grew up with violence. Fred Trump took no guff from him. He has admitted that he was smacked around at military school. Today, when he's angry, violence laces his Tweets and speeches. Is it possible that the man who became President of the United States has been a domestic abuser? According to the legal record, yes.

It took investigative reporter and author Harry Hurt, researching his 1993 book, *Lost Tycoon: The Many Lives of Donald J. Trump*, to extract from an anonymous source, who had access to some hidden part of the Trump divorce record, a statement that revealed just how cruelly Ivana had been treated.

Under oath, according to the document Hurt obtained, Ivana told of how while the marriage was falling apart, Donald flew into a fit of rage due to pain from a scalp reduction surgery, performed by the same plastic surgeon who a year prior had made Ivana look fifteen years younger. The alopecia reduction, a surgery that involves cutting the bald spot out and sewing the remaining skin back together, leaves a man with a tightened scalp that can cause headaches and swelling. Donald was in agony.

The couple were in their room in Trump Tower. They hadn't had sex in sixteen months.

"Your fucking doctor has ruined me," Trump supposedly shouted. He then committed a "violent assault." According to Ivana's deposition, Donald held back Ivana's arms and began to pull out fistfuls of hair from her scalp. He tore off her clothes and unzipped his pants.

"Then he jams his penis inside her for the first time in more than sixteen months. Ivana is terrified. . . . It is a violent assault," Hurt writes. "According to versions she repeats to some of her closest confidantes, 'he raped me.'"

Ivana spent that night behind a locked door, sobbing. The next morning, Hurt reported, she emerged. "As she looks in horror at the ripped-out hair scattered all over the bed, he glares at her and asks with menacing casualness: 'Does it hurt?'"

With the legal deposition in hand, Hurt was allowed to publish this description of what Ivana had said under oath, but lawyers forced him to also publish a statement from Ivana, for the book, pulling back on the rape allegation. "During a deposition given by me in connection with my matrimonial case, I stated that my husband had raped me," the Ivana Trump statement said. "On one occasion during 1989, Mr. Trump and I had marital relations in which he behaved very differently toward me than he had during our marriage. As a woman, I felt violated, as the love and tenderness, which he normally exhibited toward me, was absent. I referred to this as a 'rape,' but I do not want my words to be interpreted in a literal or criminal sense."

Ivana's statement, according to the "Notice to the Reader" in the Hurt book, "does not contradict or invalidate any information contained in this book."

In 2015, she again publicly denied that part of the deposition, calling it "totally without merit."

There is no doubt that there is a violating, physical element to Donald's approach to women. After his "grab 'em by the pussy" confession to Billy Bush went public, nineteen women came forward, many describing rough, invasive behavior that could, in most states, be legally defined as sexual assault. A *People* magazine reporter on assignment at a Mar-a-Lago recalled that he pushed her up against a wall and stuck his tongue in her mouth. A woman who'd sat next to him on an airplane reported that he groped her "like an octopus," and she called the incident "a sexual assault." Another recalled that he grabbed and kissed her at a Mar-a-Lago Mother's Day brunch. An adult film actress reported that he grabbed and hugged and kissed her "without permission." If these women he barely knew are to be believed (he has called them all "liars"), then his wives, his most intimate partners, might have stories of their own. But like Ivana, they have too much at stake. Another report of such behavior—also in the Hurt biography—is that at least one of his many fights with Marla Maples was physical. On his forty-fifth birthday, the couple had a violent argument in a suite at one of his Atlantic City hotels. In the morning, according to what Marla's friend Tom Fitzsimmons told a Trump biographer, the door to the suite was off its hinges. Marla doesn't remember it. He has also attacked two women—journalist Marie Brenner and hotelier Leona Helmsley—by pouring wine on them at public events.

◇◇◇◇

Privately, Donald was a wreck. As his marriage was breaking up, he occasionally spoke to Ivana about suicide. Before they split, Ivana had decided couples therapy might be a good idea. Trump reluctantly agreed, but he told her, "only if you think it will fix what's wrong with you." Donald attended only one session.

For Donald, the divorce also offered the kind of challenge he loved: he could hone his media manipulation skills. For the first time, he weaponized publicity, pretending to be his own PR man on telephone calls with reporters. As "John Miller" he told *People* magazine that Trump was dumping Marla for the Italian model (and future French first lady) Carla Bruni.

In his distinctive Rat Pack syrupy croon, he continued talking to the *People* reporter, who was not fooled but stunned: "He really didn't want to make a commitment. He's coming out of a marriage, and he's starting to do tremendously well financially. Have you met him? He's a good guy, and he's not going to hurt anybody. . . . He treated his wife well and . . . he will treat Marla well. The biggest misconception was that Donald left Ivana for Marla. He didn't. He leaves for himself."

He intimated that Donald Trump was a pearl of great price, a prize women might claw each other's eyes out to win. "He's living with Marla, and he's got three other girlfriends," he told the *People* writer. "When he makes the decision, that will be a very lucky woman. . . . Competitively, it's tough. It was for Marla and it will be for Carla."

(Carla Bruni, reached soon after, called the dating claim "nonsense," and scoffed at the notion of competition, adding that Trump was "the King of Tacky" and "obviously a lunatic.")

News of the romantic swerves of the Marla-Donald relationship flickered in and out of the news for several years. "In the annals of celebrity reporting there has never been a story like this," Liz Smith told *Vanity Fair*. Trump would later return the favor to Liz, stating, "She used to kiss my ass so much that it was downright embarrassing."

Before the internet, TMZ, YouTube, and television gossip "magazine shows" like Billy Bush's, the gilded love triangle was mainly catnip for millions of tabloid newspaper readers. But this story frenzy jumped to broadcast and major television networks. News about the scandal grabbed headlines to the exclusion of worldly events: when South Africa released Nelson Mandela from prison, for example, Trump's divorce garnered more headlines in the US.

Almost nothing the couple did was too insignificant for coverage. Donald banned Marla from his Taj Mahal's grand opening, and the tabloids knew it was because "his family was freaking out over his plans to show her off there." They also knew that Marla had ordered a sequined dress for the soiree, and they knew that she was still going to accept it from the designer, whether or not she got to the ball.

A few weeks later, the *Post* ran the headline TEARFUL CALL BRINGS AFFAIR TO BITTER END. The paper reported that "the Don bid a sad adieu to the starlet in a brief and tear-drenched call Monday from his recently moved into bachelor pad at Trump Tower." The paper even knew from "a reliable source" that Donald had changed his private number so Marla could no longer reach him at home. Marla's PR man shot back: "They're still friends. Some people are going to have egg on their face if they write that."

And they did.

◇◇◇◇

Many biographers have charted the course of Donald Trump's midlife implosion, his downfall, and his miraculous return from the land of business failure and personal disaster. But few of them have identified the true nadir of that period. It is a point that involves his mother, Mary.

On Halloween 1991, a few months short of the two-year anniversary of the Aspen Incident, and with the divorce still not finalized, Mary Trump was seventy-nine years old. She was frail, and had never really recovered from the midlife surgeries. She was suffering from osteoporosis and had been hospitalized six months prior for an allergic reaction. But she and Fred—on the verge of being diagnosed with Alzheimer's—still lived together in the house he'd built for her in Jamaica Estates, where the kids had grown up. The house and its immediate environs remained as pristine as ever, but beyond the gates of the subdivision the neighborhood had deteriorated in the 1970s, and now the streets were rough and seedy.

On that fall morning, Mary Trump left Fred behind and was

walking to the A&P grocery store with $14 in her purse when a teen hoodlum named Paul LoCasto, playing hooky from school because his parents were worried about his involvement with Halloween vandalism, spotted the old lady with a purse and jumped on her, knocking her to the ground. Before he could steal her purse, a bread truck driver delivering loaves to the store spotted the incident and the perp ran off, leaving Mary unconscious, with a broken arm, a fractured pelvis, and a brain hemorrhage. One witness who tried to help reported: "Her whole face was bleeding. It looked like her eye was coming out. I turned her over and told her everything was going to be alright. I told her to squeeze my hand if she understood me, and she did."

The hero of the story was Lawrence Herbert, the bread delivery man and part-time school bus driver, working two jobs. "I saw this kid come up from behind and grab her bag, fling her around and throw her to the ground," said Herbert. "I thought to myself that woman is hurt, she could be my mother."

Herbert chased down the assailant and dragged him out of an underground parking garage "where an angry crowd gathered." The hero then handed LoCasto off to grocery store guards and, according to the *New York Post*, "raced off to pick up a kindergartner who was waiting to be picked up for school."

Mary slowly regained consciousness in a hospital bed, surrounded by family. All her children were present and accounted for except for one—the one who had made their name world famous. When his mother needed him most, Donald was absent, and reportedly in three vacation spots at the same time. The papers—who had been looking for him as avidly as his own kin—reported him to be either in Hawaii with Marla, or "basking in the sun" with her at Mar-a-Lago, or just too busy with plans for a prizefight and casino commission hearing in Atlantic City to get back up to the hospital in Queens.

"She was calling for Donald," the *New York Post* reported, but he wasn't there until the second day.

It was a rough month for the elderly Trumps. Days later, Fred Trump was admitted to the same hospital, Booth Memorial in Queens, for hip surgery. Maryanne Trump Barry told the newspapers that Mary only remembered walking and had no recollection of the event.

When reporters reached him, Donald, now operating off the new "All PR Is Good PR" playbook he was refining during the divorce, seized the moment to make a bold statement—about something other than Mary Trump. He shot off a comment about the effect of the incident on the city's reputation. New York City "is going to hell," he told the *New York Post*. "It's a negative thing about the city that went out on the news all over the world. This is a plague that's devastating all of our cities, not only New York. It is a sad commentary on life in America."

Back in New York a few days later, Donald took his showmanship a step further and invited the hero (black) bread truck driver to the Edwardian Room at the Plaza for dinner. This was the kind of event that New York media lived and breathed for—billionaire plus common man, in unusual harmony. As Donald waited on the red-carpeted stairs of the Plaza, a mob scene of paparazzi gathered and grew, waiting to record Herbert's arrival. They then waited another half an hour for Marla to trip gaily up the steps, to join the men dining on pheasant under glass and barbecued lobster, duck, and oysters. "She's a beautiful and charming woman," Lawrence told reporters on his way out. "She made us feel warm and welcome."

When he was arrested, LoCasto, sixteen, told police he was an alcoholic who had consumed half a bottle of blackberry brandy before the attack. At his trial a year later, the judge noted that the Trump family reported that the episode had caused "a change, which resulted in a loss of spirit, spunk and a lot of what made Mary Trump, Mary Trump."

LoCasto apologized in court: "I am sorry for the pain and suffering of Mrs. Trump which her family went through and will have to go through, and my family also." The judge threw the book at him, giving him three to nine years in prison. His defense attorney complained that most teenagers without records would have received shorter sentences, and youthful offender treatment, but of course, most teenagers didn't mug a Trump woman.

The mugging came at the tail end of a wild season in the Marla and Donald affair. After months in which he'd given her an engagement ring, then taken it back, then claimed to be dating Brooke Shields and Carla Bruni, the two were back together. Two weeks before the mugging, Donald and Marla went picking pumpkins, or as the tabloids put it, "playin' in the pumpkin patch," at Pumpkintown in the Hamptons. Spies reported that Marla chose the very biggest, but as the limo driver prepared to put it into the trunk, Donald ordered her to select some of the mini-pumpkins instead.

Like the giant pumpkin, the 7.45-carat "dazzler" engagement ring he'd given her was nowhere to be seen. But earlier in the day the couple had golfed together at the Atlantic Golf Club in Water Mill, while a plane flew over the golf course, pulling a banner proclaiming "Marla I Love You."

Mary would not recover for months, and she never really regained her strength. But now Donald had his showman's game down. He loved his mother—sure—as much as he could love anyone. But the real show was just starting, and he had a new role to play. He wasn't going to be Fred, hiding his lovelies down in Miami or Coney Island and only being seen publicly with a woman aging right alongside him. That was way too Queens, way too thrifty, like choosing cheap red-brick when you could spend a lot more money and get solar glass. Mary had grown old without Fred ever seeing the point in the finer things that she yearned for. Her natural flair and sense of the regal were dampened as her firstborn son succumbed to alcoholism while living in the family home, and his slow decline left her depressed. She barely spoke during her son's last years. She and Fred owned an apartment in Trump Tower, which she decorated lavishly in French traditional style. She finally got her castle keep, but she only spent a single night in it. Fred was suffering from early Alzheimer's and the glamorous Tower apartment had never been his style. He just didn't get it. Donald got it, though. And the next thing he needed was a woman that would make other men swoon with jealousy.

CHAPTER 11

◇◇◇◇◇◇

Marrying Marla

"I just think the first moment I met him, I had a sense like I had known him before," Marla would later say about Donald. "It was much deeper than just whatever you might feel. We had a sense of like, if you believe in past lives or you don't, it was as if we had known each other. It was oddly like family."

As with all his wives, the story about how Donald actually met Marla is a tale told many ways. Sometimes she met him at a tennis tournament, sometimes they ran into each other at his book party and locked eyes. According to her, the affair actually took off when they ran into each other one afternoon in 1985 on Madison Avenue. Trump had eschewed his limo that day, saw her on the street, and proceeded to ask if they had met before. They had indeed, but now, Marla recalled, the connection was there. "I had seen him at different places throughout the years and just said hello, I was just somebody he shook hands with." After that Marla said they were both aware they "had a connection," but the timing wasn't right. Three years passed, Donald always telling her it was over with Ivana. "We'd spend a lot

of time on the telephone with each other without ever being out together in public. By eighty-eight, I knew I truly loved this guy."

Georgia Baptist Marla was raised to believe in God, for sure. But
by the time she met Trump, she was open to new interpretations of the
Great Spirit. Like that other, more recent scandal star, Rielle Hunter,
who took down John Edwards's political career when she decided they
were soul mates who had known each other in past lives, Marla's feelings for Donald could only be expressed in spiritual terms.

In the Lifetime *Intimate Portrait* she tells how she and her married
lover would meet at the Marble Collegiate Church on Fifth Avenue,
where they would find themselves together on occasion and "sort out"
their feelings for each other in the pews.

Marla eventually found inner peace in a Dixieland gumbo of
every form of late twentieth-century pop-spirituality, from Hollywood Kabbalah to color therapy and yoga, but during her years
in hiding, she got spiritual succor from *Emmanuel's Book*, in which
author Pat Rodegast, channeling an occult philosopher named Emmanuel, opines on "the limitless power of love." While tucked away
on the *Trump Princess* or in the Atlantic City suite, in love with a
married man, she found comfort in passages like this: "Love is the
only spiritual way. There is no rule that says if a heart has moved, if
a consciousness has grown, the human being must remain faithful to
something that no longer holds them in the name of society's definition of the meaning of love."

Later that year, at the US Open in New York, she wore a gold
Cartier braided band on her wedding finger, a present from Donald.
"It's what gives me my power," she said, showing it to a reporter. "I
believe I have a purpose and that there is a reason we're together."

Two years later, she invited the *New York Times* into her new apartment, and talked about how it was painted based on color vibrations.
"I've had 12 different apartments in the last six years," she told the
reporter. "To have all this softness around me, how long I've dreamed

of it! I have white and purple in the bedroom, which are magical colors to me. White is very pure, and purple is known as a color of the highest level of spirituality. It's a passionate color, too."

In the same interview, she revealed her appreciation of the supernatural theory of the lost city of Atlantis. "Color can change the way I feel," she said, pointing to the aqua suede chaise longue in the living room. "Aqua is the color of the sea, and I'm very drawn to the days of Atlantis. That was a magical time."

Mixed in with all the woo, there's an earnest and honest sweetness to Marla. She later said her years as a mistress were karmic punishment for judging adulterers as a teenaged Baptist in Georgia. She believes in political and civilizational karma.

"I'm finding more and more of my friends' moms are getting serious cancers and most often dying," she said in 2016, "and they were the young babies during the days of Hiroshima. And we can't think that what we did there didn't have fallout for all of us, I mean it just is nature. The winds blow. We can't do one thing across the other side of the world without it affecting us here. Butterfly effect."

◇◇◇◇

After some five or six years with Trump, three of them in an on-again, off-again relationship carried on in the public eye, Marla had taken to packing a wedding dress when she traveled. Because, as she put it, "you've got to be prepared."

But there were other forms of preparation she was not packing, and in February 1993, she got pregnant. When she told Donald about the pregnancy, he wasn't exactly over the moon. In an interview with Howard Stern later, he said of the new baby: "Honestly, I'm glad it happened. I have a great little daughter, Tiffany. But, you know at the time it was like, 'Excuse me, what happened?' And then I said, 'Well, what are we going to do about this?'"

Some have interpreted the question as suggesting abortion.

Trump has said he meant that he wondered if she wanted to get married. Well, is Georgia asphalt hot in July?

Donald stepped up, and was in the room when Marla gave birth to his fourth child, Tiffany, on October 13, 1993. It's hard to overstate how out of character his presence was. Donald, whose father Fred had forbade the use of the word *pregnant* in their household, has never hidden his squeamishness about female bodily functions. It's a testament to Marla's power over him that he was present in the birthing room in a West Palm Beach hospital, along with Marla's mother, Ann, and a birthing coach.

As hard as it is to imagine Donald Trump offering soothing encouragements to a laboring lover, Marla took "a spiritual approach to her delivery," her ob-gyn told Lifetime. She had filled her private birthing room with aromatherapy candles and cued up hours of New Age music. She and Donald "did a lot of kissing while I was delivering," Marla told the *New York Daily News*.

Another challenge to the imagination, germophobe Donald even cut the cord. "I was very nervous, because she was in a lot of pain," he told the *New York Daily News* after the ten-hour labor. "I tried to convince her to take something, but she wouldn't. I asked the doctor to convince her, but he knew Marla was determined not to take any drugs. She's so strong, such a strong woman. I'm amazed."

Two months later, they wed, on December 20, 1993, at the Plaza, the "*Mona Lisa*" of Trump's New York real estate portfolio. The site selection had an element of cruelty: it happened to be Ivana's great pride and joy, her last working-woman triumph as a Trump Organization exec. Donald's kids didn't come, but eleven hundred people showed up to witness Marla, in a white peau de soie Carolina Herrera dress with a "sweetheart neckline" and a demure full veil covering her face, and the something borrowed on her head in the form of a loaned $2 million tiara from Harry Winston jewelers, marry Donald Trump.

The shotgun wedding was of such grandeur that it rivaled the royal ceremonies Mary Trump was addicted to watching. B-list celebrities, all smudged with just a little corruption or scandal, packed the place to the rafters: Don King, O.J. Simpson (beloved, pre-murder), gunrunner Khashoggi, and of course the tabloid press, because in 1993, if it wasn't in the *New York Post*, and the *Daily News*, it didn't happen.

The reviews were not unanimously gushing: *Daily News* writer Amy Pagnozzi called it "tacky" and "depraved in its conception." Radio jock Howard Stern, well on his way to becoming Trump's on-air psychoanalyst, showed up dressed in what he called his "Dracula look"—purple sunglasses, dark velvet jacket—and bestowed a prophecy on the proceedings that would turn out to be closer to accurate than the lifelong happiness in standard wedding toasts. "It's probably in bad taste, but I give it four months," he told reporters.

The bride and groom looked picture-perfect, but true bliss was out of reach. A few days prior, Trump had handed the bride-to-be a prenup giving her far less than what her predecessor had just received. Marla signed it. She was, after all, now a single mother, and two-month-old Tiffany needed a daddy.

Like Ivana, who had been nervous and felt out of place and insecure at the first Trump wedding, Marla was overwhelmed. She would later claim her smiles were forced. The wedding, she would say, "didn't feel right to me." Trump, for his part, told biographer Timothy O'Brien (whom he would later sue for understating his net worth) that, as he greeted his bride at the altar, "I was bored when she was walking down the aisle. I kept thinking, 'What the hell am I doing here?'"

The honeymoon year didn't go well. The arrival of the bright Georgia Peach in 1990 had heralded a darkness. Misfortune had befallen Trumplandia, a blight ate away at business and reputation. Marla was the Avenging Angel of Trump's middle years, payback for his excess and success. As she cavorted at the US Open, giggling and handing out eight-by-ten glossies of herself in shorts and hard hat, the brand got cheesier and more laughable by the day. Later, she'd say she didn't even believe in it herself. "I was caught up in the drama. I couldn't get out. . . . I didn't know how to get out, and like he'd say, 'Well, I wasn't stopping you.' But the truth was it felt like I was swimming against the current every day. I felt completely smothered and I didn't know how to get out."

The joke was now always on Donald. Six months into their married life, a few days after Donald's forty-eighth birthday, he threw himself a party in Atlantic City, highlighted with a pay-per-view performance by David Hasselhoff. Just as the show was getting started, all eyes turned to the television screens and away from the stage. Viewers at home too were not going to be watching Hasselhoff. Every television network was focused live on a white Bronco, slowly moving through LA, as O.J. Simpson tried to elude police. The party fell apart after that, with Donald muttering over and over to anyone within earshot, "I know O.J., I know O.J.," over and over, one partygoer said, recalling that "It was like he needed to insert himself into the story."

In *An Intimate Portrait: Marla Maples Trump*—the Lifetime television documentary/infomercial filmed in the year after the wedding—Marla appears in the first and last shots au naturel, bucking the glam brand, sans makeup, clad in unflattering high-waisted mom jeans, sneakers, and with infant Tiffany strapped to her back. The camera follows her walking around the grounds of Mar-a-Lago alone, looking deeply out of place. Without the stiletto heels, without the nanny pushing the pram, and without full makeup, she looked less like a Trump wife than an off-hours Trump Spa employee allowed to stick around and enjoy herself on the posh grounds for an afternoon. Meanwhile, out of frame, up in New York, her bloated, middle-aged husband was cutting deals, and their romance was just a memory.

Watching the program reminded me of a piece of advice I received from an elegant, older woman who was bureau chief at *People* magazine in Washington in the 1990s. The staff was almost all female, and we would daily gather in her office to plan the day's coverage. One morning we found her studying a copy of the *Washington Post*. She held it up to share a photo of former Redskins owner Jack Kent Cooke and his gorgeous younger wife. The couple were on a yacht, in bathing clothes. The old man's chicken skin and sagging man boobs were in remarkable contrast to the fresh windblown younger woman beside him, who was not his daughter, but his lover. "Girls," said our experienced bureau chief. "Let me tell you something. When you marry for money, you earn it." We laughed, of course, but there was nothing really funny about Marla in her *Intimate Portrait*.

CHAPTER 12

◇◇◇◇◇◇

Ivana's Brand vs. Marla's Brand

Q: Describe your personal style.

A: Glamour, pure and simple. I love beautiful clothes—
high fashion, brilliant colors and patterns. I love being a
standout in a crowd, being noticed and appreciated for
taking the time to really put myself together.

Q: How often do you shop?

A: I don't go into shops. It's too much of a hassle for
me. People come up to talk to me, which is wonderful,
but it is not conducive to shopping. So, I do a lot
of it by catalogue. I also do 'Net surfing to shop
and designers always send me videos of their latest
collections to choose from.

Q: How did you learn your style?

A: I don't think style is learned. I think you're born with
it. As an only child, I always stood out, and as an adult,
I like the stand out fashion sense I have.

—IVANA TRUMP TO FARRAH WEINSTEIN, *NEW YORK POST*,

MAY 21, 2000

While Marla was settling into her new role as Mrs. Trump, Ivana
Trump was persona non grata at Mar-a-Lago and the Tower of T but
reigning over a new domain as the first "queen of the home shopping

network." On the screens, she was a glitzier, secular, Slavic version of Tammy Faye Bakker, whose face was the other big-haired blonde for channel surfers. There was a brand void, a market for a pretty, damaged woman selling not, like Tammy Faye, faith in God, but skin creams and affordable baubles and clothing. Ivana found it, and filled it, and the dollars flowed in, to the tune of, she once boasted, "up to $46,000 a minute."

Unschooled in business, except at the University of Donald (not to be confused with Trump U, the "fraud from beginning to end" as New York attorney general Eric Schneiderman called it, years later), Ivana, a collectivist child who'd majored in gym, proved to be a capitalist idiot savant who instinctively applied textbook marketing strategy. Perhaps recalling the unrequited longing Western brands once inspired in her and her friends in Prague, she understood that people will pay more for a brand if it has emotional content. Every brand needs a story, otherwise why not buy that same cheap silk blouse at Nordstrom?

You can still find her on YouTube, even though the product is all sold out and she's moved on. Hair piled high, pretty in pink, purring Zsa Zsa Gabor English, giggling intimately and holding up silk shirts and hand creams and fragrances with her name on them. "Welcome to the House of Ivana." Gold letters swirl on the screen, forming the words *House of Ivana*, and then there she is, hawking a *rrrromatic* scent. Or a silky white blouse, priced to sell at $79.99. Always, the 99 cents, because people will pay anything, but not a dollar more.

Unschooled but savvy, she instinctively applied marketing strategy that her own kids and their peers at Wharton would spend hundreds of classroom hours and a small fortune to obtain. People will pay more for a brand with a story, and Ivana had a good story to tell. She hired ghostwriters to tell it. She published her first book three months after her divorce was finalized. *For Love Alone* is a romance novel about a Czech skier who escapes Communism and marries an emotionally abusive but irresistible American capitalist named Adam. She would publish another romance novel, a self-help book for women facing divorce called *The Best Is Yet to Come*, and put her name to an advice column called "Ask Ivana" and another advice column for *Divorce* magazine.

Damaged, she could market what she'd learned. Everything could be packaged and sold. Dressed in a white pantsuit, exuding gentleness and a sweet charm, she hit the circuit. Hawking her divorce book on Jay Leno's show, she revealed that Donald's behavior had changed her forever. "Something in the back of your mind," she said. "I will probably never be as trusting."

She put her name on little companies, her personal branches off the Trump brand tree. In 2000, she told the *New York Post* that "House of Ivana" was launching a home products line, and "Ivana, Inc." was marketing jewelry, sunglasses, clothes, and diamonds on QVC. She was developing a cashmere clothing line called "Ivana Boutique," and she would be unveiling an "Ivana doll." All the eponymous creams, jewelry, and dressy suits generated $5 million a year in sales on the Home Shopping Network, until she cut her ties with it because she wanted a "classier" stage from which to promote her brand. She told an interviewer: "I would like to build an empire like the House of Chanel or the House of Dior, but with a line of clothing at affordable prices."

Over the years, she owned and abandoned numerous trademarks, for clothing, perfume, and even bottled water. When her ex was elected president she still had active trademarks in jewelry, eyeglasses, wine, and a website. She wrote a book after he was elected, and before its publication, filed an "intent to use" request with the US trademark office to safeguard her name for books, celebrity promotion services, television and radio shows, and motion picture production, according to government filings.

She also parlayed her brand into advertising for other brands. She portrayed herself in Kentucky Fried Chicken ads that aired in the UK, and in a pizza ad with Donald, in which the two of them suggestively looked at each other before indulging in a pie.

"I don't need the money," she said of the ads. "But I enjoy working. I can't just sit at home and look at the ceiling and have my nails polished."

But in fact, she might have needed the money too. "Need" being more than a relative term in her life. Throughout the nineties, she was always on the hustle, pitching and promoting and picking up the phone—much like The Donald—to test ideas in the public market via friendly tabloids, casting far to see whether she'd get a bite.

In 1997, she told the *New York Post* she had a "guide to elegant dining all ready to go." It would be based on what she'd learned in all the entertaining she'd done "at my homes in Greenwich and New York and Saint-Tropez" but would allow women "on a budget" to "mix and match." She also announced that she had a book for women on how to start their own business ready to go to press. Neither of those tomes ever came to be. She frequently talked about major, if vague, business deals in Europe, none of which are known to have panned out. As late as 2009, she was bragging about "major hotel developments" in Dubai, Bahrain, and Mumbai, hotels in ten cities that would be called "Le Diamond by Ivana!" and boutique hotels in the Fiji Islands. None have been developed. She did reportedly buy a 33 percent stake in Croatia's second-largest daily newspaper—with a circulation of 100,000 in 1998 (perhaps because she was spending a lot of yachting time along the Adriatic Coast). And in 1999 she launched her own lifestyle magazine—*Ivana's Living in Style*—cloning Martha Stewart's or Oprah's successful brand-named publications, but it too went nowhere.

Her lifestyle supplemented her brand, and it was key to maintain it. She almost exclusively dated (and twice married) Italian playboys, most of them with a very rollable "r" in their first or last name. One of them—a Long Island Ferrari dealer—gifted her with a red Ferrari, thus putting her into the precise demographic that Donald had once said would be the ideal condo buyer in his glass tower.

She and Donald eventually grew friendly again. She bought herself a house in Florida, on Jungle Road. She paid $4.4 million for the nine-bedroom, thirteen-bath mansion, with a lotus-shaped swimming pool and a tunnel to the beach. Moorish style, it was designed by Addison Mizner and had a name, Concha Marina. It wasn't Mar-a-Lago, but it kept her in the lifestyle. She also bought town houses in Saint-Tropez, where rich Russians, brimming over with post–Soviet flight capital, were Hoovering up properties. And she scored an elegant Upper East Side town house in Manhattan.

She invited reporters and photographers into the dwellings regularly over the years. A typical shoot appeared in *People* magazine in 2009, headlined "Inside Ivana Trump's Over-the-Top Townhouse!" Ivana, by this time sixty years old, posed lounging on a divan with her Yorkie. "In each of my homes," she said, "I have a leopard room. I don't know why, but I do. It's like my lounge next to the dressing rooms." The caption below the picture of her feline mufti on a daybed read: "The cheetah painting above her was bought while on safari in Africa."

She was making lots of lemonade with Trump's lemons. Her twenty-second cameo in Hollywood's *First Wives Club* (with Bette Midler, Diane Keaton, and Goldie Hawn as ditched middle-aged wives) offered a grim laugh to jilted women: "You have to be strong and independent and remember, don't get mad, get everything."

The Ivana brand was luxurious without being unattainable, piquant without being man-hating, and quite true to the character of its mascot, the immigrant American yuppie baby boomer everywoman.

Her rather sad fate as a working woman during the second wave of feminism—a wave she herself would never publicly embrace—was to try and fail to craft a female version of her ex. If Donald dated younger and younger models and beauty queens, she would be a "cougar" and date younger men for the rest of her life. If Donald put his name on everything from water to steak, she would plaster "Ivana" on an empire to rival Dior. But her brand aimed at multitasking women making substantially less than men, and stuck with the bulk of the housework. To them she spoke from the couch at the home shopping channels: You can still be sexy, just wear my affordable perfume and affordable silk blouse with the *rrrromantic* peephole. And if worse comes to worst and he leaves, look, just open the Chardonnay and build yourself your own little leopard room, in the ranch house you can and will win in the divorce.

The brand got her through the first post-divorce decade, but it didn't weather the test of time. "She built her own empire that didn't last as long as I'm sure she would've liked it to," said a New York friend. "There was a time with the jewelry and stuff, writing columns for the *Star*, a bigger moment. She said that 'everybody hated Marla and loved Ivana' and that they really took her side. Marla was never social. And Ivana was. Not the Jackie O world. Not Mrs. Mellon's world, but the jet-set world. Aspen and Saint-Tropez. She was a star like that."

Ivana's pals noticed that Ivana never really changed. "People who are born poor have a different outlook on life," recalled one of the lunching ladies. "Born poor stays fancy. She came on the scene right when America went into a fame thing, and with the Home Shopping Network women could shop with someone famous. Nothing changed at all with that woman. She was born poor and she married a rich man and became elegant. In person, she was the same sensitive sweetheart."

◇◇◇◇

While Ivana was off investing her divorce settlement in real estate, looking for Italian lovers, and building her personal branch of the Trump brand, Donald was trying to help Marla Maples with her brand. Donald loved to play Pygmalion with all his women, from wives to the porn star he allegedly seduced by promising a spot on *Celebrity Apprentice*. The one wife he let improve him, Ivana, had gotten too good at what he was supposed to know best, and she had to go. Helping his women get modeling contracts and parts on television became as much his avocation as building and branding Trump buildings and selling Trump steaks, wine, water, and golf courses.

Marla may have been Donald's first girl project—the first of many women he would mold to his own *Playboy* magazine Vegas showgirl ideal of female beauty and then try to sell. He insisted she pose for *Playboy* and reportedly negotiated a million-dollar fee for her, but she wouldn't do it.

Unlike Ivana, who had fourteen years and a legitimate Trump marriage with which to mold her branch of the brand, Marla was in her twenties and coming into the light after years of secret assignations with a married man. She wanted to be called an actress. But the explosion of salacious publicity, a spasm of attention, overwhelmed her. She was "the other woman," or as Ivana would call her, forty years later, still unable to bring her mouth to say *Marla*, "The Showgirl."

Marla's brand was destined to be a flash, a fad, something or someone people were aware of for a few years, like '90s tabloid diversions Octomom or Skeet Ulrich, before moving on. She would be "tabloid Marla" until she retreated from view. For a few years, as hard as it is to imagine now, hundreds of grown men and women were active participants and beneficiaries in the Marla Maples industry.

It started while she was still in hiding, somewhere between Guatemala and Atlantic City. Two months after the Aspen Incident, *New York Post* writer Matthew Flamm reviewed all the Marla Maples on-screen moments, a column that allowed the writer to exercise his cleverness like few other topics that week. There was the "small but finely nuanced role" in a 1986 Stephen King thriller called *Maximum Overdrive*, in which she appeared in a beige tennis outfit, in a car, and screamed before a watermelon rolled off a truck and smashed her. In

The Secret of My Success she played closer to type, a tennis player at a Litchfield County house party. Flamm wrote: "Maples doesn't need dialogue, running for the ball on beauty pageant legs, or tossing back those luscious locks of hair while she pretends (what an actress!) to be happy around middle aged megalomaniacs. The scene is one of those supreme moments in art when realism is suddenly real, effort seems effortless, and the viewer feels like a voyeur."

The same month as the *Post* published Flamm's pièce de snark on her acting oeuvre, *Penthouse* and *Playboy* publicly offered Marla hundreds of thousands of dollars to pose nude. She declined through a spokesman named Chuck Jones, the PR man at the white-hot center of the Marla Maples Industry for several years (until he was consumed by the chain reaction himself).

"She wouldn't do it if they offered a million dollars," Jones said. "She wouldn't take off her clothes this year or any year." (Trump would later up the ante, but the answer was the same.)

The Marla Industry didn't financially benefit Marla, at least not in the beginning, but other people were riding her name. A man named George Carpozi Jr. turned out a whole magazine called *The Real Story—Trump* with Marla on the cover. The television newsmagazine *A Current Affair* obtained an Italian ad of Marla in pantyhose and film of Marla strutting her stuff in a Hawaiian beauty pageant. A fly-by-night company called Vestry Video put out an action comedy with Marla in it.

Suddenly, her moment had arrived. With Donald playing Pygmalion, she would craft the delayed acting career out of the inescapable fame. But where to start? She did two ads for No Excuses jeans—the company that built a brand on tarnished young women like Senator Gary Hart's *Monkey Business* yacht friend Donna Rice. Marla agreed—she said—only because the company promised to let her say something about the environment. "The most important thing we can do today is clean up our planet. And I'm starting with these," she said, as she tossed into trash cans the tabloid newspapers the *Star* and the *Enquirer* with headlines about her.

But CBS and NBC refused to air the attacks on the press, so the ads ran without her message.

Paparazzi followed her everywhere, snapping her with well-heeled Manhattan playboys—not Trump—at restaurant of the moment Indochine, clad in black leather and a three-inch miniskirt. They stalked her to the Hamptons and beyond, locating her supposedly "hiding out in posh Caribbean digs." Eventually her team hired lawyers and private investigators to go after people leaking photos and videos of her, adding another level of employment opportunity to the multilevel Marla Industry.

Meanwhile an ex-boyfriend and frequent "walker" to her Trump trysts, ex-NYPD officer Tom Fitzsimmons, was reportedly producing a $10 million action film based on his experiences that would star Maples, and his twin brother, Bob, and himself. The script was called *Blue Gemini*, but was never made into a film.

She flirted with producers who wanted her to star in a Boca Raton dinner theater production of the Marilyn Monroe classic *The Seven Year Itch*. They hoped to open in the Flamingo State and then move to Broadway, but the *Post*'s review of their last effort had been headlined: "A smash in Florida, a bomb in New York." Boca was nixed.

By 1992, as she and Donald were on-again and off-again every few weeks, Marla was parlaying the media's intense curiosity into television appearances: a gig cohosting the obscure television talk show *Attitudes* with Linda Dano, a moment as "a correspondent" on *Inside Edition*, guest star spots on *Dallas* and *Designing Women*. She released an exercise video, *Journey to Fitness*.

The Marla Maples Industry hit its high point shortly before it started to tank. She got a real part singing and dancing in a Broadway musical called *The Will Rogers Follies*, which told the story of the famously affable Rogers in the form of a Ziegfeld Follies production.

The play got good reviews, and ran on Broadway for more than two years, from May 1991 to September 1993. Marla joined the cast in August 1992, and for nine months she worked nearly every day, donning a skimpy outfit and a cowboy hat, and playing impresario Ziegfeld's favorite chorus girl.

Marla would later claim she didn't take naturally to the Trump brand. She was a simple soul who craved the real. "I am basically the kid you see now," she told New York journalist Michael Gross in 1998. "I am the kid that likes to go without makeup and let my hair grow naturally, and not have to keep an image up. And once I started going out in public, an image was expected, and here goes the hair and here goes the makeup and here are all the designer dresses . . . and then you become kind of a caricature of yourself. He wanted to change me into that person, into that thing, into that social animal."

Gross pressed her about her role in creating the caricature. Wasn't it really her, "tabloid Marla," the girl who giggled to *Vanity Fair* that Donald called his Florida estate "Marla Lago" and who signed eight-by-ten glossies of herself in cutoffs and a hard hat at the US Open?

"What would you have called it?" he asked. "You give it a name."

It was 1998, the year of Monica and Bill, and the affaire de Trump was long over. She was a single mother and she was fighting for her financial life. And she was old news. The gig, which had been fun, was up. She could and would give it a name. *Sin* was what they'd call it in Cohutta, for sure. But that wasn't specific enough.

She finally replied: "It was an ugly symbol of . . . It was like the symbol of greed."

◇◇◇◇

For a while, other than her mom, Chuck Jones was her only friend, the only person she could talk to in New York, and he stayed her confidant as she hid out and then reemerged, and as her closet filled up with those designer dresses and beauty pageant stilettos that she would later say made her a caricature. "Let me put it to you this way," he would tell *Vanity Fair*. "She needed someone she could talk to, because if Marla meets some guy on the street who claims he's a producer, who's she gonna call? Not the ghostbusters!"

Marla met Chuck Jones after she arrived in New York, and before she met Trump, through a mutual friend. Jones, who resembled Bill Murray, was an ex-Marine and former head of East Coast publicity for Embassy Pictures. A New York type, he knew a little about talent and a lot about bullshitting with the media. He would tell *Vanity Fair*, in 1990, "Right now I'd say we're considering three or four major things for Marla in TV, broadcasting, and movies. If they break, I'll call you right away." *Vanity Fair* would describe him as "a vision in full taupe," sporting a gold bracelet and matching ring "copied from a little-known Egyptian prince I've long admired whose name I forget at the moment," he told the writer.

"To me, Marla's visibility is an asset at this point, but it's not something that guarantees her success. The media has portrayed Marla as a disorganized shapely bimbo, and that is not what she is." He charged her relatively little for his services, which at first were textbook: manage one of thousands of young pretty girls in the Big City looking for a break. He pitched her to Hollywood producers, got her bit parts, and when Trump entered her life, he served as her shoulder to sob on.

His Marla work ran from the sublime to the ridiculous. Quick with a quote, he ran interference for her with tabloid gossips. There was often a catfight to sort out. In 1992, Page Six reported that Marla Maples had refused to pose for a picture with Michael Jackson's sister La Toya, after a source had overheard her calling La Toya "low class." La Toya then called Marla and said: "You are nothing but a Southern piece of trash. How can you call somebody low class? How low can you get, stealing another woman's husband?"

To the *Post*, La Toya admitted making a call, but wouldn't go into detail.

Chuck Jones was called. He told the newspaper: "Marla respects La Toya Jackson."

When Marla got the Broadway part, he promised: "She'll have the same effect on audiences as Marilyn Monroe."

After the Aspen Incident, and while she was in hiding, Jones was The Man to call, whose phone number producers put on speed dial. Newspaper and television assignment desks had teams of photographers all over town, staking out his most famous client. The office phone rang off the hook for weeks. "I was wired. I served in Vietnam—as a combat correspondent. This was like a war, too—like being in combat again."

But the PTSD got the better of him. Beginning in the late 1980s, while she was still in hiding, Marla started noticing that her shoes were evaporating. From stilettos to sneakers, they kept disappearing from her closet.

"It got to be crazy," Trump said. "She'd call me and say, 'Somebody took my shoes.' I thought it was ridiculous." Donald saw for himself what was happening when he picked her up for a date one night, and saw her sneakers beside some jewelry on the way out. When they got back, the jewelry was there but the shoes were not.

A Trump security guard installed a video camera in Marla's closet, and the guard soon called Trump with the news: "Mr. Trump, I got him." Marla then watched footage of her trusted manager and friend making off with a pair of her pumps. When she confronted him, and urged him to get psychiatric help, he got belligerent. Police were called, and Jones, who shared a Greenwich mansion with a wife and two small children, was booked and jailed for three nights.

Cops searched his office and found a copy of the foot fetish magazine *Spike*, articles of Marla's clothing including lingerie, and dozens of Marla's missing shoes, some slashed down the back. When confronted with the evidence, Jones reportedly said to an NYPD officer, "You wouldn't understand."

People magazine, covering the scandal, consulted popular psychologist Dr. Joyce Brothers to explain that Jones's fetish grew out of unrequited desire for his most famous client. "It's possible he had so much emotional investment in Marla that her shoes became important as a source of sexual gratification," Brothers said.

Coming out of jail, Jones sobbed and begged forgiveness of Marla and Donald. "I love them both. I failed them both miserably." But Marla, by now able to stand on her own two feet in Manhattan's public relations mosh pit—or at least now represented by the best PR man in town, her soon-to-be husband—no longer needed Jones to write her lines.

"The show must go on," she announced. "Chuck is fired."

Her marriage to Donald lasted exactly three years, four months, and twelve days before she herself was fired. She would later say that the romance fizzled almost as soon as it went public, secrecy being an aphrodisiac and privacy being more conducive to normal intimate partnerships.

The truth was, though, that as malleable as young Marla had seemed to Donald—certainly in comparison with super-mom CEO Ivana—she really wasn't as easily controlled. She chafed and resisted his public molding, wouldn't sit still and let Trump brand her into the ideal Trump woman. She actually preferred yoga leggings and tennis shoes and jeans.

She didn't even really like the stiletto pumps that had driven Chuck Jones mad and which Donald so liked to see on every woman that he bought his own beauty pageant. There, he could order countless pairs of young female feet to assume the preternaturally arched Barbie-doll shape.

CHAPTER 13

✧✧✧✧✧✧

The Second Divorce

Twenty years later, Marla Maples "opened up," as the entertainment press likes to put it, to Billy Bush about the "Best Sex I Ever Had" headline. She laid the blame on Donald. "Let's put it this way—I think [Donald] had an opportunity to [take] that story out of the papers and he chose not to," Marla told Billy on camera. "That was pretty awful at the time. Now it's funny to look back on, but at the time it was so humiliating!"

"So you never said it?" Billy continued.

"Did I ever say it? I don't want to destroy him!" She laughed. "Maybe I whispered it somewhere along the way? But not for public domain."

More than a year after Trump was elected president, a *New York Post* reporter, Jill Brooke, would write in the *Hollywood Reporter* that she recalled hearing Trump himself, on speakerphone, urging the editor to run the "Best Sex" headline. Trump was stewing over the bad press he was getting from leaks from Ivana's side of the divorce war. According to Brooke, the conversation went like this:

"'What gets a front-page story?' Donald asked. The veteran newsman [Jerry Nachman] contemplated the question. 'It's usually murder, money, or sex.' Donald fired back: 'Marla says with me it's the *best* sex she's ever had.' Nachman's face lit up like a firecracker. 'That's great!' he said. 'But you know I need corroboration.' 'Marla,' Trump yelled into the background. 'Didn't you say it's the best sex you ever had with me?' From a distance, we heard a faint voice: 'Yes, Donald.' Only years later did we learn that Trump sometimes impersonated voices to reporters. I still can't be sure whether the voice in the room was really hers."

Whatever the sex was really like, three years after the winter wedding, Marla was alone and bored. At four in the morning on April 16, 1996, a cop patrolling a beach near Trump's Mar-a-Lago came upon a Trump bodyguard, Spencer Wagner, a buff thirty-five-year-old martial arts instructor, and Marla, a toned thirty-two-year-old in spandex leggings and a tight jogging top, hiding under a lifeguard stand on the beach. According to the *National Enquirer*, Wagner tried to tell the cop he was there alone until Marla also emerged from underneath the same lifeguard stand.

Wagner got a parking ticket, but that was just the beginning of the story.

A few weeks later the incident broke into the New York tabloids. Marla denied everything, claiming she'd been under the stand relieving herself on the sand, with the studly bodyguard posted close by for protection. A Trump spokesman scoffed at the report too. "Along the lines of Elvis sightings and Martian invasions, the *National Enquirer* has once again fabricated a wholly unreliable cover story for this week's issue."

But four months later Trump fired Wagner, who died of a drug overdose in 2012, a man ruined by the publicity, unable to revive his private security business. His widow blamed Marla for aggressively pursuing sex with her late husband. "She was out of control and he made no bones telling me that. She just loved to party a lot. She liked to go down to Miami and party when she was in town."

As impulsive as he is, Donald could serve revenge cold. On

May 2, 1997, mere months short of a date in their prenup that would have increased Marla's divorce settlement, the couple separated. Marla first learned of the separation in a *New York Post* that Donald left for her outside their shared bedroom door, with the headline DONALD IS DIVORCING MARLA.

Soon, Trump had a new Slav on his arm, a Slovenian model seven years younger than Marla, twenty-one years younger than Ivana, and twenty-four years younger than himself.

◇◇◇◇

Trump's second divorce was in some ways nastier than his first (public recriminations went on for years), but it was much cheaper. The prenup and his strategic exit timing saved him tens of millions of dollars. Marla battled in court for two years trying to break the prenup, and the couple fought in the media. In addition to his criminal lawyer Goldberg, who would "rip your skin off," Trump hired one of Manhattan's mega-divorce lawyers, Stanford Lotwin, who told the press Marla had no one to blame but herself. "She knew what she was giving up, and she certainly knew what she was getting" from the prenup, he said.

As the divorce wound through court in downtown Manhattan— where Ivana and Donald had so recently sealed their split—Marla cut off her blond locks. She stopped bleaching her hair. The paps still recognized her, coming and going from the court building, and they snapped her shorn, painfully thin, and makeup-free, just like any other white single mother in America, but under the circumstances more like Joan of Arc headed to the pyre.

She gave up her fight for more in June 1999, accepting the offer with a statement to the press: "After giving Donald two years to honor the verbal commitments he made to me during our twelve-year relationship, I decided to walk away completely under the terms of our prenuptial agreement that had been placed before me just five days before our 1993 wedding."

In the weeks before she gave up, Marla had been in another New York courtroom, listening to a now completely unhinged Chuck Jones vilify her at his criminal shoe-stealing trial. A jury had found him guilty of burglary in 1994, but a federal judge overturned the conviction, and in his retrial, he was defending himself. He would lose, spend two years in prison, and resurface again in 2012 to stalk Maples, who had to get a restraining order against him.

She soon retreated to privacy in Los Angeles, to raise Tiffany and "pursue her acting career." By fall 1999, with her ex making noises about running for president, and getting his new girlfriend deals to pose for Times Square ads and on the covers of lad magazines, Marla told the *London Daily Telegraph* that he was an "ego-driven" attention addict, suggesting he was unfit to run for president.

Trump lawyer Jay Goldberg threatened to withhold her alimony. But a New York judge forced him to pay up. "It was never our intention to withhold the $1.5 million check," Goldberg insisted. "Our purpose was to send a message that she was playing close to the fire. That should slow her down."

It most certainly did. She had promised to write a book called *All That Glitters Is Not Gold*, to be published by right-wing publisher Judith Regan, but a confidentiality clause Trump inserted into the divorce decree effectively sewed up Marla's lips for life. Marla and a ghostwriter cranked out some chapters, but lawyers refused to allow it to go forward without Trump's express approval. The sanitized version of her story wasn't deemed publishable.

Over the years, she was still able to get under his skin. She had a keen instinct for his buttons, like when she told reporters—while they were still together—that he was so embarrassed about his middle-aged flab that he insisted on turning out the lights, or getting undressed under the covers. "I saw a vulnerable man, and I like vulnerability in people," she would say on a talk show years later, while he was running for president. "I like when you have the ability to visualize and manifest. . . . Sorry, Donald, if I'm saying you're vulnerable . . . but you know, he knows how to get what he wants."

She recast the relationship as one in which Donald had pursued a naive girl, barely twenty-two (putting the start of their relationship in 1985, a full four years before the Aspen Incident).

"No one can say I had a gun to my head," she told Michael Gross in 1998. "I was romanced. I had Mister Charm all over me, and it was very hard to say no. Because the feelings were very deep and when that man wants something, he'll stop at nothing to get it."

In 2000, a somber Marla talked to a fellow parishioner at a Palm Beach Gardens, Florida, church, about her divorce. Traumatized and reflective, martyred to a titan, painfully thin, she was visibly in the middle of trying to haul herself out of the wreckage. "I think there's something in me that Donald found that was interesting, and I hoped that my faith in God would help shift him to a new place. Because he had the money, he had the power, but he didn't have the true power in here [pointing to her heart] that we know and we feel doesn't come from money. . . . And I saw glimpses of it in him.

"When you're involved with someone that powerful, it's easy for people to say, 'Oh, well she's just social climbing. She just wants to have the money, or have the wealth or have the fame.' But I walked away from that. I mean, I walked away from it because it was the emptiest, darkest place to be."

Donald's coda on the marriage was a kick in the teeth. "Marla is a good girl, and I had a good marriage with her, but it's just that I get fuckin' bored," Trump told Michael Gross. "One of those little things."

◇◇◇◇

The first thing Ivana did after her divorce was get herself a real live Italian boyfriend, the first of three, all with full heads of natural hair and trim waists (hey Donald!) and names that besides the rolling "r," would be preceded by the words "jet-setting."

Then she bought herself a yacht on which to move them around.

Her post-Donald international coming-out party was held the summer after her divorce, in London, where she was plugging her roman à clef about the champion skier and the hot but unfaithful American millionaire. Dressed in a white suit (apparently the look of choice for all newly liberated women from Hillary Clinton to Diane Keaton, Bette Midler, and Goldie Hawn in the last scene of *The First Wives Club*), she showed up at Harrods to sign books, and give owner Mohamed Al Fayed a hug. (Al Fayed's son Dodi would soon become tragically famous as Princess Diana's doomed lover, when both died in a car accident.)

After Harrods, she headed off to a party at the Queen's dressmaker's shop, Hartnell in Bruton Street, packed with London's bold-faced fashionable B List, sipping champagne and eating giant strawberries. "I don't think it is a circus at all," she told a British reporter, dispatched to cover the event. "You have to market your product. There is no difference between old money and new money. There is nothing wrong with money. I do believe money is not everything. I am not saying that I would like to be poor. That would be ridiculous."

As 150 guests drank champagne and ate strawberries, Italian Numero Uno stood nearby dapper in suit, tie, and brushed-back, luxurious hair, ready to sound like a feminist. "The press are so nasty to her," Riccardo Mazzuchelli confided to a journalist. "Maybe because it's a macho world and the men don't like to see a woman do well. Maybe people are jealous of her and they don't like it that she's done well professionally. But she was up at 4:30 this morning to prepare to go on television. I take my hat off to her."

In November 1995, she married Mazzuchelli at the Mayfair Regent in New York, wearing a pale blue satin suit and a necklace that the *New York Post* described as "a thick rope of diamonds and a gigantic piece of ice as big as the Wollman rink nestling in the décolleté." Her best friend Nikki Haskell was present, using the event to publicize her new diet candy, "Star Suckers."

Three months earlier, Ivana had splashed out $4 million for a 105-foot yacht that slept eight in four staterooms, with a Jacuzzi. She made sure Donald (struggling to stay afloat financially and unhappily married to Marla) and her crowd in New York knew about it.

"While Donald doesn't even have a dinghy . . . Ivana is in Monte Carlo kicking the tires of a spanking new vessel," the *New York Post* reported in the summer of 1995. In the same article, she let it be known that she was paying for the vessel herself. "Sisters, Doin' It for Themselves" and all.

"I make in one year three times what he paid me in a settlement," she said. "I don't need Donald Trump's money. I don't want to be in the category of women who are unhappy and trying to get more money out of their ex-husbands."

Trump saw the article and fired off a "Dear Ivana Letter"— naturally shared with the gossip columnists—claiming he understood she had paid twice what the boat was worth. "I am not particularly happy seeing you blow money on boats, town houses, etc." As for his own long-lost yacht—sold as part of his bankruptcies—Trump applied an alternative fact to history: "I was not forced to sell the *Trump Princess*" in 1991, he said. He just got rid of it because he was "extremely busy and unable to use it."

Ivana's yacht, which she named the *M.Y. Ivana*, lasted years longer than the marriage to Mazzuchelli, which ended in July 1997, just twenty months after the wedding and five months after Donald announced his split from Marla. Mazzuchelli fought back in the media for a while, complaining that he had spent $5 million on Ivana's posh lifestyle, including a Mercedes and a Rolls-Royce and homes with servants in London and Switzerland. But it was a losing battle. *Her* prenup kept her money separate. Numero Uno never got reimbursed.

Numero Due rolled in that same summer. Cavorting along the Mediterranean in the *M.Y. Ivana*, Ivana dropped anchor at Monaco and met Roffredo Gaetani di Laurenzana dell'Aquila d'Aragona Lovatelli. Gaetani, as he was known for short, happened to be president of Ferrari Long Island. He soon gifted Ivana with a custom-made red Ferrari.

Besides the Ferrari, Ivana liked that Gaetani was "from an important family" and that the Fiat chief and legendary Italian lover Gianni Agnelli "was like an uncle to him." After their first date, he sent her a case of Brunello di Montalcino from his own family's vineyard. Soon, he moved into the town house with the leopard room. He was thin, and intelligent, "really gorgeous with big shoulders and a small waist," Ivana wrote later. "Donald was chubbier." And he was a bon vivant, where Donald was a workaholic. The only problem was that he "hung out at Cipriani downtown with his Italian friends who all wore jogging suits." Ivana helped him up his style game, though, and before long, she could report with pride that he was named "one of the best-dressed men in France."

Their relationship lasted five years, but ended tragically in 2005, the same way she had lost the love of her life in Czechoslovakia. Roffredo skidded off an icy road and died at age fifty-two, while visiting his mother in Tuscany. "I cry whenever I think about him, even now, writing this chapter," she wrote in 2017. "I have no idea why I didn't marry him."

As glamorous as her branded life looked, on the inside Ivana was not all she seemed. "She stopped going to Aspen, I think because she was unhappy," one New York friend recalled.

Less than a year after Gaetani's accident, in May 2006, she parked her yacht at Cannes for the film festival and hosted a party for two hundred. Among them was "a young, nice, very good-looking, trim, stylish man with a great sense of humor." This was male model Rossano Rubicondi, and they "got along very well."

The next day, they had lunch, and soon he was cruising from Saint-Tropez to Sardinia with her on the *M.Y. Ivana*. She learned he was only thirty-four when he handed his passport to the yacht's stewardess. Ivana, fifty-seven at the time, was surprised, but decided to forge ahead. "I'd rather be a babysitter than a nursemaid" for an older man, she liked to say. "Rossano was young, gorgeous, had some money, traveled with me, went to lunch and dinners, took me to the airport, schlepped my luggage, and drove me around."

He would do fun things too, like wear a Donald Trump wig and go out to a Hollywood Halloween with her on his arm. He would compete in the Mar-a-Lago tennis tournaments—Ivana was now back in her ex's good graces and sharing time there with her children. After two years of frolic, she decided to get married at Mar-a-Lago, a big affair with fifty attendants, a $1 million diamond ring, and five hundred guests. "Donald was kind enough to waive the $20,000 fee," she wrote.

The night before the wedding, she wore a Bob Mackie beaded and pearled dress too heavy to walk in. The next day, with Ivanka as maid of honor, and flanked by her boys Eric and Don in white tuxedoes, she wore a pink silk Zuhair Murad dress and got hitched for the fourth time. Donald (by now recently married himself for the third time) stood nearby and watched. She sat him at a table with his business friends. Guests lunched on foie gras, caviar, and lamb, and the band struck up the *Rocky* theme as Rossano entered the ballroom.

The wedding day ended early—at three in the afternoon, to give Ivana time to attack the "daunting task" of choosing her selects from ten thousand shots of the event "as part of our exclusive rights deal with Getty." She changed out of her hot pink, feather-tailed cocktail dress and into a jogging suit to work on that job for the next fourteen hours.

Italian Numero Tre was not destined to last either. Even before the event, Ivana admitted to wondering if he was "using" her. She made him sign a prenup. Within days of the wedding, she flew to France and he went down to Miami. While in Saint-Tropez, Ivana got word that Rossano was in France, traveling with a Cuban girl he'd picked up in Florida.

A year later, they were divorced, without publicity or acrimony. Today they are "like family," with Rossano still hanging around, talking about opening a pizza shop in Florida or New York, and even showing up to twirl and dip her on a segment of Italian *Dancing with the Stars*. Before Rossano, she toyed with the idea of a reality show herself called *Ivana Young Man*, making a joke of her serious inclinations. Now, at sixty-nine, her delicate beauty, which never photographed well, has faded. Still, the paps snap away at her as she strolls the streets of Saint-Tropez in Pucci minidresses and slingbacks, showing off the long, athletic legs that got her out of Communism and into the luxurious West.

She might have liked to be first lady to the first husband, but he is a man who would never allow himself to be photographed with a woman who looks her (his) age on his arm. His personal Dorian Gray, Ivana is a living martyr to the "Ivana Have It All" boomer women's dashed dream of mastering the universal loss of power that afflicts women over fifty. "What's a mature woman with an attraction to younger men to do?" she mused in her book *Raising Trump*. "I'm certainly not going to marry a man who cheats or tries to control me. Since men are men, and many men cheat and control, I don't see another marriage in my future. But romance and fun will always be part of my life."

The post-divorce lives of the two Trump exes were vastly different. Ivana embraced the Trump brand and styled herself after Donald's ideal femme—primped, stilettoed, bejeweled, peroxided, bustiered, like a mistress, not a wife. She also styled herself as a mini-Donald, with her yacht, her younger men, and her voracious embrace of capitalism and "deals." Marla rejected the brand before the divorce was even final, appearing in public shorn, in flat shoes, and without makeup. Later, living in Southern California, she joined the whole grain, green juice, woo-and-crystals ranks of the state's inner peace seekers, and stayed on the periphery of Hollywood glitter. Ivana would always call her "The Showgirl," but Marla's acting career was never the same after Donald dumped her.

CHAPTER 14

◇◇◇◇◇◇◇

Buying Beauty Queens

Beautiful women are absolutely not why he bought it.
—TRUMP PAGEANT DIRECTOR JIM GIBSON

Jim Gibson, Donald Trump's future director of pageant affairs for the Miss Universe Organization, which includes the Miss Universe, Miss USA, and Miss Teen USA franchises, was working down in DC, singing at a club called Mr. Sam's, when he first met The Donald through Hall of Fame NFL quarterback Jim Kelly. It was sometime in the eighties, and Kelly and Donald were discussing Kelly possibly playing on Trump's USFL team—the one that got sacked into oblivion in 1986.

Gibson had also once dated a Miss Georgia contestant named Marla Maples. They'd stayed friends too. That's how small a world it is. In 1996, not long after that contestant, now Mrs. Trump, was caught under a Florida lifeguard stand with a Trump bodyguard, Donald Trump was for the first time receptive to Gibson's repeated suggestion that he buy himself his own beauty pageant.

"Some events I did were in casinos and as we became better acquainted, I had mentioned to him that the pageants might be a good marketing situation for him to consider, as an asset to build," Gibson recalled. "I had been working with the Miss Universe people for twenty-five years, and it was almost as if I went to Donald as I would if I had a property to renovate and modernize and make it profitable enough to sell."

Trump bought Miss Universe in 1996 from ITT Corp., which was spinning off its nonmanufacturing companies, and looking to get rid of the pageant because TV ratings were down. "Donald, as he always does, brought in CPAs and did financial reviews," Gibson said. "And he came to the conclusion that the valuation was low and there were things he could do to bring the valuation up."

Trump's plan to bring the valuation up was pretty basic. "I'll make the bikinis smaller and the heels higher," he promised. Plus it made a kind of historical sense that Trump, with his Atlantic City connections, even imploding as they were, and his skills as a boardwalk impresario, would take on a pageant. Beauty contests had been held in Atlantic City since at least 1902. So he bought the Miss Universe organization, and cut a deal with first CBS, and then NBC, to televise it.

"It was from day one a business proposition," Gibson said. "In my years with Trump, it is always a business when he's looking to purchase an asset. It is not a game. He saw a buyer's market."

The Miss Universe Organization still produces three branded big pageants: Miss Universe, Miss USA, and Miss Teen USA. The franchise now operates in between eighty and one hundred countries, each of which annually run their own smaller pageants and send a candidate to compete. After Trump got hold of Miss USA and Miss Teen USA, they began to consistently rank among the most watched television programming in the world, according to the organization.

Like all competitions at the higher levels of American capitalism, Miss USA and Miss Universe are not competitions in the strictest sense of the word. That fact is a problem that has occasionally erupted into bad publicity and at least one lawsuit. Under Trump, the contestants were said to understand the economic model for the pageant was to make money, and thus, the selection of girls wasn't left entirely to chance. The organization reserved the right to select the top fifteen, and if the judges disagreed, the organization could insist and overrule them.

Sometimes, the pageant would decide it was a good idea—financially and brand-wise—to have a winner who was a minority or who had served in the military, or—jackpot!—both. For example, according to pageant coach Bill Alverson, who has many Miss USA and Miss Universe contestants under his belt, "That's attractive and that's marketable and that's where the business model comes into it."

Viewed benignly, the pageants are part of American folklore, our way to create royalty. They also provide a herd of pretty women for men to ogle. And Trump naturally gravitated toward the business of sashes and pretty lasses, a business that allowed him to do one of the things he liked best: to make his own queens—hundreds and hundreds of them.

"A lot of people say pageants are horrible for women," Alverson said. "But *life* is a pageant. You put on makeup when you go out to a bar, and men, why do you brush your teeth? You are being evaluated and you are evaluating all the time. We have eyeballs for a reason."

New bachelor Donald began his new midlife in a playpen of gorgeous women. Within the first year of buying the franchise, he was taking liberties, *droit du seigneur*. Mariah Billado, Miss Vermont Teen USA 1997, and three other contestants from that year recalled that he wandered into their changing area backstage. "I remember putting on my dress really quick because I was like, 'Oh my god, there's a man in here,'" Billado said. Miss Arizona Tasha Dixon recalled the same activity at the 2001 contest.

"He just came strolling right in," Dixon said. "There was no second to put a robe on or any sort of clothing or anything. Some girls were topless. Other girls were naked. Our first introduction to him was when we were at the dress rehearsal and half-naked changing into our bikinis." Dixon said employees of the Miss Universe Organization encouraged contestants to pander to Trump. "To have the owner come waltzing in, when we're naked, or half-naked, in a very physically vulnerable position and then to have the pressure of the people that worked for him telling us to go fawn all over him, go walk up to him, talk to him, get his attention . . ."

During the 2016 presidential campaign, when the women came forward, a certain segment of the American voting population (bluestockings and killjoys) were appalled. But for a decade on Howard Stern's show, Trump regularly bragged about checking out the beauties in his franchise, like a man inspecting the teeth and legs of a horse. "I'll go backstage before a show, and everyone's getting dressed and ready and everything else," he told Stern, in one of the sex-related reveries the radio deejay elicited from him. "You know, no men are anywhere. And I'm allowed to go in because I'm the owner of the pageant. And therefore I'm inspecting it. . . . Is everyone okay? You know, they're standing there with no clothes. And you see these incredible-looking women. And so I sort of get away with things like that," he said. (Trump sold the Miss Universe Organization to talent and marketing agency WME-IMG in 2015 as his political career took off.)

When Trump bought the pageant, he belonged to a group of wealthy international men who also used leggy beautiful women to show off to one another, and to close business deals. Access to the girls made the men bigger in one another's eyes, and certainly in Donald's. Trump's ownership of an actual pageant made him enviable indeed in this particular crowd. The fact that he could offer the winners an apartment at Trump Tower, for example, kept some of them in his orbit.

The line between crime and marketable female beauty is thin sometimes. Andrew Dice Clay, in a monologue at one of the casinos, thanked Donald Trump for the Atlantic City hookers. Just a joke, of course. Trump toed the edge at the pageants too. He put a mob-affiliated crony named Joseph "Joey No-Socks" Cinque on as a Miss Universe judge. Cinque needed a new paying gig: in 1989 he had been convicted of possessing stolen art in his apartment overlooking Central Park.

Besides mobsters and local millionaires and billionaires, rich Russians moved among the men in Trump's set who shared this habit of professionally ogling women. Russians—post-Soviet Russians—loved pageants almost as much as they loved vodka.

Trump's desire for Putin's best friendship had existed for some time. In 2013, Trump managed to cut a deal with Russian billionaire Aras Agalarov to host the Miss Universe pageant in Moscow. Agalorov's son Emin is a Russian pop star, and he was represented by a British publicist named Rob Goldstone. Goldstone would go on to gain fifteen minutes of political fame for shooting an email to Donald Trump Jr. during the 2016 campaign, offering to share Russian intel on Hillary Clinton. Among the VIPs at the 2013 Moscow pageant was a former Trump Tower denizen, Alimzhan Tokhtakhounov, indicted but never captured by the FBI for alleged mob activities in the United States, including running a gambling ring out of Trump Tower. Tokhtakhounov hit the red carpet within minutes of Trump. (He is now living in Russia and has never gone back to the US.)

Trump announced the venue in June 2013, saying Russia had beaten out seventeen other countries. "Moscow right now in the world is a very, very important place," he said. "We wanted Moscow all the way." Trump added of the Agalarovs: "One of the great families in Russia is our partner in this endeavor."

After announcing Moscow as the 2013 pageant venue, Trump tweeted, "Do you think Putin will be going to The Miss Universe Pageant in November in Moscow—if so, will he become my new best friend?" He reportedly had even tried to manipulate the outcome of the 2002 Miss Universe pageant to award the title to Oxana Fedorova, then rumored to be Vladimir Putin's mistress.

It had been twenty-six years since Trump's first "fantastic" 1987 tour to Moscow and St. Petersburg (then called Leningrad) with Ivana. He returned at least three times, not counting visits to pursue business deals in Czechoslovakia when it was still part of the USSR. A lot of water over the dam, a lot of Russians had bought Trump condos, a lot of Slavs in his life. So many that private investigators like Glenn Simpson (whose company produced the infamous Steele dossier) and investigative journalists like Craig Unger were piecing together evidence that Trump buildings all over the world were literally a washing machine for dirty Russian flight capital and mob money. They found connections with ultra-violent Russian mafiosi, and patterns of hidden buyers buying and selling and rebuying Trump condos in New York (as early as 1984), Florida, Panama, and even more remote corners of the planet. On this trip, for the 2013 pageant, Donald didn't bring his new third wife. He traveled with a desiccated billionaire buddy from Vegas named Phil Ruffin, seventy-eight years old at the time, another ancient modelizer and casino magnate who, like Donald, had married a stunning Slavic model, his young enough to be his granddaughter.

Putin did not attend the pageant, despite Trump's plaintive tweet in advance of the gala. Putin didn't show, but according to Christopher Steele, Putin's spies were paying keen attention to the doings of their Big American Guest.

<><><>

The link between crime and beauty has many levels. The global mafia traffic in debt-bonded Eastern European or Asian or African girls. Another kind of transaction plays out in the open, in posh hotel rooms and glittery clubs, in big cities and resort playgrounds— wherever rich, bored men with disposable income find themselves in the mood for a graceful gazelle.

Donald Trump was a player in the Manhattan model game from way back: he was hosting parties on his yacht for Look of the Year contestants while he still had the boat and was still married to Ivana. The biggest player on the scene then was an agency called Elite, operated from the 1970s through the 1990s by a notorious Lothario—John Casablancas—who would ultimately go down under accusations of pedophilia for his predilection for sex with barely menstruating models (and be saved from unemployment with a Trump Organization job in Brazil). In the mid-nineties, as Trump became single again, Casablancas had something that Donald started to want. Not just the girls, but the power to control them, brand them, show them off, and move them around to impress other modelizers.

One of Trump's accusers, Lisa Boyne, described a typical night out at Raoul's, a favorite with Trump during those years. With Boyne sitting between them, Casablancas brought along four or five models, and Trump asked them to walk on the table so he could look under their skirts. They obliged—partly because walking over the tables was the only way they could leave, being literally trapped, sandwiched into the banquette by men on both ends.

For a man in Trump's position—single again, dating beauties he could select from his own pageants or from his pal Casablancas's menu—owning his own models started to make sense. Why rely on Casablancas? Why not cut out the middleman?

Trump was accustomed to hanging out with celebs and rich men in Manhattan who used off-duty models as lures, bait, prey, and baubles with which to decorate themselves and arouse the envy of their peers. Even before Donald split from Marla in 1997, he had returned to the circuit, sipping Diet Coke at parties arranged for self-styled players like himself, stocked with herds of lovelies chauffeured around by drivers hired by the agencies. According to some witnesses who partied at the Plaza and on his yacht, he'd never really left the circuit, even while married to Ivana.

According to a short documentary that ran on the BBC in July 2018 called *Trump: Is the President a Sex Pest?*, the number of women at the parties he attended and hosted vastly outnumbered the older men, and sometimes the girls were as young as fourteen or fifteen years old. One American model who spoke to the BBC about the parties she attended with Trump present also said she believed the youngest ones were "from Europe."

Another former model Heather Braden, recalled being at a party with Trump in Miami when she was twenty-three. She said she was one of the older women present, and was one of fifty women, with four men.

The men at these parties, one of the attendees recalled, "were there to get laid" and of Trump specifically, this source said, "This guy was like a predator in action." The same source recalled that Trump would later brag about it and it would get around that he "scored" with "maybe one or two girls at a time, which is what he loved to do" and that there were "very few girls above the age of nineteen" at many of the parties. He recalled watching Trump "ogling" girls as young as fourteen and fifteen. (The BBC noted that there is no evidence Trump had sex with underage girls.)

As former model Braden put it to the BBC: "I felt I could have very well have been auctioned off in a sex slavery ring. That's how I felt. I felt like a piece of meat at a meat market."

After Marla, Trump dated at least one top model, Kara Young, and dallied with countless lesser-known beauties. He then decided to get his own. He teamed up with an Italian businessman named Tommaso Buti, who had run a failed chain of restaurants called the Fashion Cafe, to start Trump Model Management. It quickly took its place in the scene. Leonardo DiCaprio famously described it as "one-stop date-shopping." It remained in business until after Trump was elected president, when the fashion industry's loathing of all things Trump sent it into a death spiral.

Trump also perfected the practice of using gorgeous models to lure clients and close real estate deals. The "meet and greet" parties Trump threw in a suite at the Plaza Hotel for his wealthy friends, high-rollers from his Atlantic City casinos, and potential Trump condominium buyers were always stocked with models wrangled by cooperative owners of lesser agencies, or by his own. Designers and photographers who were part of the scene at the time recalled that model agents would use the promise of an A-List model at a party to "bait" men over. They would then send one famous supermodel, who would leave the venue after five minutes, and a dozen of the lesser models ("show-room girls" as one Manhattan model agent, Paolo Zampolli, called his) who would stay for the evening—and maybe longer.

Zampolli, who would play a role in the legend of how Donald met his third wife, has never denied that some of his models were ferried to parties specifically to hook up with rich guys, but he said he had nothing to do with it. He blamed the hired drivers, who he said operated as pimps. "They would say, 'Hey baby, I'll drive you around and then at night we'll have a kind of dinner and we'll party, yeah? And then tomorrow I take you to the castings.' And the poor girl says it's okay, 'we'll go to the free dinner. And then after three drinks we'll go to the nightclubs.' And that was my biggest nightmare, my biggest problem was the girls go out, because if they go out, they don't make money. So it means I lose money."

Paolo Zampolli scoffed at DiCaprio's assessment of Trump's model agency. "Mr. Trump never was involved in that. Other than owning the agency, I never heard of any of his influence inside the agency. It was run by very professional people. I think Leonardo DiCaprio is kind of uh, has a little bit more to worry about than to go criticize the president. He shouldn't have worried us. There's a few FBI documents on him." (Zampolli said he was referring to allegations that the DiCaprio movie *The Wolf of Wall Street* was financed with dirty money laundered from Malaysia.)

The truth about rich men and models is that they did then and still do often inhabit a zone between prostitution and professional-ism. Model Jazz Egger blew the whistle on the practice as recently as August 2017. She described prostitution as commonplace in the in-dustry, where models are encouraged to work as actual "escorts" with powerful men, for easy cash and to bolster their careers.

"It's not only female models, also male models," Egger told Fox News. "Modeling can involve paid trips, paid nights out, paid din-ners, etc. But besides that, they get promised that they can become super-established by sleeping with wealthy men. We all know sex is a big topic, especially in the modeling scene. But once money is flow-ing, it's no longer just sex, but prostitution."

Egger, twenty, shared texts with the *Daily Mail* of a booker trying to talk her into a "private meet" for money. One invited her to a pri-vate dinner with a "famous actor"—and advised that she would need to be comfortable with the "natural intimacy" that followed:

> Thursday 17th private meet with one of my best clients, in the chiltern firehouse hotel, young handsome Iranian guy, drinks, talks followed by natural intimacy.
>
> client is a famous actor, name cannot be disclosed, girl required to wear heels and nice dress.
>
> behaviour must demonstrate exquisite class.
>
> fluent english only. PAY: £2000 time:1–2 hours

Egger replied that she was "a model and not an escort." The agent responded that "It's the most normal thing in the industry, everyone does it." The booker also told her that one of the most established modeling agencies in the world was a "partner client" of the company that had approached her for sex work. He then told her she was being naive.

"You are young so I understand this might all be a bit surprising," the booker texted. "But most models got to where they were through something like this. You meet amazingly wealthy people that can assist and propel your life in whatever direction you want. It is up to you where you want to end up."

He concluded, "All of these modeling agencies are run by hedge fund managers wanting to meet girls," and signed off with "what pride is there sleeping with 100 guys for free?"

PART FOUR

Melanija Knavs, The Third Mrs. Trump

Donald's third wife, like his first, hails from a Communist-era Slavic family that longed for the luxuries of the West. Unlike Ivana, Melania would be quite satisfied with whatever Donald offered, and did not need to be her own financially independent person, the working wife. She needed nothing more than pampering, security, and a sanctuary—in the form of several Trump condos—for herself and her parents and older sister. When Donald met her, Melania was twenty-eight—already too old to become a supermodel—and she was only too happy to let him take control of her modeling career. She was a malleable goddess, gorgeous and silent, trained to be looked at, the perfect accessory as Donald sailed into his sixties. She understood the rules, and she played by them. But when he ran for president, and she had to teeter out onstage not just to pose in her four-inch Manolo Blahniks, but stand on them and speak, he broke the rules.

She did not sign up to become the First Lady of the United States of America.

CHAPTER 15

◇◇◇◇◇◇

Growing Up in Sevnica

The hometown of Donald Trump's third wife and the First Lady of the United States is, like Ivana's hometown, situated at the very base of Maslow's hierarchy of human needs. Its people made shoes. The factory is gone now, but an eerie disembodied giant wooden shoe at the entrance to the hamlet commemorates its shoe-making history. And although more diversified industry moved in—Europe's largest lingerie manufacturer and a furniture company—Sevnica (pronounced sow-neet-suh) remains a community built by and for people whose life and work are focused on the foundation of the human motivational pyramid.

Sevnica's most famous former resident long ago stopped needing to worry about meeting basic needs. But, like her predecessor, Trump's first First Lady as Ivana calls herself, Melania Trump—born Melanija Knavs—puts physical comfort and luxury above matters higher on the hierarchy of needs. It is a hard habit to break.

The baby girl was born on April 26, 1970. It was a Sunday, and, as the nursery rhyme predicts, she would be a child full of grace. She was born into modest means, the second and last daughter of a factory worker mother and chauffeur father. Life was peaceful if not luxurious within the Alpine borders of this tiny sliver of Eastern Europe, but on another hemisphere, where her future husband was already almost twenty-four years old, social unrest rocked America. Two days after her birth, President Nixon announced he was authorizing the military to expand the Vietnam War to Cambodia, provoking mass antiwar protests. Later in May, the National Guard shot dead four students at Kent State in Ohio, shocking the world. Her future husband didn't side with the protestors. But neither had he signed up to fight the war: he took five draft deferments, four for college and one for "bone spurs" on his feet.

In 1970, Slovenia was still a republic of Josip Broz Tito's Yugoslavia, a union of six Slavic nations into one. The tiniest of those nations, Slovenia shares a border with Italy, meets Austria to the north across an Alpine edge and Croatia to the south. It is the most Italian of the Slavic nations. No part of it is more than a few hours' drive to Trieste and the Italian Adriatic beaches. It belonged to the Roman Empire in ancient times, and was settled in the sixth century by the Alpine Slavic people who are the forebears of modern Slovenians.

The breakup of Yugoslavia was still two decades away when Melanija was born, but in the years just before her birth, dissent was growing. Students in Belgrade and other Yugoslavian cities joined the worldwide protests of 1968. In April, the so-called "Croatian Spring" was under way, as protesting students in Zagreb, a few hundred kilometers to the south, demanded greater civil liberties and Croatian autonomy. The movement came to an end in December 1971 when hundreds of supporters were rounded up and arrested.

In 1977, when Melanija was in the first grade in Sevnica, the town was even more isolated than today. Only a winding two-lane road led to the capital, Ljubljana, and the drive could take several hours, through pine trees, rolling hills, and farmland planted with wheat, corn, and pumpkins. Her world was circumscribed by the Sava

River behind the main street, a few shops, and the friends and neighbors in the gray slab of an apartment building where she lived in a two-bedroom apartment with her older sister, Ines, and her parents.

Melanija's mother, Amalija, was a farmer's daughter who had spent part of her childhood as a refugee in Austria during World War II. For most of her life, until she retired in 1997, Amalija worked as a pattern-maker at the state-owned clothing factory in town, Jutranjka. Amalija stood out in meat-and-potatoes Sevnica as a fashionable woman, always elegantly turned out. She had her eye on something higher, more beautiful, less utilitarian. An avid consumer of Western fashion magazines, she passed an interest in fashion down to her daughters. The real-life fairy tales Melania and her sister consumed as girls were between the covers of international *Vogue*, where a young Catherine Deneuve was a style icon, and the glam rocker look was sweeping the West with glitter and chubby fur coats, miniskirts, and boots. The preferred silhouette for models was a plunging décolletage, unbuttoned blouses, skinny braless breasts on display. The look in the models' eyes of this era was straight out of Joan Didion's *Play It As It Lays*: passive, receptive, slightly dazed, perhaps strung out on uppers and downers, possibly used and abused, but definitely liberated.

In the Knavs household, mother and daughters formed a feminine triad at a remove from burly gearhead Viktor Knavs. His career résumé is a bit blurry. In Sevnica, people tell stories about him that are as unflattering as they are unverifiable. He's known to have been a driver for party officials, and had a repair shop or a Mercedes dealership—depending on whether one reads the official biography or Slovenian journalism. All agree that he had a great fondness for Mercedes cars. He was successful enough that he owned a small collection of Mercedes, along with a rare Maserati.

Unlike the Czechoslovakians, the Communist Party did not have a firm hold on the Slovenian people. Yugoslavia was socialist, but officially nonaligned. Only 5 percent of Slovenians were official Party members. Viktor Knavs was one of them. During the 2016 campaign, Trump people told journalists that Viktor was "never an active member," and this could be true, since his membership probably speaks more to his networking savvy than to any ideology. Party membership simply enabled access to luxury goods and travel. Whatever he was, Viktor's connections enabled Amalija, sometimes with her daughters in tow, to attend fashion shows in Milan and afford makeup and regular visits to a hair salon. The small Knavs family's apartment was in a building overlooking the factories and river. They shopped on a tiny main street, and the stylishly dressed little girls walked from home to the tiny neighborhood primary school named after Savo Kladnik, a Yugoslavian World War II resistance fighter. One childhood friend, now the school principal, remembered that little Melanija was so shy she had to be coaxed into the playground games. But she was also a peacemaker, the kind of kid who would step in to solve disputes.

She wasn't too shy to model her mother's designs. Photographs of Melanija and Ines and their friends, in culottes and other styles of the time, can still be found online, although they have become more rare since Melania hired a Slovenian lawyer to maintain control over youthful images and unauthorized uses of her brand.

Growing up in that small town, Melanija and her friends listened to Duran Duran, Simple Minds, and Queen, studied Western celebrities in *Bravo* magazine, and if a family happened to have Coca-Cola—still a luxury from the West—the girls took tiny sips and shared it. They connected lengths of woolen string to their friends' balconies around the little apartment building and sent written messages to each other with clothespins.

Childhood friends recall a family dynamic in which Melanija, Ines, and Amalija were under control of Viktor, the "big boss of the family," a somewhat fearsome presence, whom the girls kept at a distance. "He was tough. He was like a businessman," recalled Petra Sedej. "She, her sister and her mother were very close together."

During the 2016 campaign, a reporter named Julia Ioffe went to Slovenia following a tip that Viktor had fathered a son, now an adult, out of wedlock, before he married Amalija. After first denying the story, then claiming never to have heard it, Melania conceded the truth when the man himself was found, along with papers proving Knavs had gone to court to fight the mother. Marija Cigelnjak gave birth to a son, Denis, in 1965, and although a court-ordered paternity test proved Knavs the father, Knavs fought the order to pay all the way to Slovenia's highest appellate court, Ioffe found. Eventually Melania told Ioffe "I've known about this for years," and then asked the reporter to respect her father's privacy.

For that journalistic discovery, published in *GQ* magazine in the spring of 2016, Ioffe earned an onslaught of vile, anti-Semitic emails and tweets, among the earliest—but not the last—public evidence of the real sentiments in Trump's base of nationalist "anti-globalists."

Another old Knavs family friend in Sevnica told Slovenian television that Melanija "married her father" in Trump. The two men are only a few years apart in age, and look alike, both rotund, given to bellicosity, and otherwise all business. Melania's lawyer threatened her with legal action for talking to the media.

Melania herself has commented on the similarities between Viktor and Donald, though. "They're both hardworking. They're both very smart and very capable. They grew up in totally different environments, but they have the same tradition. I myself am similar to my husband. Do you understand what I mean? So is my dad. He is a family man, he has tradition, he was hardworking. So is my husband."

Both men appear to share a habit of attracting legal cases and scrutiny. Besides fighting the child support order in the courts for years, Viktor reportedly "aroused suspicion for illicit trade and tax evasion" while working as a salesman for a state-owned car company in the 1970s, when Melania was a child. Journalist Ioffe reported that she saw the police files in 2016 that have since become unavailable even to Slovenian journalists. The papers showed, Ioffe reported, that in 1976, Viktor was charged with a tax offense. The record was expunged after the statute of limitations expired, and I was not able to find them. When Ioffe asked Melania about the reports, the future first lady replied, "He was never under any investigation, he was never in trouble. We have a clean past. I don't have nothing [*sic*] to hide."

The Knavses have, in any event, been a fairly secretive little clan. Melania apparently stopped communicating with her Slovenian friends after she moved to Milan. A few months before she became first lady, she hired a lawyer there—who now monitors uses of her name and keeps track of the inquiries of local and foreign journalists, and old friends who would talk to the media about her past. A close family friend was afraid to communicate with journalists after appearing in a POP TV documentary in 2017 and backed out of an appointment with me minutes before our planned meeting.

The prohibition against use of Melania's name on products stings Slovenians the most. It's one thing for her to refuse all requests to speak to Slovenian television, but to forbid her little country the use of her name seems churlish. Slovenians have got around it by using "First Lady"—a moniker that Melania can't claim to own. The Sevnica tourist office on the little main street sells "First Lady honey," made by local bees, and First Lady wine (red), made of local grapes. A few uses of Melania's name have slipped in. The Julia patisserie on the shopping strip does a good business selling a white confection of almonds and white chocolate called the Melania torte, displayed beside the apple strudel. A "Donald Burger" can be had at the nearby pub. Other than the cake, though, the lawyer has clamped down hard. When an English-language school in Croatia put up billboards advertising its services with a picture of Melania, the first lady's lawyer had it taken down with a single call.

The other Knavs family members—Amalija, Viktor, and Ines—now divide their time between Trump apartments in New York and lodging in suburban Maryland, near Barron's school. Viktor still owns a house in Sevnica, on one of the terraced streets just up the hillside from the main strip. The white split-level has cameras affixed to the roof, and a mailbox printed with the words "US Mail." Viktor is the only family member regularly seen there. He has been known to chase journalists away on foot and in his Mercedes cars.

◇◇◇◇

On Melania's sixteenth birthday, a terrible accident occurred that arguably helped bring down the Soviet Union and damaged a vast swath of the Eurasian environment. The Chernobyl Nuclear Power Plant in Ukraine, then part of the Soviet Union, melted down in the world's worst nuclear disaster. Chernobyl is nearly a thousand miles from Ljubljana, but the meltdown spewed radiation all over Europe. The catastrophe hastened the breakup of the Soviet Union, a geopolitical cataclysm that would alter the lives of everyone, including beautiful and ambitious women in Eastern Europe.

Uninterested in world events, half-engaged in high school, doodling fashions and checking out cute guys on Vespas in the Ljubljana main square, Melania experienced her sixteenth birthday as personally significant for another reason. That year she was tall and skinny, with striking aquamarine feline eyes and black hair, and in January 1987, she caught the attention of a photographer who produced her first modeling portfolio. Stane Jerko was not just any guy with a camera, but Slovenia's premier fashion shooter. He spotted the teen lounging by a gate outside a fashion show in Ljubljana, where Melania and Ines had been living for two years.

Ljubljana is a charming miniature of classic Italo-Slavic cities. It's so sweet that it feels like a toy town. The main square is anchored by a pink church with white pillars and adorned by the words "Plenia Gracia" (Full of Grace). Small cafes line the walk, crisscrossed with a triangle of three little white bridges, along the Sava River. The snowy peaks of the Alps shimmer in the distance, and sunsets can be spectacular. The food is Italian enough to be good, people bicycle everywhere Scandinavia-style, and the remnants of the socialist system mean there's not a lot of poverty. In short, it's a charming place, and in the 1980s, it was safe enough that the Knavs parents felt comfortable sending their girls there to live alone in an apartment while attending high school.

The sisters attended the city's high school for design and photography, while Amalija held down her clothing factory job on weekdays and visited on weekends. Sometimes Viktor, on work travels, checked in on them, but the sisters were basically on their own. The girls were disciplined and responsible enough to cook for themselves, take the bus for the six-minute ride to get to school on time, and do their homework every evening.

Friends recall them as extremely close, with Ines more reticent, and in the habit of wearing "long black clothes," while Melanija, also introverted, was dressed a la mode and went everywhere perfectly made-up, with subtle amounts of foundation and eye makeup. Every morning at ten, the girls would leave school, go to the same store, and buy yoghurt and bread for a snack, then return to class. Melanija's social life consisted of hanging with a few friends, sitting in front of the school, and watching cute boys ride up on Vespas. Her first boyfriend would be one of the guys on the Vespas, an athletic guy a little older who would eventually become a male model. Remembered high school pal Petra Sedej: "She always liked good-looking guys."

But she was no partier. Her life was calm, uneventful, and lowkey. The sisters were homebodies who spent evenings in their apartment with a few friends, drinking juice. Neither girl showed much curiosity about or aptitude for languages, history, science, or current events (although Melania would much later say she learned about the world watching CNN International). They lived for fashion and drawing.

The girls were more well traveled than the average Slovenian in the 1980s. Ines and Melanija had gone on vacations beyond the borders, and were still visiting Italy fairly often with their mother during high school. But teenaged Melania wasn't yet interested in living abroad. She and Petra went on double dates with their boyfriends and spent their downtime looking at fashion magazines.

"She drew fashions all the time, and was really into looking at English or Italian *Vogue*," Petra recalled. "Everything she wore was designed and made by her mother or her sister. I still remember the pink swimsuit she wore to our graduation trip to the beach in Dubrovnik, homemade by her mother, a two-piece, pink with a little white elastic."

During high school, Melanija started taking modeling lessons. Her friends remember watching her practice the catwalk walk. She wasn't a natural on camera. Photographer Jerko recalled her first photo shoot with him. She turned up with a basket of her mom's homemade designs. She was nervous and stiff. But Jerko thought she had the basic elements of a successful fashion model. He eventually produced a portfolio for her. "She was never euphoric. She was quiet, kind, hardworking, did not complain, which is why she did not attract attention," he recalled later. "But I recognized a potential in her that is difficult to describe. It was clear there was something about her, some energy that she has."

The source of her energy lay primarily in her unusual coloring, black hair and vivid blue eyes. "She was a special kind of beauty, not the classic type," a former friend from Ljubljana told Ioffe. "She had eyes that were kind of psychedelic. You look in those eyes and it was like looking in the eyes of an animal." Although she had some training and the portfolio, Melanija didn't head straight off to the catwalks of Milan after high school. She still regarded modeling as a side gig, not her vocation, and after she graduated from school with a specialization in industrial—not fashion—drawing, she took the entrance exam and got accepted to the University of Ljubljana, entering the school for architecture and design after graduating from high school in 1988.

An older architecture student and former teaching assistant assigned to proctor one of Melanija's earliest architecture exams recalls what happened next. "I was working at the university. I had been there for four years. And I remember her because she was a bomb. The other girls were average-looking girls—there were no good-looking girls applying for architectural studies! And when she came in, wow. She was wearing jeans from Italy or Paris, cut so you could see the meat, with chains, and sunglasses on top of her head. Nothing wrong, just stylish and nice."

The first year's first architecture exams were divided into different segments. In the morning, the students were tested together as a group, asked to draw perspectives, which they had studied. The afternoon session was individualized. It assessed creativity and imagination. Students came in one at a time, were handed a sheet of paper, and were asked to draw, on the spot, a rendering of the buildings and features of the town where they came from.

"The question was, just try to put on paper how you would present this place where you lived and studied," recalled the proctor, now a Slovenian architect. "If you are going to be an architect, you would put in this river, this church, the castle, and do it with some energy."

The proctor gave Melanija the assignment and waited, but quickly became alarmed. "Oh my God, after about fifteen minutes, there was nothing on the paper. It was still completely white, and she was standing there, with all her beauty, against the wall, just shaking and shaking, trembling, nervous. Knowing, I think, that she couldn't pass the exam. She was sad. She didn't talk with any energy. It was almost like depression."

After that, he says, "she was not at the school. She vanished." (Melania has denied that this incident occurred and says that she left school to pursue her modeling career.)

Before the Republican National Convention in 2016, Melania's (she dropped the j in her name after she left Slovenia) website stated that she had graduated with a degree in architecture "at University in Slovenia." But reporters who looked into it found no "University in Slovenia" or a "University of Slovenia." And the University of Ljubljana had no record of Melania graduating with a degree in architecture.

Nine days after the election, the new President-Elect Trump's website contained a new account of Melania's college years. The official government website bio stated that Melania "paused her studies to advance her modeling career in Milan and Paris." It did not say whether she graduated.

Her bio also says—and reports about her have often repeated—that she speaks five languages, including French, German, and Italian besides Slovenian and English. But friends in Ljubljana don't recall her having any aptitude for languages, and in the years ahead, she did not converse with Italians when she worked with Italians, or in French with French photographers. It is, however, common for international models to speak what is called in the business "Model French" and "Model Italian"—a Euro-patois that gets them around restaurants and public transportation in Paris and Milan.

Melanija's big break out of Slovenia coincided with the breakup of the former Soviet Union and Yugoslavia. In 1989, the Berlin Wall fell and the USSR started breaking up, followed by Yugoslavia. On June 25, 1991, Slovenia declared independence and won it, in a relatively bloodless Ten-Day War.

As capitalism flooded in, fashion talent scouts came too, scouring Slovenia and other Eastern European backwaters for exotic rural Slavic beauties. By the early nineties, Ines and Melania had both left Slovenia to start careers in Milan. There, Melania worked as a fashion model while Ines tried to break into fashion design.

After some moderate successes, including a shampoo commercial, Melania returned to Slovenia in 1992, to compete in the tiny new nation's first "Face of the Year" contest. The contest, which mimicked the larger contests annually held in Europe and New York, pitted young beauties against one another on the catwalk, judged by designers and fashion magazine editors. The winner got a modeling contract and would be catapulted into the higher realms of global fashion in the West. *Vogue* magazine covers, New York and Paris Fashion Weeks, and huge fees—all, until very recently, unimaginable to Yugoslavian girls—awaited the lucky one.

Slovenian fashion magazine *Jana* sponsored the contest at the Adriatic resort town of Portorož. Melania, now twenty-two, tied for second place, losing to a much younger model in her teens. She was crushed, and her father, Viktor, was predictably furious. He believed the contest was fixed. But the truth was that Melania, striking and disciplined, just had unlucky timing. If the Wall had fallen a few years earlier, the teen might have received a different quality of attention and professional training and become marketable at a more nubile age.

CHAPTER 16

◇◇◇◇◇◇

The Sexualization of Modeling

M elania came of age in the modeling industry during a decade when Slavic women, from Moscow to the steppe, across the myriad nations that had been behind the Iron Curtain, or associated with Communism, were released from decades of asceticism, devotion to comradeship and the regimes, drab, utilitarian lives in cheap shoes, whether they were factory workers or professionals. After decades of peeking through the window of Western luxury brands, and at *Playboy* magazine and advertising that relied on women's bodies to titillate commercial senses, the post-Soviet world went into a sugar shock of cultural sexualization.

Soviet media under glasnost primed this cultural trend by moving to feature sex, nudity, and erotic imagery as soon as state censorship rules loosened. "Many scholars have amassed evidence of a general 'eroticization' of the country, in which 'criticism of culture and politics increasingly included analysis of sexual behavior and relied on sexual metaphor,'" wrote scholar Katherine P. Avgerinos in a 2006 article examining the "normalization" of prostitution in the former Soviet Union and Eastern Europe. "The use of female nudity and semi-nudity to sell products or entertain—already familiar to the

Western public—became increasingly prevalent in the USSR. Stores with imported Western sex toys or pornographic material became common and strip bars like the Hungry Duck were in high demand."

One survey in the 1990s found that post-Soviet women ranked prostitution eighth in a list of what they felt to be the top twenty most common employment positions in the USSR. Another survey found that 60 percent of high school girls in Moscow said they would exchange sex for hard currency. By the 2000s, 1 million prostitutes were operating in the Russian Federation—more than the combined total of doctors, farmers, and firemen.

"The sexualization of Russian culture had normalized promiscuity and broken down the formally conservative social mores," Avgerinos wrote. "Women could now transgress sexual boundaries they previously would not have crossed."

Newly rich men from formerly Communist regimes also associated their hard currency primarily with sex. According to Eliot Borenstein, a Russia expert at New York University, "the accumulation of money was not driven by the need to accumulate investments but for the sake of pleasure, and sexuality was one of the major manifestations of this pleasure. . . . Buying love was now the most desirable way to attract the opposite sex."

The beauty contest industry, imported from the West in the mid-1980s, played a role in the transformation. Contestants were usually from modest families, and while many had had access to higher education, they were relegated to menial and low-paid jobs anyway. Even post-Soviet psychologists supported beauty pageants for women, because "feeling beautiful improved a woman's sense of well being and her work performance."

But the Russian beauty contests had a darker transactional aspect. Women were often expected to trade sex with fashion photographers, modeling agents, and pageant organizers for higher profile work. By 1998, a flood of Slavic beauties, conditioned by post-Soviet mores to view their bodies as marketable commodities, were flooding the world's brothels. *New York Times* writer Michael Specter published a feature called "Traffickers' New Cargo: Naïve Slavic Women." He compared the trafficking to enslavement, and wrote that "few ever testify" for fear of being killed by the increasingly violent and powerful Russian mob that pimped them.

⬦⬦⬦⬦

Melanija Knavs entered the international modeling world just as the sexualization of Eastern European women was going global. She may have adapted by trying to Germanize herself. Very soon after leaving Slovenia, she changed the spelling of her name from Knavs to Knauss and from Melanija to Melania. But her accent, and her family roots in Yugoslavia, soon to be ravaged by a grisly civil war, marked her to many as belonging to a set of trafficked, sexualized, and sometimes truly desperate women, being abused at a phenomenal rate. She could never escape that perception, no matter how disciplined and healthy she was, no matter how often she pretended be Austrian.

In October 2017, Finnish writer and playwright Sofi Oksanen dared speak of this elephant in the Trump room. Oksanen wrote an open letter to incoming first lady Melania Trump, published in several Nordic newspapers, accusing her of failing Eastern European women in general by failing to publicly stand up to Trump for his public declarations about sexually assaulting women and his other oafish behavior toward women.

"The desire to seem more Western is the convenient explanation for why you changed your name from Melanija Knavs to Melania Knauss. But I'd wager there's more to it," Oksanen wrote. "By then, Eastern European girls had developed a certain reputation. In the West, women cast them suspicious glances, and men ogled them, all of which came as a complete surprise to the newcomers, presumably including you."

Oksanen said Trump's election had made Melania a visible symbol of the Eastern European woman's dream—and its dark side. "You are the First Lady of the United States of America, but whenever you hear a familiar accent on TV, the woman on-screen is a prostitute, a stripper, or a mail-order bride. And she doesn't get many lines, either, because what would be the point?" Oksanen wrote. "Each new article about the indignities you've endured in your marriage sells more bachelor getaways, attracts more customers to the dating apps and interpretation services. That's why your silence isn't a private matter. It affects the lives and opportunities of countless other women."

Melania never responded publicly to that challenge, and there's no reason to believe she did so privately. Her own modeling career in New York was essentially fading fast before Donald Trump encountered her, and made her not just his girlfriend but a Trump brand deal. (In fact, when he said to Howard Stern about Melania that "I got a good deal," he was actually referring to getting her a deal on a giant Times Square cigarette ad.) Melania arrived in New York in August 1996, and according to documents shared with the Associated Press during the campaign, she earned $20,056 for ten modeling jobs in the seven weeks before she got her work visa in October. At around $2,000 a gig, those earnings were far from supermodel money. Like Ivana in Canada twenty years prior, but a few steps above, she modeled for a department store, Bergdorf Goodman, and a fitness magazine. She worked as a spokesmodel for Panasonic television commercials and eventually did lingerie ads—although not the coveted Victoria's Secret catalog that potentially catapulted girls into supermodel status. Her first real big New York modeling breaks only came after she connected with Donald Trump in 1998. Almost all the work cited in her White House bio—*Vogue, Harper's Bazaar, British GQ, Ocean Drive, Avenue, In Style, New York* magazine, *Sports Illustrated* Swimsuit Issue, *Allure, Vanity Fair,* and *Elle*—is post-Donald. As her personal Pygmalion, Trump would go on to oversee her career. Because of that ironclad control, it is plausible that Trump himself either leaked or approved when Melania's lesbian nudes were published by the *New York Post* during the campaign, a paper owned by one of his pals in Yacht People World, Rupert Murdoch.

◇◇◇◇

By the mid-1990s, Melania was no longer living in Milan, but in a Paris apartment with a Swedish athlete and former Miss Sweden named Victoria Silvstedt. The aspiring models would drag their books to twelve "castings" a day, spending hours on the Metro, running from location to location, trying to find work. Judging from the available photographic record, she didn't get a lot of jobs—certainly not high-profile campaigns. Life was hard at this level of the modeling industry, and not glamorous at all, especially since neither one spoke French, Silvstedt recalled.

"This was the time before cell phones. We were in a different country without speaking the language and it's not easy to move in with a stranger coming from two different countries. We really, really got along very well. She would never go out and want to party. She was very determined, very serious in her work."

Silvstedt went on to become a "prosecco entrepreneur," and a European TV commentator and swimwear and lingerie designer. She recalled her years with Melania as a period of youthful ambition and permanent dieting. "When you move to Paris, the first thing your agent tells you is, 'Lose weight, lose weight. Don't do sports. Don't even take the stairs because it will make your legs big.'" The women ate tuna salads at home every night, and then would run up and down the stairs to burn it off. "We didn't care that they told us not to build up muscles because we had to burn the calories."

In those days, Melania—still a shy and somewhat stiff introvert—harbored the unlikely ambition to be a famous actress. She had competed in a Cinecittà competition in Rome, but it hadn't gotten her anywhere. "One day, I will be famous like Sophia Loren," Silvstedt recalled her saying. "Melania's style icon was always Sophia Loren. That was the idol she had in her life—the look, the beauty, her mystery."

She was doing okay in Paris, but she was definitely not on a supermodel track or about to become the next Sophia Loren when she went to Fashion Week in Milan in 1995 and ran into fate in the form of an Italian businessman with a colorful résumé who had launched his own modeling agency in New York.

Paolo Zampolli, according to his own life story, grew up rich as the son of an Italian businessman who tested and imported American toys, including the first Star Wars dolls, and sold Italian versions of them. The American Easy-Bake Oven became the Dolce Forno in the Zampolli brand. Then Paolo's father died in a skiing accident when Paolo was eighteen, and the younger Zampolli went into the toy business. Soon, he sold his company to Silvio Berlusconi's megacorporation, and ventured forth to test the waters in the wider world.

A handsome bon vivant who slicks back his black hair and wears crisp white shirts with monogrammed cuffs (sometimes with "TRUMP" cuff links), Zampolli likes food and beautiful women. While he was looking for a way to combine business with pleasure, he bounced around Europe and New York. On one visit to the United States, he first encountered Trump Tower, and then, networking around Manhattan, met "Mr. Trump," as Zampolli would forever call him.

In the legend of how Donald met Melania, Paolo Zampolli plays a central role. He eventually, briefly, worked for the Trump Organization (hence the Trump cuff links). He then went on to start his own real estate company—Trump wasn't doing real estate as much once he became a TV star and there was nothing to sell. Zampolli's Paramount Group developed a high-class business clientele showing luxury apartments and properties via Rolls-Royce and helicopters. He also used former models as brokers to sell the apartments. "The gorgeous ladies," he said on CNBC. "They meet the most rich and powerful people of the world, and some of them, they keep this connection."

Zampolli's connection to Melania paid off nicely for him. Trump's election propelled him back into the news cycle, his happy place. He told and retold the story of how Melania and Donald met under his watch, and on the less welcome side, played a starring role in a lawsuit that Melania filed against a UK tabloid that made unsavory allegations about his role in her past. Zampolli definitely prefers parties to courtrooms, and plus, he has other matters to tend to these days, as one of Dominica's ambassadors to the UN. It's an appointed position. His wife Amanda Ungaro-Zampolli, another former model, is an appointed ambassador for Grenada at the UN. Together, they live and work out of a town house in New York from which they fly the pale blue UN flag and the flags of their Caribbean affiliations.

◇◇◇◇

In the early 1990s, Zampolli opened a model agency, Metropolitan, in New York. It was a small player in the fashion world, and Zampolli personally worked the various Fashion Weeks, looking for girls. He eventually stocked it with about two hundred beauties. Zampolli was at Fashion Week Milano on the lookout for prospects when he ran into Melania. "She was stunning, she was beautiful," he recalled, but she was twenty-five—an age considered much too old to start a modeling career in Europe. She had a few ad campaigns on her résumé, and she had done catalog work, but she was still hopeful that someone might make her the next Sophia Loren.

Zampolli said he knew right away what he was looking at. A workhorse. Melania wasn't one of the super-young ones, or the strange-looking, "edgy" ones that every agency needed just one of. She also didn't look like she was going to be trouble.

"She gave me the impression of someone with their head on their shoulders," he recalled. "And as an owner of the agency, my biggest problem was that these young girls will go out every night with all these free things, free dinners, free clubs. And the next day they would call in sick because they'd been drinking until five in the morning at some club which, in another part of the world, they would not have had access to. I could see that Melania was someone with her head on her shoulders. So basically I told her, 'Would you like to come to New York?' And she said, 'Well how do you think it would work?' and I said, 'Well I think you are very beautiful and you have to try the American market, I think you can do well.'"

Around 1996, she arrived in New York. Paolo put her up in an apartment on Union Square, with a male photographer roommate, and Paolo paid the rent. He also arranged for her to work on an H-1B visa—the same visa system that Trump would try to destroy as soon as he got into office, arguing that it took jobs away from qualified Americans. The Trump camp vociferously denied that Melania worked illegally in the US at first, but the AP never retracted its story. She would have to wait until 2001, well into her romance with Donald, to gain permanent residency in the United States with a green card granted under the so-called Einstein visa program, normally granted to individuals who have demonstrated "extraordinary ability in the sciences, arts, education, business, or athletics through sustained national or international acclaim."

Besides helping her with the apartment, Paolo gave her a friend—his own then girlfriend, a model named Edit Molnar. Soon the pair were "doing girly stuff" together, Zampolli said, eating healthy model food, going to the gym and pool in the building, and seeing movies. Paolo did what he could to get Melania jobs.

Zampolli knows what they say about Slavic beauties in the

1990s flooding the New York market, and how there were so many gorgeous photogenic women looking for work that the value fell and pretty soon they were doing other things, things that maybe weren't supposed to be captured on camera. He doesn't deny this was true—although he has never included Melania in this category.

"At the time, once a month, I would have some guy calling me, putting pressure on me, saying his girlfriend should've been a model. And most of them, they were from Eastern European countries, because they had a visa problem. And you know, the girls would be beautiful. But they're not model material, you understand. It's a very different thing, is to be model material, or to be a girl you take out, or do other things. Okay. And in the nineties, New York was overflowing with these—those things—you might say. But this is not what happened in model agencies. Because in model agencies, we wanted to make money left and right."

To accommodate the influx and see whether he could make money off it, Zampolli opened a division for the nonprofessionals. "We called it 'People,' and they said, 'Why do you call it People?' and I said 'Because they're not models, they can get little jobs, but they have to understand, they're not models, they're not fashion models. For me, they are people.'"

Paolo said his People division was roughly equivalent to what other agencies called a Showroom division—basically lower-tier models who were contracted to designer showrooms.

Zampolli girls were also sometimes employed by what he called "party promoters"—as tall, glamorous human decorations. "But these are not models. They are beautiful girls with a stunning body that fits the clothes and their face is okay, but nobody gives a shit about the face because you just need somebody to wear the clothes." He called them "clothes hangers."

Sometimes he would send a dozen of his showroom girls to an "event," Paolo recalled. That didn't mean he expected them to stay out all night, he said. He chalked those incidents up to the "party promoters."

"My biggest enemy was the party promoters," he said, recalling his agency days. "How it worked was, the model's promoter, this night-club, needs them more than the dinners. So, the nightclub would take them from twelve o'clock to, I don't know, whenever they close. And the party promoter, they have to keep the girls busy from dinnertime to twelve o clock."

Zampolli described the party promoters as like Uber drivers with second jobs stocking nightclubs with lissome babes. "Remember this was before Uber. I had drivers driving them around in SUVs."

Zampolli's business with the People models synced up quite nicely with his personal style, which was super-social, involving lots of par-ties and almost weekly mentions in the *New York Post*'s Page Six gos-sip column for his appearances at various boîtes and clubs frequented by the international oligarchy and Manhattan's richest. His buddy network eventually included billionaires like magnate Ron Burkle, who became famous for flying ex-president Bill Clinton on a model-packed private jet that gossips nicknamed Air Fuck One.

CHAPTER 17

◇◇◇◇◇◇

The Sexualization of Melania

Plastic surgeons and tabloid journalists go together like cattle and cowbirds. Theirs is a symbiotic relationship. Journalists give before and after photographs to doctors, who apply the professional eye to the photos and diagnose what work has been done. Journalists publish their conclusions, attracting more clients. Doctors prosper. Dozens of plastic surgeons and dermatologists have handed out professional assessments of the facial transformations of Melania and other Trump Queens. The best guesses on Melania, looking at teen pictures compared to after 1998, are that she had lip fillers, nose work, and breast enlargement. "You know about the work I'm sure," said a New York friend. "She's had work. Work, and extensions, hair extensions and balayage." *Balayage* is a French word for expensively hand-painted blond streaks.

But when Julia Ioffe asked her point-blank about a boob job, Melania denied it. "I didn't make any changes. A lot of people say I am using all the procedures for my face. I didn't do anything. I live a healthy life. I take care of my skin and my body. I'm against Botox. I'm against injections, I think it's damaging your face, damaging your nerves. It's all me. I will age gracefully, as my mom does."

But her roommate in New York when she first moved there, photographer Matthew Atanian, remembers otherwise. In fashion modeling, age twenty-six is deemed too old. Melania was being farmed out to alcohol and tobacco ads, jobs that younger models were not allowed to take under industry guidelines. She complained about the unfairness of it incessantly. "She aired frustration over the work issue," Atanian told Ioffe. "She wasn't working every day. She was going to castings every day and not succeeding every day." Her desire for work reached a point during her early New York years that she even allowed Jarl Alé de Basseville, a Paris-based photographer, to take nude pictures of her—some in bed with another nude model—for a French men's magazine.

She went away for a two-week vacation, and, Atanian recalled, she returned with a new look. "She came back, and was more . . . buxom," he told Ioffe. "She admitted it to me. She just said it needed to be done to get more lingerie jobs."

Much later, in 2000, when she was Trump's girlfriend, she would pose nude for *GQ* magazine, in a deal Trump himself cut for her. She posed nude, half-naked, hand-cuffed, clad in a vaguely S&M chain mail swimsuit, in the cockpit and cabin of the Trump jet. The pictures would resurface during the Republican primary campaign, when a Republican super PAC waved them around in hopes of destroying Trump's growing appeal with conservative Christians.

Candidate Trump wasn't worried at all. It was obvious to him what any red-blooded man thought of his wife. On the contrary, he blamed Ted Cruz and lashed out cruelly, tweeting an unflattering picture of Heidi Cruz next to a gorgeous shot of Melania and the words, "A picture is worth a thousand words."

Trump's pride in sexualized Melania is never far from the surface. He's pretty okay with showing her off, naked or in clothes. Media gossips in New York believe Trump himself gave the *New York Post* the naked photographs. "Where's my supermodel?" he shouted from the stage at a campaign event back in 1999, when he was toying with a run for president.

People thought he was kidding.

Despite all the work, which is subtle and has turned out gloriously, and the balayaged locks and her ability to look exquisite before cameras, Melania seems uncomfortable in her skin, naked or clothed. The tension that Stane Jerko noticed in his first photo session with her is always there, an almost palpable awareness of potential threat, an unease with too much exposure, always pulling the surface ever more taut.

⬦⬦⬦⬦

TRUMP: Who do you think was the best in the sack, Howard?
JOHN MELENDEZ: I say Melania.
STERN: Melania.
TRUMP: Oh, I feel like Melania.

According to legend, Trump was fifty-two when he first spotted animal-eyed Melania, at a New York Fashion Week party in the fall of 1998 at the Kit Kat Club. The host was Paolo Zampolli, who was throwing a big party to celebrate one of his models, who had been selected as a Victoria's Secret "angel"—a gimmick the lingerie company was using in its ad campaigns at the time, in which they put feathered wings on the back of a particularly shapely girl otherwise clad in a thong and push-up bra.

"For a modeling agency to have Victoria's Secret attention is a big deal," Zampolli recalled. "So out of how many models, we had a Victoria's Secret angel, and a Victoria's Secret angel makes hundreds of thousands of dollars." He threw a party, made sure all his girls knew about it, and invited, among other modelizers, Mr. Trump.

Oddly, the Kit Kat story isn't the only story of how they met. In his role as Pygmalion to unformed beauties, Donald might have been involved in her career as far back as 1997, when she appeared on the cover of *Harper's Bazaar en Español*. According to photographer Jarl Alé de Basseville, Melania and Zampolli both told him she was Trump's girlfriend at the time (1996) but that Zampolli instructed him not to let the magazine publish that information since Donald was still married. Melania's spokeswoman and Zampolli deny this. He was definitely involved with her by the fall of 1998, when Melania, who had ignored Slovenian friends for years, suddenly showed up in Paris at an event to which seven Slovenian journalists were invited, to talk to her about developments in her modeling and acting career. (She had been claiming to be Austrian for some time, causing a small protocol question for the Slovenian Embassy in DC when Donald squired her into the tabloids.)

At the Hotel Lutetia in Paris, Melania told the Slovenians that her three best traits were "honesty, precision and professionalism." She announced that she was about to start shooting a movie with Mickey Rourke, to be directed by Craig Singer. "To me this means a new challenge, a step further," she said in her scripted remarks. The movie never got made. She did appear on TV later, long after she and Trump were together, as a celebrity judge for Miss USA 2003 and on a show called *Fashion Week Diaries* in 2005.

The Kit Kat story is that Trump arrived with another woman on his arm, but was immediately captivated by the exotic twenty-eight-year-old Melania. While his date was in the bathroom, he sidled over and got right to business, asking for her number. Melania refused, and instead asked Trump for his contact information.

Melania was not immune to the charms of the billionaire. "We had a great connection, we had great chemistry, but I was not starstruck. And maybe he noticed that." She turned him down. Melania would later explain her calculation. "If I give him my number, I'm just one of the women he calls. I wanted to see what his intention is.

It tells you a lot from the man what kind of number he gives you. He gave me all of his numbers."

She walked away with his personal phone numbers at the office, at home, and at Mar-a-Lago, and few days later, she called him. He took her to Moomba, and like his other wives, she would later say he captivated her with his "energy." She broke up with him once, early, which brought him to heel. "She had some trust issues with him at the beginning," her roommate Atanian told *GQ* magazine. "She was telling me that she wouldn't have it, he was back to his old ways. She kept her apartment to have her own space because of this." A family member says Melania's breakup "provoked his competitive streak."

Within six months they were back together—and have been together almost ever since, with a short and unexplained breakup during one of Trump's presidential explorations in 2000 (reportedly, she was not up for politics). Photographs of them during their dating years show the younger Melania without the iron facial self-control she has now, sometimes grinning widely, in a way she never does anymore, at other times looking wary and tense. In several pictures, her legs are tightly crossed and aimed away from him, hands covering her torso protectively, as he leans in, his hot breath on her neck, a paw on her back or thigh. These pictures are almost painful to look at.

But one body language expert concluded that Melania in those moments might be uncomfortable when cameras were aimed at her in genuinely intimate or sexualized situations—not necessarily uncomfortable with her older man. "She might be taking measures not to be seen as a sexual being," body language expert Patti Wood told *Cosmopolitan* magazine after Trump was inaugurated and the internet was flooded with commentary on how unhappy Melania looked.

In any case, Melania stuck with him, and according to Trump, when he finally asked her to marry him seven years later, they had not had a single disagreement. "We have literally never had an argument:

forget the word 'fight.' We never even had an argument. We just are very compatible. We get along."

Unlike Marla, who demanded Trump make an all-encompassing spiritual commitment to her, and a spiritual commitment to doing good works, and unlike Ivana, who had morphed into a female version of Donald, Melania purred with contentment, was happy to stay indoors, and as she would say in many future interviews, she had no interest in changing Donald. It didn't hurt that she met him just as she was about to age out of the all-too-short life span of a working model and faced an utterly chaotic and uncertain future. "It's about all that power and protection," one of Melania's old friends from Ljubljana said. "I think she needed a strong man, a father figure."

Trump was soon handling her career. Paolo was out of the picture. No more *Vogue Bulgaria* for her. Soon she was on the cover of *New York* magazine and *Tatler*. In 2000 she appeared in a bikini in the *Sports Illustrated* Swimsuit Issue. Trump bragged that he "got a good deal" for Melania on a Time Square billboard. His publicity minions "bombarded" *GQ* editor Dylan Jones to shoot Melania in 2000, and Jones acquiesced. "Given that she was obviously so keen to be featured in *GQ*, we came up with a rather kitsch and camp story for her to feature in," he said. The resulting work of art was Melania lolling butt-naked inside Trump's gold-plated jet.

The rewards of submission to Donald's "vitality" and whims were great. Ensconced in the gold-plated triplex with servants above, and Tiffany and Gucci down below, and a chauffeured car to move her around Manhattan, plus the summer home in Bedminster and the winter mansion in Palm Beach, Melania soon forgot what it was like to shop at Crate & Barrel—which she had done to fill the Union Square pad. Of course, there was a small price to pay to keep the wolf of financial mediocrity at bay. There was a role to play. If Marla had played tabloid Marla, Melania would play sex kitten Slovenian.

Trump put her on the phone with Howard Stern, and she purred on cue.

> STERN: You are so hot. I see pictures of you, I can't believe it, you're a dream.
> MELANIA: Baby.
> STERN: I want you to put on your hottest outfit. What are you wearing?
> MELANIA: Not much.
> STERN: Are you nude?
> MELANIA: Almost.
> STERN: Ahh. I have my pants off already.

When Stern asked if she went to Trump's every night to have sex, she replied yes, adding "even more."

Stern then asked her if she ever "steals money from [Trump's] wallet" and finished with a compliment, telling her she had a "nice chest for a model."

In exchange for allowing herself to be subjected to humiliations like a lecherous Howard Stern interview, Melania reaped benefits. First, by letting Trump handle her career, she got the kind of modeling gigs at top-shelf magazines and even in Times Square that had been out of reach when she was working for Paolo and shopping for her own food and furniture in Union Square. And by 2005, Donald had made an honest woman of her, as they used to say, granting what would be a lifetime sinecure to her and her little family inside the safety of a gilded cage, if she could maintain her chill posture in the face of untold humiliations to come.

CHAPTER 18

◇◇◇◇◇◇◇

Marrying Melania

The Last Great Trump Wedding was held on January 22, 2005, at the Bethesda-by-the-Sea Episcopal church up the road from Mar-a-Lago, and it was the Trumpiest yet. "Supermodel" Melania wore a $100,000 hand-beaded duchesse satin Dior dress with an "oceanic" veil, and looked exquisite—and for the most part, really happy. Unlike the previous wives, Melania had had seven years to get used to life in Trumpworld. She was an active participant in the wedding plan, something the others were shut out of. She proved up to the task of allocating a small fortune.

The dress she chose had a thirteen-foot train and had taken laborers 550 hours to make. The insane Marie Antoinette–ness of it won The Dress (and Melania inside it) the cover of *Vogue* with the headline "How to Marry a Billionaire." On the wedding day, her personal valet and attendant was *Vogue* style editor Andre Leon Talley, who would later call her "the most moisturized woman I've ever met."

She asked for and got a full orchestra, plus an opera singer. She hired a New York event designer to create "a very classic, very white" wedding with a five-foot-tall centerpiece candelabra "to give the room height" plus thousands of dollars' worth of roses, gardenias, tea roses, orchids, and hydrangeas. The ballroom itself, reports were always keen to mention, had cost Trump $35 million to renovate in the years prior to the wedding. He blew a million on the wedding.

The cake was the most preposterous cake ever made, a wasteful folly. Five feet tall, built around a wire cage, it was covered with tiny sculpted sugar roses that had taken the baker two weeks to make. It was a real cake, flavored with Grand Marnier, but it was inedible, because it was impossible to slice through the wire scaffolding. Guests ate miniature versions of it made for each table. After the party was all over, hungry staff devoured the larger cake, taking it apart with their hands.

Melania's hand sported an emerald-cut, ten- to fifteen-carat Graff diamond wedding ring that Trump claimed he got for half price. The company's executive later denied that he gave Donald such a deal, although Graff had advertised on *The Apprentice* the year prior. There was one Trump brand extension Melania declined. Trump had wanted to broadcast it all. Melania nixed it.

Trump's sons Eric and Donald Jr. were the groomsmen, in white tie and tails. Melania's sister, Ines Knavs, was maid of honor in white strapless.

As with Donald's other two weddings, friends of the bride were hard to find in the bold-faced crowd. The Knausses were the only Slovenians in the ballroom, where former president Bill Clinton and Hillary mingled with current governors and senators, supermodels, pop music celebrities, television anchors, and sports stars: Barbara Walters, Russell Simmons, Kathie Lee Gifford, Arnold Schwarzenegger, Rudy Giuliani, Chris Christie, Matt Lauer, Leslie Moonves, Jeff Zucker, Shaquille O'Neal.

Elton John, Paul Anka, and Billy Joel each serenaded the couple.

"Let me tell you something," Sandra Rose, the bandleader's wife, told a reporter. "If someone had dropped a bomb on that place, it would have wiped out an entire generation of famous Americans."

Melania couldn't walk in the beaded dress, so she changed into a strapless white satin gown for the reception, where guests dined on shrimp salad and beef tenderloin. The honeymoon was a staycation at Mar-a-Lago. Donald couldn't think of a better place to hang out.

After the wedding, the Slovenians began spending more time in New York. Ines would stay in the Trump Park Avenue, the same building where Ivanka and her husband would live. Ma and Pa Knavs would stay in a condo inside Trump Tower, a few floors down from the Versailles triplex. The Knavses weren't citizens, but a New York immigration lawyer always made sure their papers were in order. Viktor Knavs was by late 2007 listed in public records as residing at Palm Beach, in Mar-a-Lago. In February 2018, Melania's immigration lawyer, also working for her family, responded to questions about the family's status. "I can confirm that Mrs. Trump's parents are both lawfully admitted to the United States as permanent residents." But he would give no further details on how they had managed to get their status. "The family, as they are not part of the administration, has asked that their privacy be respected, so I will not comment further on this matter." An anonymous source revealed to the *Washington Post* that the Knavses were "awaiting scheduling for their naturalization oath ceremony," indicating that they have probably held green cards for some time. Permanent residents must have had green cards for five years before they can apply for US citizenship. In May they were spotted at the New York federal building for a hearing on their application.

Inside this secure bubble, the sisters grew even closer. But aside from her own family, she appears to have shut out all Slovenians. Except for Melania donating $25,000 to the hospital in Sevnica, there is every indication that she turned away from her homeland, journalists and friends included, and almost never looked back. Journalists in Ljubljana who have covered their most famous subject are routinely ignored and beg American journalists (like this one) for help with access.

When her childhood and high school friends were organizing a high school reunion seven years ago, a group of them found her on-line through a PR firm and emailed her. Crickets. "Yes. I understand this now when she's the first lady," said one old friend. "But before. When we just wrote an invitation. We expected just a feedback. Not from her. Just something, 'Thank you for invitation. Melania will not come.'"

Another childhood friend, now the local grammar school prin-cipal, recalled another example of Melania's staunch turn away from her homespun childhood. Mirjana Jelancic recalled for the *New York Times* a conversation she had with Amalija Knavs. Melania's mother told Jelancic that she had asked her daughter what to do with all the sweaters she had knitted as a child. "Throw them away," Melania told her mother, who said she told her: "Come home, pick some out and throw them away yourself." In the end, Jelanjic offered to take the sweaters and add them to an exhibit of relics related to the school's most celebrated graduate.

Melania did not give up her mother tongue, though. Besides in-teracting in English with Donald and the occasional social event in New York or Palm Beach, she spent her days and nights talking in her native language with her sister and family, a little quartet of im-migrants. In 2001, she had obtained a self-sponsored green card based on "extraordinary ability." Her immigration lawyer said the designa-tion was based on large-scale ad campaigns (she had appeared on a Times Square billboard for Camel cigarettes).

In 2006, she took the oath of American citizenship. She has re-fused requests to release the documentation. Her attorney has also de-clined to clarify the status of the extended Knavs family's presence in the US, saying only "they are here." But under US law, Melania could have applied for her family to be allowed to come and stay for long periods, a situation known as "chain migration" that Trump nativists would like to eradicate.

◇◇◇◇

Even more than Melania herself, her older sister, Ines, is a mystery woman. In her hometown, there are rumors of depression. She has left maddeningly few clues about herself on her Facebook page, except for a photo in a white, strapless gown at the Trump wedding. The rest of her posts are about sister Melania, with baby pictures of "M," as she refers to her, and the occasional online slap at ex-friends back in Ljubljana who tell tales out of school about M. When one ex-boyfriend gave an interview about Melania in the Slovenian-language press, Ines posted at him: "We all have good memories & lies are not good karma."

Like Melania, Ines didn't spend much time outside in New York City, unless incognito. One of the few who have spoken out about her is photographer Jarl Alé de Basseville, who shot Melania nude in New York in the 1990s. "Ines wasn't like the other girls you would meet there, who behave like queens," he recalled. "She was really polite and very mellow."

One of her few known friends, Milan-based fashion designer Luisa Beccaria, who attended the Trump wedding, visited the Trumps in New York after Melania gave birth to Barron, in 2006, and reported that the Knavs/Knausses were all present. "I realized that Melania was very close to her family when I saw them all there supporting her after Barron's birth," Becarria told the *New York Post*. "Melania had all the professional help she needed at that point, but it was her sister she trusted."

To fashion-conscious farmer's daughter Amalija and to Melania's sister, Ines, who had wanted to be a designer herself, but somehow didn't make it, Melania's wedding was the culmination of a lifetime of gazing in from the outside at the West's fashion magazines. Amalija, the pattern maker who walked across the Sava River bridge in heels every day to the factory, was on the inside of an *American Vogue* fashion event, and would soon be ensconced in Trump Tower. The two sisters had spent their adolescence and early twenties doodling and drawing beautiful clothes. Besides witnessing her sister in one of the most gorgeous confections created that year, for Ines, Melania's wedding day meant that she too would have an apartment in New York. To the little clan, and especially to her sister, "M" was nothing short of a hero. And the goose that laid the golden egg.

◇◇◇◇

Prada. Louis Vuitton. Chanel. Bulgari. Harry Winston. Gucci. And Tiffany.

She spent so much time there that a rumor started about her having an affair with the Tiffany head of security. The clerks at Gucci knew her better than her peers, the moms at Barron's private elementary school. "Melania is always shopping at the shops around the Tower," one of her New York friends mused, trying to explain what life was like before Trump ran for president.

Melania and Donald's separate bathrooms keep the marital mystery alive. The separate toilet areas also accommodate Donald's well-known germophobia, plus his fear of menstrual blood and, presumably, since he's gained even more weight since Marla said he liked the lights off when he disrobed, a place for him to hide his body.

In a 2003 *Howard Stern Show* interview, Trump bragged about Melania's discretion.

"Does she make doody?" Stern asked.

"Isn't that amazing? In years, three and a half years she's never . . . wow," Trump replied.

Melania was the Virgin Mary of the toilet—immaculately relieving herself without sound.

Holding in the gas was not too high a price to pay to remain sixty-eight stories above Fifth Avenue, doodling jewelry designs and listening to the sound that pearls and diamonds make clacking together on a polished marble table.

While Melania was pregnant with Barron, in 2006, Trump marveled to Stern at how large she grew—but in all the right places. There's no indication she invited him into the birthing room the way Marla had. A scene of birthing gore would have been the quickest way to dampen whatever remained of Melania's portion of his ardor.

Even before the baby was born on, March 20, 2006, Donald was by several accounts casting around for someone else to manage his manly needs. During an interview and photo shoot at Mar-a-Lago, a few months before she gave birth, Trump allegedly assaulted reporter Natasha Stoynoff, dispatched by *People* magazine to cover the couple's first wedding anniversary. While Melania stepped away, Donald took the journalist on a tour. According to Stoynoff, he led her into a room, shut the door, and stuck his tongue down her throat, insisting that they would have an affair back in New York.

With Melania postpartum, Donald allegedly propositioned a few porn stars for sex. One of them, Stephanie Clifford, who went by the nom de plume Stormy Daniels, says she actually got in bed with him at a golf resort where she'd been hawking her videos. During the 2016 campaign, a Trump lawyer, Michael Cohen, paid her $130,000 for her silence.

Trump was already president, the government was chaotic, and at first, hardly anyone besides the media pack noticed or cared, when the *Wall Street Journal* revealed the payoff and Stormy hired a lawyer to bust out of the agreement. "Picture this, Donald Trump chasing me around the bedroom in his tighty-whities," Stormy had reported to a girlfriend about the encounter. Another porn star, "sex educator" Jessica Drake, claimed that Trump offered her $10,000 to have sex with him, also in 2006. A *Playboy* bunny came out of the woodwork to claim that American Media, publisher of the *National Enquirer*, had paid $150,000 for her story of a year-long affair with Trump, also while he was married to Melania, just after she gave birth.

The alleged encounters—which arguably led to a raid on the office and home of Trump lawyer Michael Cohen—seemed to be the norm, not an aberration. Steve Bannon later claimed that Trump's lawyers paid off "a hundred women" during the campaign, buying a lot of silence.

The claimed timing—while Melania was pregnant and postpartum—certainly fits the pattern of his phobia. He was raised in a household where his own mother managed to bear five children without ever uttering the word *pregnant*. He has a well-known revulsion toward the details of female biology. Hence, his choice in women— porn stars and *Playboy* bunnies whose airbrushed parts and fake sexuality are geared toward tricking men into a male-centric version of female sexual pleasure.

What Melania knew or cared about of this is impossible to know. Trump's own theory of their successful relationship—about which he liked to brag before he got elected president—was not just separate bathrooms, but keeping separate lives. After two tries, and countless girlfriends, he'd say he finally discovered the key to a happy marriage. The couple went weeks without seeing each other, easy enough to do when one has access to a private jet and lives in a Fifth Avenue triplex.

Melania herself seems to have been perfectly fine living without Donald for long periods of time, staying in the triplex or her parents' apartment with her son, and making the occasional trip (by car) to visit her sister a few blocks away, or to shop the luxury shops around the Tower. She even purchased another Trump Tower apartment after her husband was elected. This no doubt encouraged the rumors about her affair with the head of security at Tiffany, rumors which have never been verified. The very public nature of the humiliation around the later revelations about porn stars and bunnies and hush money changed her and sparked still more rumors. Her New York friends believed she was then living in Potomac, Maryland, with her parents, in a house near Barron's school. "Her friends are worried about her," one New York pal said. But she maintained her silence.

For Melania, never an outgoing personality, a retreat to the cabbage-scented warmth of Slovenia was always her first choice. In the high-rise heart of haute Manhattan, Barron learned Slovenian first, and spoke English with an accent.

Inside the Slovenian bubble, in the Tower, Melania's English didn't improve. Curiously, the few Slovenians she deigned to see after her marriage were stunned that she would insist on speaking her halting English with them, instead of their shared native language. Back in Sevnica, Viktor Knavs did maintain a home, and sometimes bragged in the pubs about how Trump himself would deliver the paper every morning to the family condo in Trump Tower. In a documentary made by POP TV on the first lady, a family friend named Mrs. Dernac told journalists that when Melania's sister, Ines, came back to finally sell the family apartment, after living near Melania in a Trump property in New York for several years, "she was withdrawn and uncommunicative." As for Melania, who did not come back to Sevnica after one short visit to introduce her parents to Donald before the marriage, Dernac opined that she too seemed unhappy. "She has never uttered the word 'happy' when she has talked about Trump. I felt sorry for her, she should have got someone equally gorgeous and her age. This one's not ugly, but he's not right for her."

Besides shopping, Melania had an assistant and chef do basic errands. For almost ten years, life was cozy and luxe. The cradle rocked, but the marriage never rocked. The price of the nest was to be a good brand shill when called upon. Michael D'Antonio, author of *The Truth About Trump*, published in 2015, conducted numerous interviews with Donald before Trump cut him off (after Marla Maples reported to the Trumps that D'Antonio was asking sensitive questions).

D'Antonio witnessed Donald at Trump Tower scripting his wife. "He begged her to praise him [to me] as a husband. . . . Literally, he said, 'Tell him I'm a really good husband.' She looked at him, and he repeated himself. And she said, 'Yeah, he's a really good husband.' It was being dragged out of her," D'Antonio said.

The truth about Melania is that, as Stane Jerko noticed, she was never really comfortable being exposed. She trained herself to it, and approached the job with rigor. She could balance on four-inch heels and maintain posture, without ever looking down; she could take off her clothes or pose nearly nude on a facsimile of Trump's jet, if that's what it took. "Her world is very, very small," said one New York friend. "Melania only wanted red-soled shoes and a roof over her head. And she got this." The posture and the posing for the camera and in public always masked wariness. But now, with eyes on her all the time, it leaks out as unsmiling tension.

◇◇◇◇

In February 2017, with Trump in the White House, Melania Trump's name was still listed as CEO of Melania Marks Accessories Member Corp, the holding company of Melania Marks Accessories LLC. The companies managed between $15,000 and $50,000 in royalties from her accessories lines, according to the Trumps' May 2016 financial disclosure filing. Melania LLC was also still active, though the Trumps had listed it as having less than $1,000 in value and producing less than $200.

Two more Melania skin-care products companies were listed in the same financial disclosure as having little to no value or income. One of them was a miracle anti-aging cream made of caviar that crashed and burned in a lawsuit. Seven years married to Trump, Melania signed a deal with New Sunshine LLC, a Midwest skin-care holding company that also held contracts for a Kardashian bronzer, to license the cream, which, according to the brand's now defunct site, was specially created by researchers with caviar imported from the South of France.

The Trump publicity machine churned into gear, booking Melania on *Celebrity Apprentice* and *Good Morning America*, and getting write-ups in various women's magazines. The miracle fountain-of-youth product, whatever it really was, never got to stores. The co-owners of New Sunshine LLC, two Trump millionaire pals, got into a fight that disintegrated into a highly entertaining octopus of litigation. Dirt flew. One of the owners accused the other of trying to lure his wife—named "Tomisue"—into a threesome, saying he "no longer liked working, was tired of pleasing his customers, and had decided he wanted to live his life fully and fulfill his sexual urges."

Eventually, one of them sued Melania too. The caviar cream never got to retail. The product and its weird history became another scrap of Trumpiana, lying inside the overflowing bin that goggle-eyed journalists were pawing through day and night as the candidate churned toward the presidency with his own trademark chaotic political hell style.

But a good brand is a hard thing for any Trump to relinquish. Melania was still hawking eponymous "affordable" jewelry and "timepieces" in the spring of 2016. And she was having some success. According to a fawning interview published in luxury *DuJour* magazine, "her QVC line of sparkly jewelry sold out in 45 minutes."

The next time her brand made news was in another lawsuit, filed just as "FLOTUS" was about to add immeasurable value to the brand.

◇◇◇◇

In August 2016, a Slovenian magazine called *Suzy*, and then the British newspaper the *Daily Mail*, published claims that while working with Zampolli Melania had been a high-end escort. The Trumps hired libel lawyer Charles Harder, fresh off laying waste to the Gawker media company, a man whose very name struck fear into the hearts of editors and publishers.

The paper retracted the story within days. "To the extent that anything in the *Daily Mail's* article was interpreted as stating or suggesting that Mrs. Trump worked as an 'escort' or in the 'sex business,' that she had a 'composite or presentation card for the sex business,' or that either of the modeling agencies referenced in the article were engaged in these businesses, it is hereby retracted, and the *Daily Mail* newspaper regrets any such misinterpretation."

In February 2017, Harder filed suit in New York, demanding $150 million in damages from the *Daily Mail.* In the claim, Harder suggested that Melania's *brand* had taken a severe hit. She "had the unique, once-in-a-lifetime opportunity, as an extremely famous and well-known person, as well as a former professional model and brand spokesperson, and successful businesswoman, to launch a broad-based commercial brand in multiple product categories, each of which could have garnered multi-million dollar business relationships for a multi-year term during which Plaintiff is one of the most photo-graphed women in the world," Harder claimed, adding that the spuri-ous claims about her past affected her ability to market her branded apparel, accessories, jewelry, cosmetics, hair care, and fragrance.

In April 2017, the paper agreed to pay a reported $3 million to settle both the UK and US suits. The Slovenian magazine, source of the original published claim, also settled for an unreported sum. The actual source for the story, a Slovenian journalist named Tomaz Mihe-lic, settled and apologized after Melania sued him for defamation and making false and unverified statements.

He is now participating in an unrelated Slovenian reality show.

PART FIVE

Ivanka Trump, First Daughter

Of all the Trump Queens, Princess Ivanka was the only one to the American manor born. The line of aspirational immigrants, from Elisabeth Christ, to Mary Anne MacLeod, to Ivana Zelníčková, has been integrated in her towering, soigné form into the ultimate Trump female. Her mother officially branded her when she was still a young teen, filing papers to patent her name for selling clothes and jewelry. Her destiny is to take the name and remake it into her father's image of what he would call classy—against all the challenges presented by his outrages and buffoonery. In politics, she provides a measure of cognitive dissonance, a soothing faux-feminist, empowered by the best that money can buy. She is smarter than all of them, instinctively strategic, and a lifelong student of power and how to wield it.

The Trump brand will succeed or fail in her.

CHAPTER 19

◇◇◇◇◇◇

Ivanka at Choate

"It was insane, so offensive, so upsetting." That's how silken, dignified adult Ivanka Trump would remember the year of her parents' divorce, and the tabloid circus. Her dad moved out, her mom was sad, her older brother wasn't speaking to her father.

But the experience of living inside a tabloid scandal, in third grade, looking up at the wall of paparazzi every time she stepped outside, branded Ivanka internally. "It was the darkest, most difficult period in my young life," she wrote. Besides losing her dad to Marla Maples, within a year her grandfather died and then her beloved nanny Bridget Carroll, who died of a heart attack while she was minding the children in the Trumps' Greenwich mansion.

In hindsight, Ivanka decided that the childhood catastrophes made her a wiser adult. "I firmly believe that without those heartaches, my life might have been just a little too easy."

After the divorce, she lived with Ivana, whose lifestyle was rocket-fueled with divorce cash and the money she was earning from books and the home shopping empire. Ivana would take her daughter with her to Paris to look at the shows, to Saint-Tropez, to Milan, to the

Alps, and on extravagant jaunts around the world. The kids summered on their mother's yacht, usually with Italian men—some stepdads, some not—along for the ride. "All through childhood, there was one adventure after another to typical jet-setting-type hot spots, remote, undiscovered haunts, and everywhere in between," Ivanka wrote. "My childhood summers spent globe-trotting with my mother gave me a tremendous worldview. . . . I went to France, China, Argentina, Egypt. . . . My mother would get excited about some part of the world she'd never seen or experienced, and off we'd go. It was wonderful! Outrageous, really."

At age fourteen, she was bundled out of New York and off to boarding school. Not just any boarding school, but John F. Kennedy's alma mater, a finishing school for some of America's most privileged kids. Being banished to the New England countryside wasn't her choice. She'd rather have stayed in New York. She was a city kid who had known how to hail a taxi since she was in primary school. Waiters at Le Cirque and the Four Seasons knew her by name and her favorite meal.

"The dorms at Choate were the first buildings I lived in that didn't say 'Trump' somewhere on the facade, and I remember thinking that this was worth noting," she recalled. Even among children of great privilege, "this wasn't a common dilemma," she wrote, and "it struck me as symbolic." Surveying her new digs, she decided she would try to look at the world from a whole new angle. "Even if it meant living in a building named for someone else!"

Choate was the "first class section" of American schools. At home, the Trump kids were surrounded by fine things, but so were most of the other students. The difference was in degree of ostentation and celebrity. Other kids were rich, and maybe also well traveled. But Trump life was different. What other girl could say that Michael Jackson had come to see her perform *The Nutcracker* with the School of American Ballet at Lincoln Center? Who else had been ringside at a prizefight

in a girly dress with a bow and little satin Mary Janes, flecked with the
flying sweat of heavyweight boxers?

"We . . . enjoyed a kind of front-row seat before the world stage,"
she realized. There was something else too. A degree of entitlement.
Unlike other Choate kids, Ivanka's parents had insisted that "our big
bold advantages come as the result of their dedication and determination and that they were never to be taken for granted."

In other words, they were not to the manor born. But she was.

To ease the transition from New York life to the bucolic lawns
of academia, she opted for one of the Trump family traditions—
modeling. "I was all of a sudden in the prison of boarding-school
life, and all my friends in New York were having fun," she told *Marie
Claire*. So she started modeling. "I had no interest in being a model. I
just wanted to get the hell out of Wallingford," she said later.

Chipmunk-cheeked, her hair a dishwater shade of dark blond, in
a silvery sequined dress, her lips clotted with sticky gloss, she was still
in an awkward phase when she made her television debut as a cohost
at the Miss Teen USA pageant in August 1997. She muffed her lines
and looked lost and nervous, like a regular kid.

Her parents came to watch. It was believed to be the first time
Donald and Ivana had sat together since their divorce.

Despite her clunky look, a major agency, Elite models—helmed
by Trump pal Casablancas—picked her up. Donald and Ivana both
made noises about not being too pleased (perhaps because of Casablancas's well-known predilection for teen models), but having a hot
daughter was going to burnish the brand, and Donald didn't object
too strenuously. Mom and Dad consented as long as Ivanka promised
to put her studies first.

During her brief career, Ivanka was featured in *Elle, Marie Claire*,
on the cover of *Seventeen*, and in ad campaigns for Thierry Mugler,
Tommy Hilfiger, and Sasson jeans. She finally gave it up in 1999, after
walking the runway in the Paris and New York Fashion Week shows.

Eventually, Ivanka redefined her modeling years and the special Choate exemption she got for trips as an early sign of her tyro deal-making. She was just like Dad. "I've been negotiating for as long as I can remember," she wrote in *The Trump Card: Playing to Win in Work and Life*. "When I was a student at Choate, I negotiated off-campus privileges to allow me to pursue my modeling career in New York—no easy feat in the traditional boarding school lockdown environment. The school officials were lined up against me on this, but I made a compelling argument." The argument was that another student had been released to train for the Olympics. Afflicted with born-on-third-base syndrome, Ivanka didn't wonder whether the Choate pedagogues actually believed modeling and the Olympics were equally valid reasons to give a student special privileges or whether a call from Trump Tower had helped them decide.

Her Choate classmates remember Ivanka belonging to a popular, mostly blond clique, a closed circle of girlfriends who were more athletic than artistic. She was private and aloof. "She wasn't mean, she just didn't mingle," one classmate recalled. And she wasn't around much, often flying off to do fashion shoots. She didn't date much, nor was she a party animal, on a campus where parties were not infrequent.

On occasion, her tone-deafness erupted in a way that even other rich kids noticed. One classmate, who found her "arrogant and spoiled," recalled an English teacher recommending that the class see a new Monet exhibit traveling from Paris to either Boston or New York. Ivanka cut in, "Well, you really should see it in Paris."

No one seems to remember seeing Ivana on campus at all, but faculty and students do recall a visit from Donald Trump, who brought Melania to Ivanka's graduation in 2000. One classmate recalls that Trump—probably on that visit—also brought Tiffany and left her with Ivanka, who was not interested and tried to get a classmate to babysit for her half sister.

Choate faculty remember a good, smart student. "My impression of her was that she was hardworking, sharp, socially skilled, and a good kid," teacher Jim Davidson recalled.

Fellow classmate Stephen Farrell said during the 2016 campaign that he never noticed any Trumpian arrogance in the daughter's personality. "I would never want her smeared with the same paintbrush that is smearing him because she is very different from her father. She is a very wise woman, and I would advise people to distinguish between them," he said.

Years later, working for the Trump Organization, Ivanka made it clear that she was never really interested in the life path that led her stepmother from Slovenia to Manhattan. "Modeling was not an endgame for me. I didn't particularly enjoy the act of it. It's as ruthless an industry as real estate—the people you meet in that business are just as fricking tough. I used it as an excuse to travel. I used it as a way to break up the monotony. It was great, but it is an annoying source of confusion at this juncture in my life," she told *Marie Claire*, when she was starting out at her dad's company. "People still constantly ask me, 'How's modeling going?' That's how they remember me, and I want to be a little bit more serious than that, ha ha!"

◇◇◇◇

Despite avowals to the contrary, Ivanka did learn some very useful skills during her modeling years. All the Trump Queens know that being camera-ready is a prerequisite for appearing in public with Donald. They walk the extra mile in stilettos for him.

Ivanka transformed herself into exactly the kind of woman he would be photographed with. Most young people go through an awkward phase. Ivanka modeled through hers. So the photographic evidence of her transformation is in the record.

Her development from gawky teen to soigné adult came with a remarkably subtle and supernatural reorganization of nose, cheeks, lips.

It's possible that somewhere between the ages of fifteen and twenty-five, her nostrils shrank, her nose bridge narrowed, and the tip of it got less bulbous.

Based on photographic evidence, the nose job occurred between 2004, when she still had her childhood nose, and 2005, when she stepped out with a Barbie-doll version.

It's also possible that she ballooned naturally from a B cup to a D+ cup overnight. It happens to nursing mothers. But she was not pregnant in January 2007, when she wore a tight, white dress to the Golden Globes that showed off a suddenly much larger bosom. Gawker pointed out that Ivanka "took her mini boobs into a surgeon's hands and emerged with giant funbags" for the event. "Ivanka shocked everyone when she arrived with some, er, golden globes of her own," wrote one review. "A white clingy one-shouldered gown, with melons on her chest." Around this time she also appeared in a *GQ* photo shoot, and her new chest was the talk of the New York media crowd.

Ivanka's brother Donald Jr. has scoffed at the rumors, saying that his sister is "100% real." But her future husband Jared complained to people about "all the plastic" in the years when they were dating.

But whatever she did, she didn't do it for Jared or her brother.

"I think even Ivanka wanted her father's attention," said a friend of the family. "And from a very young age, she knew he liked beautiful women, he liked beauty, he liked elegance, and she wanted to be a model."

The same friend claims that for her surgeries Ivana took her daughter to Florida, where "she had breasts, nose, chin, cheeks, is my understanding." In Palm Beach, the word is that Ivanka underwent two boob jobs. The first round wasn't sufficient for The Donald, who saw her sunbathing in a chaise and at Mar-a-Lago and cracked that she wasn't big enough. She then showed up at the Golden Globes with "melons."

The amount and kind of plastic surgery she underwent as a teenager and young woman is a matter of pure speculation, since she denies it. But Donald's very specific, *Playboy* bunny/porn star ideal of big-boobed and sanitized female beauty, plus the example of her own mother's increasingly dramatic efforts to stave off natural aging, must have left a mark on the young woman's self-image. Not necessarily in her view though. "There's no doubting my father values beauty, but in my formative years, I never thought he valued it to the point that it should make me uncomfortable," she told *Harper's Bazaar* in 2007, while brushing off questions about plastic surgery—without, in this instance, denying them.

Today, Ivanka might be a millennial style icon for young Republicans, the self-styled working mom with a branded Instagram account of snaps of her playing with her children while wearing stiletto pumps, but she still dresses not for the girls or even for Jared, but as an extension of her father's brand.

CHAPTER 20

◇◇◇◇◇◇

Ivanka in Love

After Choate, after attending Georgetown and then transferring to her father's alma mater, Wharton, and earning a degree in economics, Ivanka was back in Manhattan, among the children of the city's moneyed nobility. After a half-year stint working for a real estate concern in Queens, she returned to the Tower. Donald knew what he had in his daughter. She was loyal. She was strategic. And she was a tall, poised blonde, perfectly proportioned as far as he was concerned, with just enough modeling experience to be able to walk into a frame in the sexiest stilettos, and still keep a hard hat on her head at ribbon cuttings.

She was never a wild child like some daughters of the men in her dad's set—never a PR disaster like famous-for-being-rich Paris Hilton, or a family tragedy like the drug-addicted Johnson & Johnson heiress, or even one of the countless private family problem kids she'd known since primary school who were doing tours in expensive Florida or Minnesota rehabs. And her stability was real. "I can tell you that I know people who've been in a room with only the family, and Ivanka is always poised, always picture perfect, always on record, and on brand," said a family friend. "There are no stories of her dancing on tables. She's always been on target."

When she finally took her place in a small suite of offices with a pink conference room in the Trump Organization in 2005, after a short stint working for another New York real estate firm, she also took her place in millennial generation New York society, a claque that included other famous men's daughters who would show up at philanthropic events and otherwise kept a low profile, like Georgina Bloomberg and Chelsea Clinton. She hobnobbed with style mavens who kept her supplied with their designs and got her photo shoots at *Allure* and *Marie Claire*, and she sometimes dated celebs (actors John Cusack and Topher Grace for a New York minute each). She started collecting art.

She arrived in Manhattan after college with a veteran publicist's instinct for image control. When a boyfriend, society scion Bingo Gubelmann, teamed up with his childhood friend Jamie Johnson (another heir to the Johnson & Johnson fortune) to make a movie, *Born Rich,* about the children of the New York rich, eventually aired on HBO, Ivanka agreed to appear. She showed off the view from her Trump Tower childhood bedroom, and talked about her childhood and growing up rich, in a self-effacing and thoughtful way. In the finished documentary, she comes off as unspoiled, decent, perhaps the most together rich kid in the whole movie. It helped that she had made sure she was in the editing room when it was being made, but the appearance wasn't far from the truth.

Still, the outer shell of the marvelous construction that is Ivanka encloses a woman who has sublimated a childhood of trauma as the daughter of a megalomaniac whose very public antics exposed his family to humiliation in the greatest sex scandal of the late twentieth century. Even among the famous-for-being-rich children of the Hilton/Kardashian sex tape age, it would be hard to find a soul mate who could relate to all that.

Then, along came Jared Kushner.

A real estate developer introduced them, thinking of it as a business networking opportunity. Ivanka later called it "the best deal we ever made." Tall, brown-eyed, with adorable dimples, from a major real estate family, he possessed, civilians who met him noticed, a social awkwardness that was almost autistic. He was a man-child whose career was predicated on his ability to hand off the details, and "let my people take care of it." The couple had in common something deep: his dignified bearing concealed the still raw scar of a dad-caused trauma that rivaled Ivanka's from her own father.

Charles Kushner, son of Holocaust survivors, was a millionaire real-estate developer who had raised his family in a pampered, but Orthodox Jewish, New Jersey household. Jared grew up knowing Bibi Netanyahu, attending yeshiva school, learning Hebrew, and following the Sabbath rules. He also wanted for nothing. Like Ivanka's, Jared's family had drivers and servants, and the children got expensive educations and life in a graceful—if not Versailles-level—suburban mansion. Money could do just about anything: an average high school student, Kushner was accepted at Harvard after his father donated $2.5 million.

But there was something money could not do: stop a federal investigation. A year after he started law school, the young man's pampered world exploded. Charles Kushner, in a fight over family funds with his siblings, had hired a prostitute to bait his sister's husband (aka his own brother-in-law) into sex to be videotaped at a motel. Kushner then sent the videotape to his sister. The family reported this to the feds, who were already looking into his political donations. Kushner was arrested, charged with illegal campaign contributions, tax evasion, and witness tampering, pled guilty, and was sentenced to federal prison in Alabama for two years. (He left a bit early after claiming he was an alcoholic and submitting to serve part of his sentence in halfway-house rehab.)

Given what their fathers had inflicted on them and bequeathed them, it's hard not to imagine Ivanka and Jared realizing they were soul mates from the minute their eyes met.

Your dad headlined the sex scandal of the last century.

Your dad hired a hooker to destroy his sister's marriage and went to jail.

And we're both tall, attractive, young, and worth hundreds of millions of dollars.

They fell in love. It was real. Even a Trump enemy, Rosie O'Donnell, after running into them at a New York restaurant, was moved to poetry. Rosie wrote: "i watch them / stunned by her face / and his calming charm / . . . oblivious to all seeing them / love works like this."

There was an obstacle: the Kushner family adheres to a strict Jewish sect, and Jared would not marry outside the faith. They broke up. After they'd been apart months, Wendi Deng, a pal to both of them, still married to leather-faced septuagenarian Rupert Murdoch, invited Jared to spend a weekend on the Murdoch family yacht, without letting Jared know that Ivanka would also be there.

True love prevailed.

A former *New York Observer* writer who worked with Jared beginning in 2006 recalled that he was "very friendly, social, personable" and made a point of trying to seem like a regular guy. "He always wanted to meet at places like Katz's deli. He'd never, say, pick up lunch at the Four Seasons the way other young monied moguls did. He seemed bent on cultivating this down-to-earth image even as the media reported constantly on how much money he had and his business dealings."

After Ivanka entered his life, he seemed to get more comfortable embracing his wealth. Out on the social circuit, they were an odd couple, or at least an example of opposites attracting. Jared was quiet and reserved, while Ivanka was chatty and engaged. "She came off as being much more intelligent and savvy than he was. He was a bit of a deer in the headlights about most things—except real estate," the former *Observer* writer recalled. Around this time, the couple started spending a lot of time with Yacht People Murdoch and Deng. "Eventually, he talked more about real estate, and more and more about Murdoch, their friendship, Rupert's yacht," recalled the *Observer* writer. "It seemed like Rupert Murdoch was kind of his only friend, and had become a father figure, and was very influential over Jared and important to him."

Later, when it was all worked out, Ivanka told *New York* magazine: "One of the jokes I first started making when Jared and I first started dating is, I'm a New Yorker, I'm in real estate. I'm as close to Jewish, with an 'i-s-h' naturally, as anyone can start off." But it wasn't enough.

By 2008, Ivanka was studying Judaism with American Modern Orthodox rabbi Haskel Lookstein, who presided over a well-heeled congregation on Manhattan's Upper East Side, where congregants give a lot of cash to Israel but don't tarry with fundamentalism.

The Supreme Rabbinical Court in Israel has deemed at least one of Lookstein's conversions less than kosher, but Ivanka takes her Judaism more seriously than do many American Jews. She is raising three children according to Orthodox tradition, keeps a kosher home, observes all Jewish holidays, and assiduously keeps the Sabbath, when observant Jews turn off electronics and take twenty-four hours off from Friday to Saturday—although the word in Washington is that they just dictate to their servants who hold their iPhones during that period.

"It was very brave of her," said her mother's friend Nikki Haskell, who has known Ivanka since birth. "And she is very, very strict about it and keeps a very tight ship."

Jared's Orthodoxy provided Ivanka with a stable core that was missing growing up around her chaotic father. In an interview with Britain's *Mail on Sunday* in 2000, when she was nineteen, Ivanka said: "I never, ever want to get divorced. I think I'm quite good at judging what people are like, and I could never be with someone whose motives I was constantly questioning. And I certainly couldn't stand worrying about whether he'd run off with the first blonde who came along once I got my first wrinkle." The fact that Jared's sect is also deeply patriarchal (women cannot be rabbis, and at the far conservative end of the community, women wear wigs to cover their hair, similar in concept to the hijab, and men are forbidden to touch women to whom they are not related, lest they be menstruating, a primeval taboo) probably also appealed to the daughter of a man horrified by female biology.

For love, Ivanka also subdued her style, which had included some risqué magazine photo shoots and off-color jokes with friends about things like "mulatto cock"—an anecdote Ivanka denies, although her friends and some journalists have witnessed her tendency to be profane in private. She took to wearing sensible shoes and conservative clothes in private and still does so, and on Jewish holidays and Saturdays, and the paparazzi occasionally catch her out wearing a little beanie to cover her head, in covered-up coat dresses or long skirts. Her conversion and subsequent marriage and motherhood all coincided with Ivanka becoming more conservative, said Dirk Wittenborn, one of the producers of the documentary *Born Rich*. "I think she's someone who understands the responsibility of her position," he said. "She understands the role she has to play. She understood the role she had to play in 2002 and the role changed. I think the success of their reality TV show changed everything. It opened her horizons and the financial shift in the empire."

Ivanka did not completely abandon Trumpian style. Pregnant with their first child, she showed up in the pages of *Harper's Bazaar* showing off her bump and boobs, posing as a *Playboy* bunny. She was always proud to show some leg on the campaign trail, and as the first daughter she daily swans in and out of the White House in spike-heel pumps and a different floaty Zara dress (she wore a bit less haute couture after taking a White House gig, unlike the first lady, who continued to appear in couture).

The couple announced their engagement in July 2009, and were married that October before a rabbi at the Trump National Golf Club in Bedminster, New Jersey, in front of family and their New York friends. "The wedding was hardcore Zionist," a guest recounted. "There was a really conservative rabbi talking about Israel and hostages and terrorists, while they stood there holding hands. He even said something like, 'don't forget the little boy butchered in Israel.'"

Charles Kushner, out of jail, cleaned up and in a tuxedo, "was a real asshole, and gave a nasty toast, almost like he was snubbing the Trumps," the guest recalled. The father of the bride, by contrast, behaved himself. "Trump was gracious, especially to his ex, Ivana, who had been really difficult throughout the wedding planning," behaving like the Motherzilla of the Bride. "She was dramatic and driving him crazy, but he talked about what a great mother she was."

New York society, who had expected less of Trump, were surprised. "We had expected him to sell memberships to his club or charge for food, so the bar was low, but that was a point in his favor." (The expectation about being sales marks might have been heightened by the fact that the Trump wedding invitation included either a flyer for Trump's golf courses or an offer of a free round of golf at one of them.) Wedding favors included a book in Hebrew and flip-flops with "Ivanka" and "Jared" on the insoles, and a tag that said "A Great Pair."

To the blue bloods, the wedding was "two tacky families" coming together to enlarge their empires in the dirty world of New York real estate. "To our parents, he was like Kim Kardashian," sneered one of the society friends. "I don't think anyone believes Trump really has any money. I knew at seven years old that Ivanka was a real estate developer's daughter and that those people were not allowed into the golf clubs. Also, we were told that he cheated at golf, which in those circles is like being a pedophile."

The smirks of the New York blue bloods at the wedding bound the bride and groom even closer. Ivanka and Jared grew up rich and powerful, but with no generational distance from the dirty mining of money.

In fact, that no longer mattered.

◇◇◇◇

In the end, it does not really matter what the millennial blue bloods in New York society, descendants of the swells of yesteryear, think or say about Ivanka and Jared. The couple came of age in a new society, one remade by their dads and other men who got super-rich in the 1980s after Reaganism ripped the regulations off Wall Street.

Their dads had made Greed Good Again.

The sheer size of the new fortunes dwarfs the old. The energy WASP ancestors had possessed to amass the family fortune has been dissipated into heirs who want to make art, or do good, or simply drift and enjoy their trust funds. The Trumps and Kushners belong to a different, more energetic set, stained with recent scandal and reeking of reality show celebrity's cheap perfume maybe, but bursting with dash and vitality that cast out the old regime.

Ivanka's best friends are the new Yacht People, who float, anchors aweigh, on oceans of cash. She has much more in common with the daughters of the Nigerian kleptocracy than she has with the trust-funded great-granddaughters of the Gilded Age. National borders mean little at this stratum. Ivanka shares more of a worldview with British royalty and the wives or daughters of Russian oligarchs or third-world dictators with loot in Swiss bank accounts than she does with most of her American peers.

The yacht is a significant motif in Ivanka's life. Some of her earliest memories are of scampering around as a five-year-old on the *Trump Princess*, anchored at the "Trump Marina" in Atlantic City, where her father would soon be hiding his mistress. She spent summers on the Adriatic and the Mediterranean, on the *M.Y. Ivana*, anchored at Cannes, Saint-Tropez, Sardinia, Dubrovnik, with adults popping champagne and stripping to dive off the sides.

Ivanka and Jared's Yacht People are different from Ivana's old Saint-Tropez Tan crowd. They float around with real power. They cemented their love on Rupert Murdoch's yacht. The octogenarian media titan and father of Fox News has served as a father figure (without a criminal record) to Jared. Murdoch was such a role model that his example might have been a factor in Jared deciding to buy himself a newspaper, the *New York Observer*.

The summer Donald was campaigning for president, Ivanka and Jared—*sans enfants*, apparently—took some time off to relax on Democratic mega-donor and movie mogul David Geffen's yacht. The pictures of that grouping confused the plebeians: How could Donald Trump's daughter be yachting with David Geffen, a man who had so loved Obama that he gave up Hillary for him and raised millions for his campaigns? Less than a week before Paul Manafort was forced to step down from her dad's campaign, Ivanka jumped off the yacht long enough to post an Instagram photo of herself with Deng, Dubrovnik's old town as their backdrop.

To the Yacht People, political labels are for the civilians.

Besides Wendi Deng, one of Ivanka's closest Yacht People friends is Dasha Zhukova, the younger, art-collecting estranged wife (since August 2017) of Russian industrialist billionaire and Vladimir Putin pal Roman Abramovich. Abramovich's reported net worth is $10.8 billion.

In the tense last months of the 2016 campaign, while Donald was prepping for his first debate with Hillary Clinton, and the October Surprise Billy Bush tapes were still secretly wending their way toward the *Washington Post*, Ivanka and Jared were with the Yacht People again, on land, in the VIP seats at the US Open. They shared a box with Wendi Deng, David Geffen, Princess Beatrice of York, and the ubiquitous Dasha, still married to billionaire Putin pal Abramovich.

After Trump was elected, stunned investigators and journalists were moved to start looking into rumors of Russian links and spies. In January 2017, US counterintelligence officials warned Jared Kushner that Wendi Deng might be actively working for China. The Yacht People were also buzzing that Deng was dating Putin (recently divorced and worth an estimated $200 billion). "I've never met Putin," Deng told *Vogue* in the summer of 2016. She'd been spotted a few months earlier boarding Roman Abramovich's *Eclipse*—the world's second-largest private yacht, with twenty-four guest cabins and two swimming pools—while it was docked at St. Barts.

In 2016 it was revealed that Abramovich had given Putin a different, $35 million, 187-foot yacht as a gift.

It only has room for ten guests.

CHAPTER 21

◇◇◇◇◇◇

Ivanka's Brand

Perception is more important than reality. If someone
perceives something to be true, it is more important than
if it is in fact true. Let the other guy think what he wants.

—IVANKA TRUMP, *THE TRUMP CARD*

The brand was there before there was a product to attach it to.

In 1997, Ivana Trump trademarked the name "Ivanka." The real
Ivanka was just fifteen, a prep school teen with pouty lips and chip-
munk cheeks. According to her application with the US Commerce
Department, Ivana, as her child's "guardian," wanted to protect the
Ivanka name because she planned to use it on a line of cosmetics
including pressed powder, lipstick, a "mini-lift and repair lotion,"
bronzer, and a jewelry line. She also reserved it for a possible Ivanka
clothing line, and the application left out no sartorial possibility, listing everything from anoraks to skorts.

In her book *The Trump Card: Playing to Win in Work and Life*,
Ivanka uses the word "brand" sixty-eight times. She and her brothers are "ambassadors of our *brand*." They work to "grow the Trump
brand." "I believe in the Trump *brand*." We "build the value of our

brand." We "were able to purchase, develop and *brand* a number of properties around the world." She writes about "*brand* recognition" and "building and extending our *brand.*" And that moment, shortly after his reality show *The Apprentice* took off, when her dad "looked up and realized he had become a *brand*" because "his celebrity couldn't help but enhance the Trump *brand.*"

Like House of Ivana, Ivanka was bred to be a branch off the Trump brand tree. By the time Ivanka was old enough to apply her own brand, reality TV had juiced the trademark *Trump* like A-Rod on steroids. "You're fired" went global, Trump went global. The Trump kids, Dad's emissaries to foreign countries (*shitholes* and the nice ones) that Donald personally avoided because he is a man of habit, felt it right away. "Because of our roles on the show, people were suddenly inclined to take us more seriously than they might have otherwise," Ivanka noticed, as she traveled to third-world nations, Trump-branding new developments. After *The Apprentice* was franchised to more than a hundred countries, "when I travel to work on a deal, it becomes a big story. Forget the deal itself—the mere fact of our interest in a region or a particular property is now considered newsworthy in some parts of the world."

The brand she's been honing since college is not the photogenic doll you see on Instagram. It's working mother, canny dealmaker, hot wife. "She is going to be able to narrate her own story," said a New York friend, estranged because of Trump's politics. The movie that she is writing of her life is as "a developer, of growing up and hanging out on construction sites."

In real life, Ivanka's "deals" were about labeling and licensing and promoting the Trump brand, from Panama to the Arab Gulf States and the former Soviet Union, without asking too many questions about business partners. Like her affable Rat Pack Dad, but with a different shtick, Ivanka's soigné, cultured persona has provided for dubious characters the brand cover they need to invest their money. All of this provided fodder for journalists as they examined her and his deals in the wake of his candidacy.

And really, it was thrilling and exotic to be so young and so important in third-world countries. Unlike her father, who grew up around squinty-eyed men who played hardball and who surrounds himself with thugs and goons, Ivanka missed that crucial part of her dad's education. She's not the person in the room who gets handed the bag of cash. In "deals" with sketchy characters from countries like Azerbaijan or Malaysia, she is the figurehead, and she enjoys the reverence, standing two heads above the small brown people who are still scrabbling for cash, an enterprise she has not had to dirty her hands with in quite the same way as her dad and grandpa. Cutting a deal with a notorious family in Azerbaijan, the Mammadovs, in 2014, she posted a picture on Facebook, giddy. "I'm in Baku, Azerbaijan . . . and will reveal why next week! In the meantime, check out this cityscape view." Later she told an interviewer for *Baku* magazine that she couldn't wait to visit the hotel's Spa by Ivanka, which she praised as "a huge spa area."

Everyone was just so nice, and she was nice in return.

Is Ivanka as oblivious to the truth about the Trump Organization's seedier partners as she appears? Alexandra Wrage, of TRACE International, helps American businesses vet foreign partners to avoid violating the 1977 Foreign Corrupt Practice Act, aimed at curtailing American participation in corruption and bribery in foreign countries. "In the world according to me," she said "I don't think there is any way Ivanka could have operated in these circles for as long as she has, in the shadow of her father, with these thuggish characters and not have had questions about the qualities of her business partners. The whole pitch she has made, and her father has made on her behalf," she adds, "is that she is this flinty businesswoman with her own brand and a supply chain in China."

A former US government official and expert in money laundering was more blunt. "All you have to do is watch *The Godfather*," he said. "This is an organized crime family and you are not trusted unless you are inside it. Ivanka is her father's alter ego. When she is present, people know it's 'I am Donald Trump and I approve this transaction.'"

While she was making foreign deals for the Trump Organization and working alongside convicted felon Felix Sater on a Manhattan project called Trump Soho, Ivanka was also planning her eponymous personal brand, which she launched in 2011—aimed, according to its website, "to fill a void in the market by creating a line of chic, affordable, easy to wear pieces for modern women." On the company website, Ivanka promised to help her consumers "architect" their lives.

The chief Trump ambassadress developed her own brand, selling Ivanka Trump clothing, shoes, and jewelry, just as her mother had envisioned decades earlier. Ivanka and her team licensed Chinese-made affordable clothes and shoes and bred the products with a lifestyle, giving them a story—Ivanka's story—as a working Everywoman. As her father's improbable and proudly misogynistic campaign for the Republican nomination started taking off, Ivanka's company was hatching a new hashtag, #womenwhowork, on social media. The campaign, asking women to "join the conversation," heralded a second book by Ivanka Trump, to be about, well, women who work, and how that happens.

The potential of politics to boost the Ivanka Trump brand became clear when she wore a powdery pink Ivanka Trump sheath to introduce her dad at the Republican National Convention in Cleveland. Outside, vendors were chanting one of their best-selling T-shirt slogans: "Hillary Sucks But Not Like Monica!" Indoors, Ivanka talked about child-care tax credits and working mothers, sounding suspiciously Democrat to the star-spangled crowd assembled fresh off chanting "Lock Her Up!"

Twelve hours after that appearance, her father now the official

Republican nominee for president, Ivanka tweeted a link to the $138 dress. It sold out within a day.

But politics also proved a tricky way to boost brand value. Ivanka officially stepped down from her company in January 2017, but not before one last promo. She wore a fetching gold cuff bracelet for a *60 Minutes* post-election interview. One of her marketing minions blasted a "style alert" to fashion journalists advertising the $10,800 item. Outrage ensued. Her company apologized and announced she would use her social media accounts only for personal messages. All new social media accounts promoting her brand would henceforth use the handle IvankaTrumpHQ.

Meanwhile, a grassroots movement called #GrabYourWallet urged shoppers to boycott stores that carried her brand. After Nordstrom dropped her line, citing "low performance," now-President Trump and "alternative facts" counselor Kellyanne Conway went on offense, telling the public to buy Ivanka.

The spectacle of a White House hawking family products sent ethics lawyers and Democrats sputtering, outrage upon outrage. By then, Ivanka and Jared were in Washington, settling into a rented mansion on Kalorama, not far from the Obamas. After her father was elected, Ivanka had called Anna Wintour, editor of *Vogue*, an executive at Condé Nast, a mentor and friend, and asked, "How can I use this to further my brand?"

Anna wasn't helpful, although she would reportedly swallow her declared opposition to Trump and offer herself to be ambassador to the Court of St. James (she has denied this). Anna's chill might have been the last straw. The Trump-Kushners decided to get out of New York. They had been "exfoliating friends" throughout the campaign, as Jared put it. Just as Melania's being first lady added to her brand value, offices in the White House could do something for the Ivanka brand that no one in New York—no marketing people, no fashion maven, no hedge fund wives—ever could.

But the presidency attracted too much attention to seamy details that diminished the brand story—to consumers who read the *Washington Post*, anyway. While Donald Trump was urging Americans to "Buy American," the *Post* revealed that in China, Ivanka Trump's company was paying workers even less than the spartan Chinese minimum wage, half what the average Chinese manufacturing laborer made. The Ivanka Trump CEO told the paper it was economically impossible to produce Ivanka Trump in America.

Inspectors made a two-day visit to the Chinese factory where G-III Apparel Group was licensed to make clothes for the Ivanka Trump brand, and found workers had five days of paid leave annually. The inspectors also found that the factory didn't have a union, and was deficient in safety procedures and training.

None of this alarmed the Chinese. On the contrary, not long after the revelations, the Chinese government granted Ivanka Trump's company approval for three new trademarks, giving it monopoly rights to sell Ivanka brand jewelry, bags, and spa services in the world's second-largest economy. The day China granted the trademark, Ivanka and Jared dined on Dover sole and steak at Mar-a-Lago with Chinese president Xi Jinping.

But stateside, the Ivanka brand took a hit in inverse relation to the number of Trump's days in office. According to Lyst, growth in the number of orders dropped 288 percent in March 2017, then 114 percent in May, and 6 percent in July. As of August, the volume of growth had shot down to a negative 1 percent in comparison to August 2016.

Some stores were selling Ivanka: Goodwill and thrift stores. A fashion resale website found that in 2016, users listed 223 percent more Ivanka Trump–branded items compared to the same period a year earlier. That trend continued into the presidency. Trump-haters were dumping their Ivanka. Retailers like Nordstrom, T.J. Maxx, and Marshalls had pulled the line after Trump's inauguration—blaming falling sales after a boycott campaign. Just before she shuttered her line, Hudson's Bay, a Canadian department store giant that owns Lord & Taylor and Saks Fifth Avenue, announced it was dropping the brand as well.

Turned out, this didn't matter so much anymore. In July 2018, she abruptly shuttered her company. Inside the White House bubble, Ivanka had other branding to consider: her own political brand. "After seventeen months in Washington, I do not know when or if I will ever return to the business, but I do know that my focus for the foreseeable future will be the work I am doing here in Washington," she said in a statement. "So making this decision now is the only fair outcome for my team and partners." She is a woman who makes a plan, who thinks ahead, much more strategist than opportunist. She disappeared for a while, keeping a low profile while Jared was securely and officially appointed. And then, precisely at Day 60 of Presidential Year Trump One, she started off-the-record lunching with selected journalists, talking on background.

As an official, but unpaid, senior advisor to the President of the United States, she treated her 4 million plus Instagram followers to regular peeks at playtime with her adorable children—Arabella, six; Joseph, four; and Theodore, two—sometimes while clad in high heels and affordable dresses from Zara, more often in her own brand. The pictures were always delicious to look at. She 'grammed little Theo's first crawl in the White House State Dining Room in January. There was middle child Joseph pressing his face against the window glass in the Oval Office in February. There was daughter Arabella running down the White House steps. Ivanka's aim was to give the American public something royal, or at least something like the Kennedys. (She has given all three of her children Kennedy names.)

Of course there would be the critics. But Trumps were used to that. A *Wall Street Journal* investigation looked at the impact of Ivanka's outfits in her Twitter, Facebook, and Instagram postings over six months between March 29, when she officially started as White House advisor to her father, and October 31, 2017. They called her a billboard for her brand, a walking conflict of interest. "Every time she steps out sporting Ivanka Trump merchandise, Ms. Trump—wittingly or not—is . . . an example of the conflicts that arise when government employees have both public and private professional interests," the *Journal* wrote.

Trump nemesis Walter Shaub, a lawyer and former government ethics watchdog who resigned over nepotism and other violations of norms, called the arrangement "the definition of corruption" and warned the Trump White House that such actions come close to ethical violations. "We're in this situation because she is one of the rare government appointees in the White House who has not divested her financial interests," Shaub said on CNN.

Shaub and the *Wall Street Journal* were no different than the Democrats and trolls obstructing Trump's presidency. They did not get it: if the person *is* the brand, how does one divest? Trumps know a strong brand identity can withstand a lot of "fake news." Better to focus on the love. And there it was: by early 2018, Instagram had dozens of Ivanka Trump fan fiction accounts. Teen girls were harvesting photographs from Ivanka's personal profile and news outlets like the *Daily Mail* that publish daily paparazzi shots of Ivanka and Jared. The Instagram accounts chronicle Ivanka's outfits and moves with captions like: "More than grateful for having such an incredible role model to look forward to." They use political hashtags too, like #ivankaforpresident. The Instagram site @alwaysivanka had more than fifty thousand followers in May 2018. Its founder was a sixteen-year-old from Tennessee who told a reporter she "almost started crying" the day Ivanka followed her account.

On Instagram, it is summertime and Ivanka is in the Rose Garden in a floral off-the-shoulder dress. She is swinging Arabella, a happy mother-daughter moment just visible behind a hedge of green.

Behind that hedge, Trumps were talking of a dynasty. Sixteen years of Trump.

Eight of him. Then eight of Ivanka, the first female president.

CHAPTER 22

◇◇◇◇◇◇

The Sexualization of Ivanka

You've seen the pictures. If you have not, just Google "creepy pictures of Trump and Ivanka."

There she is on his lap; he is in a white linen suit, she in a miniskirt, a leggy colt, about fourteen years old. Her hand is cupping his chin; his hand is on her lithe, pubescent waist.

There they are on a bed, indoors. Trump Tower? A five-star hotel room? He's in a tuxedo with a phone on one ear. She is in a little black dress, clinging to him, long legs draped over his lap. She's about twelve.

There they are again, his hands on her shoulders. She's dolled up like Honey Boo Boo, in a shimmering gold dress, gold large-link Chanel chains, and bleached blond, straightened hair. She's about nine.

And there they are again, onstage at the Republican National Convention in Cleveland, after she's introduced "my father" in a flawlessly delivered speech. He's whispering in her ear; his hand is on the top curve of her sheathed hip.

Trump-hate was so visceral that by the end of the campaign, his foes, especially his female foes, cringed at the thought of his hands touching *anything*, from a White House doorknob to a Miss Teen USA crown to his own daughter. Viewed through that lens, one can read a lot into photos of budding pre-woman Ivanka, sliding into the Italian sports car with Daddy, on his lap, on a bed.

Journalist Julia Ioffe, after months on the receiving end of vile and—at the time—unprecedented anti-Semitic trolling from Trump supporters, went there. After Trump was elected, she tweeted: "Either Trump is fucking his daughter or he's shirking nepotism laws. Which is worse?" The tweet linked to a news report that claimed Ivanka would get the White House office space traditionally reserved for the first lady. (The report was wrong: Ivanka took an office in the West Wing.)

The journalist was soon filled with remorse. Some things, even in the era of Trump, remained off-limits. Accusing a politician of incest was one of them. "It was a tasteless, offensive tweet that I regret and have deleted. I am truly and deeply sorry. It won't happen again," she wrote. But it was too late. *Politico* terminated her contract. Speculating on incest is as off-limits as the subject of Barron. Of course, as Alex Jones would put it on Infowars, "people were asking . . ."

Ivana Trump wrote in her book *Raising Trump* that Donald's much photographed hands-on involvement with Ivanka was no different from the loving and close relationship she had with her own father. Entirely wholesome. But Donald and Ivanka do have a special relationship. She reveres him and works for him and seems to genuinely believe the Trump brand PR about her father: a decisive businessman, media impresario.

"She does believe that he's a genius," *New York Times* writer Maggie Haberman said. "She believes that there are things that he can intuit that other people can't. And she is very riveted by it."

When Ivanka looks at her father, she does not see an ethically challenged, coddled rich kid and bully, a cutter of corners. She sees, first and most viscerally, the Great Man who built the Tower in which she passed her own princess years overlooking the glorious realm of Manhattan, and second, the man who runs the real estate empire she will inherit pieces of, and if she plays her cards right, might even preside over, with or without her brothers. Ivanka has worked hard crafting an image of herself as a subtler, calmer version of the man, a female "entrepreneur" who has learned by careful study how to "negotiate the best deals" and who dreams as big as the Manhattan skyline. And with her father in the White House, she is his female alter ego, as angered by the slights and as certain of her rectitude and instincts as he is.

She calls him "my father" in public, rolling the two words off her tongue with a dignified, reverential cadence, throwing an upperclass twist on the vowels. In private, she sometimes calls him "Daddy" though—which he apparently prefers. During an appearance in Mandan, North Dakota, selling his tax reform plan two hours north of the site where cops and private mercenaries earlier that year had broken the back of the long-running Native protest at Standing Rock, which came to naught after his election, Trump made news talking about how much he likes being *Daddy*.

"Daddy, can I go with you?" Trump said, quoting his daughter. "And I said, 'Yes you can.'"

Onstage, at first, Trump said Ivanka called him "Dad." He then paused to correct himself—twice—and repeat that Ivanka had referred to him as "Daddy," adding, "I like that."

Trump-haters lob the "pedo" charges at him all the time, because of his own recorded ogling of half-naked Miss Teen USA contestants and his known predilection for young models. He has made myriad jokes about Ivanka's desirability. Is he joking? Or is he like Jim Carrey in the movie *Liar Liar*, a man who blurts out the truth uncontrollably?

Early in his campaign for the Republican nomination, in 2015, he told a *Rolling Stone* writer who'd just met Ivanka and praised her,

"Yeah, she's really something, and what a beauty, that one. If I weren't happily married and, ya know, her father . . ."

Once on TV, asked what he and his daughter both consider their favorite things, Trump answered, "I was going to say sex, but I can relate to [golf and real estate]."

He has publicly free associated on how he'd feel about her appearing in *Playboy*, and concluded that he'd probably be dating her. "Ivanka posing for *Playboy* would be really disappointing . . . not really. But it would depend on what was inside the magazine. . . . I don't think Ivanka would [do a nude shoot] inside the magazine. Although she does have a very nice figure. I've said that if Ivanka weren't my daughter, perhaps I'd be dating her."

He's lavished oodles of praise on her body and taken credit for it himself—a crucial aspect of his relationships with all his women is playing Pygmalion, and his daughter is his finest work of art. "You know who's one of the great beauties of the world, according to everybody? And I helped create her. Ivanka. My daughter, Ivanka. She's six feet tall, she's got the best body."

"She's actually always been very voluptuous . . . she's tall, she's almost six feet tall . . . she's an amazing beauty."

In 2004, when Ivanka was twenty-two years old and fresh out of college, Trump told Howard Stern that it was okay to characterize his daughter as "a piece of ass."

Donald liked to joke that he would date her if she wasn't his child, but when she posed in a see-through top and tiny bikini bottom for *British GQ* when she was eighteen, Trump apparently hit the roof. The *New York Post* reported: "Making dad steam even more was the description of his darling daughter as 'a nymphet.'" Trump was conciliatory when reached. "Those are not my favorite pictures in the world. But it is a highly reputable magazine."

If she's present, Ivanka smiles, chuckles, shakes her head. He appeared on *The View* and told the ladies that "if Ivanka weren't my

daughter, perhaps I'd be dating her." Ivanka called the media after-
math of that "a nightmare," but she still didn't take it personally. "I
mean, I've even heard him say that before," she said. "He loves seeing people's reaction, when they're flabbergasted. Plus, he was obviously making fun of the fact that he has a tendency to date younger
women."

Ivana and Melania and Marla all married their dads in Donald. If
you lined all four men up together and corrected for height, it would
be hard to pick them apart. They fall into the same general category:
swarthy, tubby, and white.

But Ivanka, clearly, has not got that kind of issue with her father.
Her choice of husband—dark, slender, silent, and calm—couldn't be
more different than Daddy.

Ivana always takes credit for how well the Trump kids turned out,
but Ivanka was close to her dad, long before her mother handed off
what she called the "finished" kids. Her parents' divorce "brought me
closer to my father," Ivanka wrote in her first book, because once he
moved out, she made a point of stopping at his office every day after
school. "Not incidentally, all that time in my father's office was well
spent," she wrote in her book.

She was always either darting into his office on her way home
from school, or hiding in a janitor's closet during recess to secretly dial
her dad, who would put her on speakerphone with whomever happened to be in his office. "It was colleagues, it was titans of industry,
it was heads of countries," she said, and she soaked it up. "He'd always
tell everyone in the room how great a daughter I was and say cute
things and ask me about a test I took."

Ivanka is much closer to her father than the business colleagues
and titans are. She's seen him at his worst, certainly, and loves him
still. "She knows better than anyone that he's not fit for the job, she's
seen his deceitful, destructive side, and I honestly believe she's trying
to hold it together" in Washington, says one of her New York pals.

"Ivanka knows better than anyone that her father is totally wrong for the job."

Or maybe not. Maybe she really believes Daddy was a great dad and is good for America too. She does grant that her dad might have a kind of supernatural power. She recalled a boarding school girls' trip to a jewelry store where she and her friends planned to get belly-button piercings. "Luckily, I didn't go first," she wrote. While she was listening to her friend shriek, her phone rang, Donald on the line. "It was my father, calling to check in and see what I was up to," she wrote. "They always had great timing, my parents. Somehow, throughout my childhood, they managed to thwart most of my bad or impulsive decisions before I could even make them. It's as if their antennae were set in just the right way."

As an adult, in the White House, she is on record to the *New York Times* saying her father is a genius. She admires and emulates his business style, without the boorish edge. While she doesn't agree with him on some issues—climate change and, presumably, his treatment of women—she's been mostly silent in public when she disagrees. This led to the early accusation of complicity. However, she—being her father's daughter—is strategically using his presidency to advance her husband's politics and ambitions, including the Kushner family's support of a Jewish single state, and Jared's general success in his various global tasks. Last but not least, her father's position affords her the chance to do exactly what a good businesswoman—in her playbook anyway—would do, which is network her way to the very top of not just the corporation but the global power structure. Her access means an ever-growing contact list of world leaders who will, presumably, still be running whole nations if and when her father steps off the stage.

She wrote her first book in 2009, a setup for the greater Ivanka brand, piggybacking off celebrity from appearances on her dad's show. She first appeared as a judge on *Celebrity Apprentice* in 2006, then joined her dad on the show at the beginning of 2007, replacing Trump exec Carolyn Kepcher, a veteran businesswoman who had been Trump's sidekick from the beginning. Trump fired her from her post at the Trump National Golf Club and *The Apprentice* after he decided she "lacked focus." But Trump was actually making room for family: he also started having monosyllabic Donald Jr. fill in for real estate lawyer George Ross.

On the show, Ivanka perfected a thousand-yard glare and practiced the cruelty that made "You're fired" such a hit with aggrieved couch potatoes across America. In her first episode in the new role, she ripped into Martin Clarke, an Atlanta-based attorney trying to save himself from getting fired. "I don't see you fitting in with our company," she said, tartly. "I don't see you working side by side with me and my father." Clarke protested, but Ivanka held her ground, cruelly personalizing it. "I don't like the way you talk . . . the way you project yourself . . . I feel everything you say is rhetoric . . . no hunger, no passion, no fire."

The colosseum roared for more.

Ivanka's sense of filial duty has never publicly wavered. She is the battle-scarred survivor of a traumatic childhood at the center of the media swarm Donald attracted. She was just nine when reporters shouted to ask her to comment on whether her father was good in bed. Having come through that, she could be relied upon to maintain her composure and sense of humor when he said on live TV, with her sitting next to him, that what they probably had in common was "sex—okay, golf and real estate." Sitting beside him, she tossed her hair, snickered, and flicked a nanosecond of a benign, almost maternal *oh you naughty boy* look at him, even as the ladies on *The View* were making appalled noises.

CHAPTER 23

◇◇◇◇◇◇

The Women of the Campaign

"My daughter and my wife Melania,
they love the women, and the women love them."
—PRESIDENT TRUMP, FARGO, NORTH DAKOTA, JUNE 27, 2018.

The women closest to Donald Trump during the campaign, the *family* women—not Kellyanne Conway or Hope Hicks—were two very different Trump brand extensions, each perfectly suited for a different political demographic. For the Christian Evangelicals, the gamer bros, and other toxically masculine men fed up with female power chipping away at the patriarchy, there was Melania, the Silent Partner, gliding like a Barbie doll that God's hand moved around beside or behind the candidate. And she was hot AF. If they Googled her, oh man, there were those naked lesbian pictures. Silent and smokin': The Perfect Woman.

For white suburban women and their husbands who weren't full-on misogynistic but who didn't trust "Crooked Hillary," there was the daughter. Polite, reasonable, groomed, and respectful, and blond—if Trump was such a misogynistic ogre, how could he possibly have spawned a daughter like that, who so obviously loved and supported him? She talked a good game about child-care tax credits, and female entrepreneurship, and taking responsibility—code for not blaming men for your date rape, or your single mom poverty, or just being a lazy poor person.

Obviously, here was a white woman who worked, like so many women did, and who was a parent, *just like us*.

At rallies from Altoona to Reno, these two poles of American femininity flanked The Donald. What woman could watch and not secretly appreciate their beauty and poise, their stunning clothes and their perfect hair? You could pick your favorite one, like when you chose between Betty and Veronica, or the three Charlie's Angels, or blond Barbie and brunette Barbie.

Melania gave three speeches during the campaign. It was obviously painful for her to speak English in front of crowds, and that garnered her some sympathy. She'd been beside him for months, but Donald finally rolled her out to the podium by herself on a cold early spring night in Wisconsin. "She's an incredible mother, she loves her son, Barron, so much," he said. "And I have to say, she will make an unbelievable first lady." The crowd went wild. "I'd like to introduce my wife. Melania," he said. "Come."

The introduction was much more dignified than the one he'd bellowed from a stage in 2000: "Where's my supermodel?"

Melania crossed the stage in front of the crowd of Cheese State Trump supporters all bundled in their lumber jackets and road salt–crusted hobnailed boots. Long, lean, world-class beautiful, and Mar-a-Lago-tanned for early spring, she wore her signature Manolos, which might literally have not touched Wisconsin pavement. She ticked off her husband's qualities from a prepared list. "He's a hard worker. He's kind. He has a great heart. He's tough. He's smart. He's a great communicator. He's a great negotiator. He's telling the truth. He's a great leader. He's fair. As you may know by now, when you attack him, he will punch back ten times harder." Wild applause. "No matter who you are, a man or a woman. He treats everyone equal."

She emerged again in Cleveland, at the Republican National

Convention, delivering a painstakingly read and ultimately disastrous speech quickly exposed as a piece of plagiarism, stolen from Michelle Obama. The campaign had been giving Melania sole credit for the speech, but when the similarities to Mrs. Obama's speech were detected, they threw a Trump ghostwriter under the bus.

Melania laid low after that, and didn't give a speech again until five days before the election, when she went to suburban Philadelphia to condemn cyberbullying at a rally. "We have to find a better way to talk to each other, to disagree with each other, to respect each other," she said. The media eye-rolled its way through that one—excuse us, have you been paying attention to your husband's campaign?—but she might have won back a few suburban white women who were wavering post–Billy Bush.

Melania's role as one sort of Trump brand extension was really secondary to her stepdaughter's. Ivanka hit the campaign trail with him early as Active Millennial, Instagramming herself on breezy tarmacs from Maine to Nebraska, pregnant for part of the time, reliably and confidently high-heeled, speaking in measured, perfect diction about child-care tax credits and personal responsibility, not a blow-dried hair out of place.

Ivanka was the official face of Trump's apparently well-hidden woman-friendly side. Anyone watching them together could see that the candidate adored his daughter. He let her handle "the woman stuff," whenever those squirmy questions came up. While husband Jared ran things behind the scenes, racing out to Silicon Valley to get a crash course in Facebook advertising, Ivanka showed up at rallies, spoke, and was a key figure behind the scenes herself. She used her influence judiciously, and to effect. New Hampshire hockey bad boy Corey Lewandowski, pugnacious campaign manager, shoved a female reporter, after months of outrageous comments, and Ivanka leaned on Trump to sack the top aide. Ivanka was rumored to have acted not because Lewandowski had manhandled a female reporter but after rumors swirled that he was trying to plant negative stories about Jared.

Ivanka sat down with her dad and gave him an ultimatum: Corey, or me.

Dad chose "The Vonk."

In September, just before the Billy Bush tapes emerged, Ivanka cut a Trump campaign ad aimed right at women. "The most important job any woman can have is being a mother, and it shouldn't mean taking a pay cut," she said in the thirty-second spot. She said that if elected, her dad would support child-care tax credits, paid maternity leave, and subsidies for stay-at-home parents. "Donald Trump understands the needs of a modern workforce. My father will change outdated labor laws so that they support women and American families. He will provide tax credits for child care, paid maternity leave, and dependent care savings accounts. This will allow women to support their families and further their careers."

Back in New York, in their Trump Park Avenue apartment outfitted with Eames chairs and Murano glass chandeliers, Ivanka and Jared were increasingly isolated from the New York society they'd once aspired to. Their friends couldn't understand how a woman who had donated money to HRC and bundled $40,000 for Democrat Cory Booker's New Jersey Senate run could be using her progressive cred to help a white nationalist get elected. "I think she likes power and the trappings of respect," said one New York pal. "She and Jared both grew up in families that were ridiculed and outcast and in certain circles even though they grew up powerful, they were 'not good enough.'"

Trump's win was a kind of vindication for the couple, even though they lost pals. "I don't think they want to be able to launch nukes, but they like the idea of power and respect, and I believe they are really trying to hold it together for their legacy and their children and lastly the country," said the New York friend. "And in Washington, she can play the role of the elegant woman. Here everyone thinks of her dad as the male Leona Helmsley."

Ivanka's unconditional defense of her father cracked only once during the campaign. When the Billy Bush audio was leaked, she begged her father—Mr. Never Apologize, Never Explain—to publicly apologize. "As she spoke, Mr. Trump remained unyielding. His daughter's eyes welled with tears, her face reddened, and she hurried out in frustration," according to a *New York Times* account of the meeting. But Trump did eventually apologize, saying, "Anyone who knows me knows these words don't reflect who I am. . . . I said it, I was wrong, and I apologize."

Ivanka was then able to make a public statement: "My father's comments were clearly inappropriate and offensive and I'm glad that he acknowledged this fact with an immediate apology to my family and the American people."

It fell to Melania, scorned wife, to go on Anderson Cooper and defend Donald, calling the tape "locker room talk." She staunchly accused the female accusers who had come forward at that point of lying. Melania also thought of herself much differently than as the gorgeous doormat she presented to the world. Near the end of the campaign, her handlers allowed a writer from *DuJour* magazine, a luxury ad vehicle, into the Tower triplex, where Melania felt comfortable enough to set the record straight for anyone who thought she was a pushover.

"To be married to my husband, to someone as successful as he is, he needs somebody who will tell him the truth," she said. "Somebody smart, you know. It's not just like I'm there and I'm just doing things for him. People say I'm not on the campaign but I'm very involved from home." She said she watched Fox or CNN every night. "I like to know exactly what's going on. I give a lot of advice to my husband and tell him how it is and how I see it. I'm not backing off. I tell him the truth."

She even suggested that she—not Ivanka—was the true shadow

female power in Donald's life. "After a speech, the kids are calling me—Ivanka, sons—saying 'Call Dad and tell him this and that. He's listening to you.' They know I could talk to him and put him in the right direction. Sometimes he does, and sometimes he doesn't. He will decide what he does."

If there was then any truth to Melania's claim to having power over Donald and serving as a conduit to his children, it fell apart once he got to the White House and she stayed home with Barron. It is of course certainly possible that his children would enlist her to inject something important into her apparently infrequent pillow talk with her husband (in the White House they have separate bedrooms). The same notion, Melania as power center in the White House, was also floated to the press around the end of the first year in office, as people who needed to reach him sometimes called Melania when they couldn't get through. But that pipeline—and political pipe dream—collapsed when Stormy Daniels showed up and Melania started spending more time at Slovenia House in suburban Maryland.

◇◇◇◇

Russians with money have always had a special relationship with the South of France. French was the language of the pre-Communist Russian aristocracy, and going back to the eighteenth century, Russians with money migrated down to the French shores of the Mediterranean for relief from their Siberian climate. Today, Russian oligarchs, with their muscular security retinues and girlfriends wafting designer scent, run the waterfront from Cannes to Èze. They sidle into the bistro chairs, sip white wine over platters of crudités aioli around linen tablecloths, the Med lapping at warm rocks nearby, super-yachts hulking on the horizon. The French Riviera is a warm and welcoming community for a Russophile woman with a taste for champagne, diamonds, and expensive perfume, traveling in the company of global moguls, supermodels, Saudi royals, and Donatella Versace.

In her flush years, riding high on the success of her cable shopping empire, Ivana bought herself two town houses in Saint-Tropez, besides her New York town house, Florida mansion, and yacht. By the late 1990s, New York designers and stylists invited in to fit her at her Florida mansion, La Concha on Jungle Road, noticed that it was furnished with what looked like leftover pieces from the casinos and hotels she'd decorated. She appeared to be having a difficult time keeping the Florida mold at bay. She had bills to pay that her home shopping network fans never had, like the $400,000 she owed to one James Mintz, the PI she'd hired to investigate Donald and Marla. Mintz sued her for nonpayment in 1998, compounding interest.

She unloaded the Miami house and sold off the *M.Y. Ivana* (not because they're too expensive, *daahling*, she just got bored). But she kept the French properties. The grubby smell of American politics hardly ever drifts into this elite playground, although one can apparently never avoid the uglier facts of life: *Page Six* reporter Paula Froelich recalled Ivana complaining about being extorted by the Russian mafia on the French Riviera for protection money. And Ivana's closest running buddy on the Med is Clinton mega-donor Denise Rich, wife of the late fugitive financier Marc Rich, notoriously pardoned by Bill Clinton in one of his last presidential acts.

Ivana's emotional life hit some rough patches as well. There were published and private reports of her approaching falling down drunk. Froelich, who covered a number of incidents, recalls furious spats with lovers, including in one instance ending in her throwing someone's clothes off the yacht. By the Obama years, while Donald was ginning up the birther movement in preparation for his own political run, Ivana was single again. Like her ex, she was pushing seventy. Unlike him, she didn't have the trophy partner, the arm candy. It was so unfair. She was still fit and couldn't keep the attention of a young Italian. Meanwhile, her ex was white and lardy, and had a new Slavic goddess on his arm. In 2013, Ivana explained to Oprah, "I have this thing for

Italians. I don't know why, but the bad boys—not all of them, but the sort of semi-bad. I'm very energetic. I don't want to worry about a bad back and bad knees."

Long before he ran for president, she and Donald had worked things out well enough so that she—often with her mother, Marie, in tow—flew on the Trump jet. Sometimes she and her mother flew on the jet with Melania on board at the same time, from New York to Mar-a-Lago, to be with the growing brood of grandchildren they shared. One diplomat flying to Florida on the Trump jet in the '00s was surprised to see Melania and Ivana and Marie Zelníčková on board at the same time. Melania told him it was perfectly normal. "Me and Donald are very friendly," Ivana told Oprah. "We have now five grandchildren and the kids, they call me not 'Grandma,' they call me 'Glam-ma' or 'Ivana-ma,' for the youngest ones. And we just enjoying [sic] our lives—you know life is too short."

During the long, turbulent American summer of the 2016 campaign, Ivana stayed mostly in the South of France, was photographed walking a tiny dog on the streets of Saint-Tropez, in a colorful minidress, hair in her signature beehive do, clutching a black bag that the *Daily Mail* helpfully sussed out as a Dior "Diorissimo" bag worth nearly $4,000, with her fourth ex-husband, Rossano Rubicondi, at her side. She told the *Post* she wasn't involved in the campaign, but that she and Donald were so close he routinely asked for her advice about how he looked on the stump. She said she advised him to "be more calm," and to adopt the motto "You think it, I say it."

The former immigrant, who as a young woman had been ambitious and wily enough to get around a great wall during the Cold War, professed to be all in for Trump's wall. "I have nothing against Mexicans, but if they [come] here—like this 19-year-old, she's pregnant, she crossed over a wall that's this high. She gives the birth [sic] in American hospital, which is for free. The child becomes American automatically. She brings the whole family, she doesn't pay the taxes, she doesn't have a job, she gets the housing, she gets the food stamps. Who's paying? You and me."

She added that Americans do need some immigrants, though. "Who's going to vacuum our living rooms and clean up after us? Americans don't like to do that."

She half-joked that if he got elected, she wanted Donald to appoint her ambassador to the Czech Republic, but when he offered it, she turned him down, saying she didn't want the hassle. "I have a perfect life," she later explained.

Perfect, except for one thorn in her side. She has never, ever forgiven "The Showgirl" who stole her first ladyship away.

◇◇◇◇

After her divorce was finalized, Marla retreated to the LA hills, seeking inner peace, raising Tiffany alone for sixteen years, stretching Donald's miserly alimony. She tried to turn her New York acting and modeling career into a second act in Hollywood. It was hard and it was sad; she couldn't shake Tabloid Marla. She sought answers within and without, became a member of the star-studded Kabbalah Center, finding her spirit animal, practicing yoga, hosting her own spiritual radio show. That's what she was doing when Trump started running for president.

She made do on Donald's checks, and kept her mouth shut after his lawyers literally withheld a million and a half dollars after she threatened to tell the world what he was really like during his 2000 presidential experiment. She had reason to complain: if Donald was an inattentive dad when his kids lived in the same building as his office, he was comparatively an absentee father to Marla's child in California. One of her New York friends claimed Donald saw Tiffany exactly four times in her life before the young woman moved to New York in 2016, after graduating from the University of Pennsylvania, his alma mater.

Trump's presidential campaign jump-started a prurient inter-est in Marla Maples, which she parlayed into a stint on *Dancing with the Stars*. There, limber from years of yoga, she proved that a woman in her early fifties can still kick a long leg higher than a Rockette. In April 2016, as her ex-husband was looking unstop-pable in the Republican primary, she moved back to New York, to be closer to Tiffany. She then appeared on *The Wendy Williams Show*, in a black, skintight jumpsuit, and updated the world on what she'd been up to.

Introduced as Donald Trump's ex-wife, Marla was visibly taken aback. "They told me they were going to drop the title," she said. "I met him when I was twenty [which would have been 1983, the year she won the Hawaiian Tropic competition in Daytona]. We were married for six years and we were together for years before that. But listen, we've been divorced since 2000." Then she said with a sweet plaint, "Can't I just be Marla Maples today?"

Sadly, she will never be Marla Maples.

After sixteen years, she had no complaints about the settlement. "I always said from the beginning I am here because I love you," she told Williams. "I have friends who say I should have fought for more. But I watched his first marriage and there was lots of fighting about money. He took good care of Tiffany. She went to the best schools."

She denied that she had ever considered writing a book about Donald. "No. No. No! I was never going to write a tell-all book," she told Williams, eyes wide.

"Look, I'm a writer, I'm writing one now about life's journey and how we overcome our negativity. No one stopped me from writing a book. The publishers wanted more scandalous stuff and I couldn't do that. I love the kids."

Wendy asked her how Tiffany was faring, now that she had Secret Service protection. "I am a big believer in the power of prayers and I surround that girl with angels every day. That's more important than the Secret Service."

Marla's sweetness, though, has always covered something with more bite. The Scorpio sting perhaps. And that's why she fell under suspicion for performing a kind of personal karma, late in the 2016 campaign.

Three pages from Trump's 1995 tax returns showed up at the *New York Times* just before the election. The tax returns had been the Holy Grail of the 2016 campaign. A single page showed that Trump had taken a $916 million loss—meaning he was immune from paying tax for eighteen years. The return confirmed what the Czech secret police had reported all the way back in the 1980s.

Suspicion quickly fell on Marla, whose personal religious practices include honoring the Jewish New Year, Rosh Hashanah. On October 2, ten days after the *New York Times* received the anonymously mailed copy of Trump's tax return, she tweeted a photo of pumpkins and hay, with the caption "#FallLove Breathe it in as if 2day's the first day of your life. The kabbalists say 2nite Adam&Eve were created. S . . . [*sic*]"

One of the Rosh Hashanah rituals is the casting of sins on the water. Observant Jews throw bread into water off beaches or riverbanks to mark the occasion. Marla, married to Trump in 1995, theoretically would have had access to that very page of his taxes. Suspicious minds wondered: was Marla puling a DIY spiritual cleansing by casting that white page of sin onto the roiling waters of the world media? In response to Marla's tweet, Marc Caputo, a *Politico* reporter, wrote, "TFW you serve up a cold plate of revenge and then appreciate fall as you think about Etz Hayim, the Shekinah & Isaac ben Luria."

She had no comment.

After being cast out of Trumplandia, she had sought and found inner peace. "You know, it all works out," she said in 1998, even before the divorce was finalized. "When you can really get through to that part of yourself that you know is real, and you can understand that this is just kind of all an illusion, then you can kind of step through the fires and move on."

In 2013, she released a spiritual healing album called *The Endless*, which featured the likes of Deepak Chopra and the fourteenth Dalai Lama. She now wore a golden eagle pendant around her neck made by her friend, a woman named Rainbeau Mars, author of *Sacred Yoga Practice*. The eagle, associated with her astrological sign, Scorpio, is her spirit animal. She told a reporter for the *Daily Beast* that she has "worked on my Scorpio, tamed it."

In the days after Trump won, she was photographed paying a call at Trump Tower, dressed in a camel-colored coat and scarf. She took the golden elevator upstairs to let it be known that she hoped he would appoint her to her dream job, a UN Goodwill ambassador to some impoverished African nation. The president, as powerful as he is, doesn't have the authority to appoint UN Goodwill ambassadors.

Marla was next heard from when a Washington stylist, Tricia Kelly, called the *Washington Post* to share emails in which Marla's rep had demanded free hair and makeup for Marla and Tiffany, as it would generate social media posts and be great exposure.

"I've turned away several things for fame," Kelly said. "But I felt like things like this shouldn't be silenced. This is about people taking advantage of you and the industry." After she went public about it, the same person who had referred Marla to her sent a threat. "You are messing with the president of the United States. I don't think you realize the power my clients have. That your reputation could just as much be on the line."

A year after Donald was elected president, Marla was active on Instagram and had her own podcast, *Awakening with Marla Maples*. She had learned much and had much to share. In fall 2017, she earned a certification in the ThetaHealing system. ThetaHealing was developed by Vianna Stibal, a naturopath who claims to have healed herself of cancer instantly in 1995, using the power of her own theta brain waves and the "cosmic all" to change herself at the DNA level.

CHAPTER 24

◇◇◇◇◇◇

#FreeMelania

The last time Melania looked like herself in public, as far as her childhood friends in Slovenia are concerned, was when the Trumps showed up on *Oprah* in February 2011 for an interview *en famille* that oprah.com had billed as "Trump Family Values." Barron still had his baby teeth and dashed around the stage joyously, far more demonstrative than he is now. Melania sat in the front row beside Donald, with a wide smile that seems to have disappeared in FLOTUS, giggling with her child in her lap. Her face moved, she was unguarded, and even kind of a relaxed counterpoint to Eric, Donald Jr., and Ivanka, seated in the back row, stiff as the Elgin Marbles.

"This was when Melania acted like herself, like the girl I remember," says Petra Sedej. In photographs and video from the late 1990s and early '00s, photographers often captured her smiling hugely, clearly content and radiant. Somewhere between the million-dollar Mar-a-Lago wedding and her husband's campaign for president, Melania's ability to convey natural happiness to cameras evaporated, replaced by a public persona that is such a robotic version of her former self, internet conspiracy theorists have claimed she employs an imposter to stand in.

Nobody really knows who first came up with the #FreeMelania slogan. It erupted spontaneously zeitgeist, on signs at the Women's March on January 21, the day after one of the worst days of Trump's career, at least as he would judge it. Yes, he was being inaugurated President of the United States, the most powerful man in the world. But his crowds were far smaller than Obama's. And his wife, his trophy wife, couldn't play the part he needed her to play.

It had been a bad day for optics. In Trumplandia, that's unforgivable.

First, he'd left Melania behind in the limo, leaping out of the car and dashing up the White House steps with embarrassing alacrity to greet the Obamas. She didn't know what to do. The cameras recorded the first lady–elect, exiting on the other side of the sedan, looking lost in her pseudo–Jackie O baby-blue suit, picking her way over to the current and future presidents on her Manolos and clutching a large Tiffany gift that matched her outfit.

She looked so lost and helpless, and had to be rescued by Michelle and Barack, who put their arms around her and walked her up the stairs. No one seemed to know what to do with the box, until the president took it.

That was bad. But a few hours later, at the reviewing stand on the Capitol steps, the cameras of the world captured the Melania smile/frown, a moment quickly reduced to a GIF for all eternity, in which, when Donald turned to her, her face lit up, then collapsed into misery the second he turned away.

Finally, there was the cringe-inducing first dance, onstage at the Liberty Ball, she in her white first lady gown, he in his tuxedo, dancing stiffly to Frank Sinatra, with Donald crooning "My Way" into her ear. Melania's face was a frozen mask and her hands literally seemed to be pressing the newly minted President of the United States away from her. Everything about her body language manifested what Trump-haters worldwide were feeling at that moment.

Revulsion.

Noli me tangere.

The FreeMelania hashtag exploded the next morning, at the Women's March. Now, the diamond-dripping former model who had dismissed Donald's fifteen-and-counting female accusers as liars, and his pussy-grabbing boast as "locker room talk," was a victim. She was the beauty trapped in a Bluebeard's castle, Trump Tower, holding keys to all the doors to the rooms filled with riches, but told to stay away from one of them, the one that's bloody and filled with the hanging corpses of his previous women.

This was a new fairy tale: Melania as in need of rescue as Rapunzel.

The pampered prize gazelle—a woman who admitted she had no idea whether Crate & Barrel still existed because, once ensconced in the Tower, she never had to shop for her own household items, a woman who had endured a night or two at Holiday Inns doing the campaign and was still marveling at how awful that was—was now a figure to be pitied. Celebs chimed in. Cher said Melania always looks "sad and sorry." Candice Bergen—who went on a date with Donald once in college—wore a "#FreeMelania" T-shirt on television. Rosie O'Donnell publicly urged Melania to grab Barron and "flee" Trump. Television host Joy Behar went on air to say she felt sorry for Melania, because she'd had to sleep with Trump "at least once."

As the months passed, for those who sought it, evidence mounted for her being an unwilling and miserable captive.

She was declining to move to the White House, remaining holed up in the Tower with Barron, costing taxpayers and the city of New York millions a day in security. More than a hundred thousand New Yorkers signed a petition demanding that she get out of town, and still she stayed.

That's how much she hated him, the story went.

Her official Twitter account favorited a #FreeMelania tweet about her marriage—a mistake, the White House later explained.

In February a cameraman captured Melania visibly shuddering when her husband touched her arm in Florida.

On their first trip abroad together, in April, there she was, slapping his hand away on the tarmac in Tel Aviv.

When she and Barron finally moved to the White House, in June, the *Guardian* ran an article headlined MELANIA TRUMP HAS MOVED INTO THE WHITE HOUSE. SHOULD WE SEND A RESCUE PARTY? Once in the White House, she was such a non-presence that she operated with half the staff of Michelle Obama—a fact that conservative media applauded.

The awkward photo moments piled up. In September, after Melania gave a brief and groggy-sounding introduction for her husband at Andrews Air Force Base, Donald *shook her hand* as he passed her going to the podium.

Joy Behar went on the air and said Melania treats Trump "like he has Zika virus."

Democratic Congresswoman Maxine Waters tweeted that even Melania couldn't trust Trump, he was such a scoundrel.

People took notice that she had taken to wearing shades—even at night.

But what if these clues are all just Trump-hating projection?

According to one of her closest advisors, while she might not enjoy all the negative publicity, Melania is still quite satisfied with her life as the pampered and idle wife of a billionaire president. "If you had a private dinner with them you would understand the relationship. It's an open relationship with conversation and kidding and laughing," said a New York style maven and pal. "I'm not kidding you. These divorce rumors. I would tell you. I would say I can't talk about it. There's none of that. I'm not gonna sit here and lie to you. I would actually say nothing. I would glide over and not even go there."

Still, on her first Christmas in the White House, when a ten-year-old visitor asked the first lady, "If you could spend the holidays anywhere in the world, where would you go?" she replied: "I would spend my holidays on a deserted island, a tropical island—with my family."

Until the Stormy Daniels payoff was revealed in January 2018, she rarely ventured out in public alone, only showing up for photo ops or in transit with Donald between the White House and Mar-a-Lago. She delivers her public remarks in a recitative way, like a phone bot or computer-generated transit announcement, where the emphases on words in a sentence don't match the emotional content because the computer can't bring meaning to the words.

Author Michael Wolff, in his book *Fire and Fury*, reported that Melania cried when it first appeared that Trump would be elected, on the night of November 8. The White House denied it, but in the #FreeMelania view, it's totally believable.

The standard public facade of the presidential marriage broke down in early 2018, after a porn star and a former Playboy bunny both broke separate election-year hush agreements and publicly talked about having sex with Trump while his wife was in her first postpartum year. The first lady cancelled an international trip, and then was seen less and less around the White House throughout winter and spring, showing up for the Easter egg roll and a few other events, but basically letting her husband hang alone. In April, at a White House lawn ceremony welcoming French president Emmanuel Macron and his wife, Trump's efforts to get Melania to hold his hand—a kind of spidery, little finger tapping motion that she brushed off repeatedly, created a new YouTube-worthy meme.

Then on May 14, without warning, the White House announced that she had checked into Walter Reed to undergo an "embolism procedure for a benign kidney condition." The procedure is usually uncomplicated and patients don't even stay the night, but she remained in the hospital for five days, and then wasn't seen in public for twenty-four days. Her office declined repeated requests for explanation, leading to wild rumors, from imminent divorce to "self-harm" to Ivana Trump—first "First Lady" telling friends that Melania was in hiding because she was taking care of her own ill mother. On day sixteen of her vanishment, a suspiciously Trump-like Tweet issued from the FLOTUS account.: "I see the media is working overtime speculating where I am & what I'm doing. Rest assured, I'm here at the @WhiteHouse w my family, feeling great, & working hard on behalf of children & the American people!"

Two weeks into her disappearance, President Trump responded to a question about his AWOL wife's whereabouts by saying she was "doing great" and pointing to a dark upper floor White House window, suggesting Rochester's hidden mad wife in Jane Eyre. After she finally reappeared at an event for military families, Trump blurted out that she had had a "big, four-hour operation" and couldn't fly, but gave no further details. By late June, however, she was back on duty, even letting her husband hold her hand on the White House lawn before they took off on a trip to Europe. On close inspection of the photo, it looked like they weren't exactly holding hands. Trump had seized and captured her wrist and balled fist in an inescapable grip.

In New York, among her set, there were a lot of rumors that she'd been paid to stick around, the way Joe Kennedy supposedly offered Jackie money to stick with her philandering Jack so he could be properly married in the White House.

"I know there were financial guarantees throughout this marriage," one pal says. "Her parents got an apartment, and I know she spends money decorating her parents' apartment. And I know that the parents said, when Trump went down to see the White House, he said, 'Well, is there enough room for my friends to come stay?' There was never any truth to the claim that she wasn't going to move down there. She's shy and look how burned she got with that speech, I mean, my God, it's a miracle she ever set foot outside again after what they did to her. And they did do that to her."

◇◇◇◇

Nothing says Trump Queen more than the vertiginous heel. The shoe is attached to the soul of the Trump movement. It and a hard hat could be the MAGA leitmotif.

During his circus of a campaign, Donald Trump's women were the acrobats, trained rare mountain goats of the right, teetering alongside him, sure-footed in the most dangerous shoes. This minor Trumpian fashion trend, the otherwise démodé, but ubiquitous, stiletto pump, went unremarked for a long time, until I wrote about it for *Newsweek* in summer, drawing down a surprisingly virulent barrage of online hate.

After January 2017, the nation and the world grew accustomed to images of Trump women teetering around Washington and the world in shoes that average women only don for a few hours at weddings or proms, before casting them off, moaning and rubbing their soles.

For Ivana, Ivanka, Melania, and the two Trump daughters-in-law, and Trump stalwarts Kellyanne Conway and Hope Hicks, Carrie Bradshaw's shoe of choice was never démodé. The female consorts and family members of the Leader of the Free World rarely step into the public eye without their feet contorted into the shape Mattel toy designers first molded for Barbie's plastic feet in the 1950s. They have officialized the footwear of the beauty pageant as the shoe of a certain type of working woman.

Stiletto pumps are the ultimate test of a certain type of femininity. Sometimes derided as "fuck-me shoes," they actually telegraph rigor. They signal a taut combination of power and weakness that conservative women must cultivate in order to survive among ideologues who demand that women be both self-reliant enough to raise alone the children of unwanted pregnancies, and weak enough to be gotten pregnant whether they want to be or not.

Trump Queens in the shoe never look downward for obstacles

that might break up their gait or send them sprawling. They have pranced in them from the tarmac to the Wailing Wall, crossed the spongy White House lawn to Marine One in them without sinking, clicked around the halls of Congress, and ascended in them to rickety risers at MAGA rallies in Youngstown and Chattanooga.

Besides the pain they cause, stiletto pumps demand a critical level of internal attention to pebbles, cobbles, sidewalk cracks, mud, grass, curbs, and stairs—all while keeping head erect and shoulders back— that has sometimes eluded even the greatest public females. Remember Naomi Campbell's famous runway spill. Or Jennifer Lawrence tripping up the steps to receive her Oscar.

The internet and YouTube are rife with tutorials about how to bear the pain (Band-Aids, gel inserts, baby powder) and walk gracefully in them. Michelle Phan's "How to Master the High Heel" tutorial has received millions of views. Her nuggets of advice include: "Your first assignment when walking in heels is to find a straight line and follow it" and "For every step you take, you need to have a general awareness of where your heel is being placed."

In late summer 2017, *Vogue*'s Andre Leon Talley believed that, other than the White House Easter egg hunt on the lawn, Melania Trump was not photographed as first lady without her feet arched into one of two brands of towering high-heeled shoes that she favors, Manolo Blahniks or the 4.5-inch-heeled So Kate by Christian Louboutin. Talley reported that the first lady picked up twenty-two pairs of Manolos in various colors before decamping to the White House the month before.

That changed after the hurricanes, when Melania arrived for a flight to Houston, to tour flooded areas, in a bomber jacket, skinny jeans, and her signature four-inch heels. The internet went wild. By the time the plane landed in Texas, someone had handed her a pair of boots.

Talley, who attended Melania at her wedding, believes the Trump women favor the stiletto because they were trained young in the rigor of wearing them. "It creates a tall, statuesque, almost ideal elegance," Talley says, but also comes with an element of risk—which, mastered, further differentiates them from the average woman. "When they are climbing the steps from the tarmac to the airplane, it is a shoe that defies gravity. It is a risk-taking shoe. If you stumble you will break your ankle. But these girls have mastered the art absolutely through rigorous discipline of daily exercise and weight loss, and when you set your foot into the toe box you have the mental knowledge that you can't make those mistakes and fall."

The stiletto is also a podiatrist's dream, or nightmare, depending on your point of view, because devoted wearers ultimately require medical attention. "As you get older in these shoes, your feet are going to have problems," Talley says. "I am not gonna say Melania is gonna have them soon, but sooner or later she is going to have to come down off that high arch."

Besides telegraphing a certain kind of athletic superiority, the Trump women's shoe choice serves another purpose, summed up in shoe designer Christian Louboutin's comment "The core of my work is dedicated not to pleasing women but to pleasing men."

Science suggests that high heels do please men. British psychologist Paul Morris and his colleagues wrote a paper describing high heels in biological terms as "supernormal stimuli," that is, a stimulus that works better than the original, biological trait in provoking an instinctive response. For example, Morris explained, the orange spot on a herring gull beak causes a chick to peck at the beak, but researchers found that a chick will respond even more eagerly to a big orange blob on a card.

"In terms of the human example we tend to find the defining characteristics of the opposite sex attractive," Morris said. "High heels function in a similar way. Males respond to the characteristic way a woman walks, i.e., the movement of the female pelvis, high heels just exaggerates the femaleness of the walk. So to deconstruct why Trump women wear high heels: they are just buying into traditional binary views of male and female."

American anthropologist and author Helen Fisher puts it more bluntly. "High heels thrust out the buttocks and arch the back into a natural mammalian courting—actually, copulatory—pose called 'lordosis.' Rats do it, sheep do it . . . lions do it, dogs do it. It is a naturally sexy posture that men immediately see as sexual readiness. [Heels] are a 'come hither' signal."

Fisher is in the camp that believes heels detract from women's power, and shouldn't be worn at work. "When women wear high heels at work, they send sexual signals that should be avoided if they want to be taken seriously."

Historically, the Trumplandian woman's shoe of choice was invented in the early Renaissance for aristocratic men who would never have to work, who didn't have to walk much, but were carried in litters or carriages. Paintings of Louis XIV, the Sun King, show him sporting red-soled heels and posing much like Ivana and Ivanka Trump have in countless photographs, with one foot forward, and pointed out.

Shoe historians say that the first *women* to wear heels were Italian prostitutes in the seventeenth century, when they adopted them, along with smoking, from their male friends. From there it became a sexual symbol. The high heel was a staple of Victorian porn, and the stiletto (dagger in Italian) was introduced into women's fashion in the 1950s. It has remained there, waxing and waning à la mode.

Among the Trump women, Marla Maples is the only one consistently photographed wearing flats—sneakers and espadrilles—a result of her inner tomboy, her post-divorce downsizing, and her former publicist's shoe fetish.

The diagnostic name for Chuck Jones's problem is *altocalciphilia*. One altocalciphilist, writing on a British website called Retifism and Fetishism, tried to explain what spike heels can do to a man (or, presumably, a woman). "The allure of high heels for some people is very strong. Subconsciously this may relate to a primal instinct to identify lame prey. Throughout recorded history limping in others has been seen both as a physical weakness as well as a sexually attractive impediment. Wearing high-heeled shoes can accentuate the limping characteristics in a very tantalising way."

Feminists have long grappled with the high-heeled shoe, and whether the stiletto telegraphs power (sexual or otherwise) or self-hobbled weakness. Younger women in the public eye sometimes say they have sworn off heels. Jennifer Lawrence called them "Satan's Shoes," Kristin Stewart wears Chucks with her gowns, and Miley Cyrus sings in "Party in the U.S.A," "All I see are stilettos / I guess I never got the memo." Actresses and critics alike went ballistic in 2015 when the organizers of the Cannes Film Festival reportedly decreed that women could not walk the red carpet in flats.

The death of the high heel is often prematurely reported. In an exhaustive essay on the topic in May 2016 Megan Garber wrote in the *Atlantic*, "Will the heel, indeed, go the way of the corset and the bound foot—an icon of femininity rendered, via the network of advances we tend to shorthand as 'progress,' obsolete?"

In the Trumpian era, the answer is no. As long as the Queens of Trumplandia have anything to say about it, the heels make the woman. And Trumpian women across America agree.

NOTE: Portions of the above shoe story were published in Newsweek *in summer 2017. Two things happened: The author received more online fury from conservative men and women than she had all year. And Ivanka appeared in public in lower, square-heeled shoes.*

CHAPTER 25

◇◇◇◇◇◇

Ivanka in the White House

Just saw @Oprah's empowering & inspiring speech at
last night's #GoldenGlobes. Let's all come together,
women & men, & say #TIMESUP.

—IVANKA TRUMP TWEET

As her dad's misogynistic campaign against Hillary Clinton, an
orgy of woman-hating for the ages, wound toward its denouement,
women—and men who were appalled—saw a glimmer of salvation
in the form of flashes of carefully ironed blond hair. For those who
wanted to see a silver lining in Donald, there was Ivanka. Not only
was she a working mother herself, she was for other working women
and even writing a book called *Women Who Work.* Throughout the
campaign, she had been preparing the field for her book with a
#womenwhowork hashtag and social media campaign, inviting work-
ing women to "share their stories."

The final product was going to be not just a book but an "inclu-
sive conversation" among us girls, "designed to be the millennials'
manual for architecting a life you love" and "recognizing that success
looks different to every one of us."

The brand Feminist Ivanka was rolled out on a steamy stage at the

Republican National Convention in Cleveland in July 2016. While vendors hawked buttons and T-shirts calling Hillary a bitch and a witch and much much worse, on the street just outside the Quicken Loans Arena, the first daughter strode to the podium and delivered a speech introducing her father that sounded suspiciously . . . *Democrat*.

She called his construction sites "incredible melting pots" and recounted how he had such a warm heart for the downtrodden that he would single out sad stories in the newspaper and have his secretary send money. But lest the assembled think that was a suggestion that the MAGA candidate believed in handouts, she reminded them that he had insisted that even she and her brothers work.

Inside at the Quicken Loans Arena, you could sense alarm building. They were applauding at the right lines, but she was suddenly talking about the gender wage gap and promising, "As President, my father will change the labor laws that were put into place at a time when women were not a significant portion of the workforce. And he will focus on making quality child care affordable and accessible for all."

Unease instantly prickled necks on the convention floor, where applause was polite but restrained. The looks on many faces seemed to say: Did I just hear her say "affordable child care"? Who let a feminazi Democrat in here? Lock her up!

Ivanka put on a game face at the convention, while spouting feminist dogma at a wall of Hillary hate. But behind the scenes, she was not as comfortable with her new role as she appeared. A few months prior, when her first "Entrepreneur in Residence," ex–Wall Street lawyer Elizabeth Cronise McLaughlin asked her how she was holding up, she replied, according to McLaughlin: "You know, if I had my way I would toss my TV out the window, throw away my phone, stop all my newspaper subscriptions, and never leave my apartment. But they won't let me."

McLaughlin, who has since cut ties with Ivanka over Trump's politics, said she never learned which *they* Ivanka was referring to.

"It was definitely a message of feeling completely trapped. There was no escape. She was eight months pregnant when she said that and one week later he had her out on the campaign trail. I am not compassionate for any of this, though. If you say you are in favor of women's rights then you don't stand in the room with people advocating separating immigrant women from their children. She is beyond complicit."

Once ensconced in the West Wing of the White House, Ivanka still talked about getting women a child-care tax credit (and her efforts probably ensured that that was added to the tax bill). But by the time her father was inaugurated, liberals had pinned so many of their hopes on Ivanka—saving the climate pact, a reasonable attitude toward abortion, compassion for LGBTQ people—and she soon showed that she had neither the intention nor the ability to squander her political capital with Daddy that way.

He was off to the misogynist races, days after taking office, reinstituting the gag order on discussing abortion in foreign aid offices, telling the IRS by executive order to back off the "religious freedom" of politically active churches, canceling a federal study of the gender pay gap.

Ivanka wasn't stopping any of that. She was instead, as *Saturday Night Live* soon billed her, in a fake ad for perfume, Complicit. As an unpaid official White House advisor, she has defined down her role to two issues. One is unstated: protecting herself and Jared from the Mueller investigation's likely forays into their family finances. The public one is promoting women entrepreneurs, at home and abroad, jetting around the planet from India to Japan and Germany, hosting panel discussions about female entrepreneurship.

Her confabs mimic the female empowerment industry that writer Sheelah Kolhatkar has skewered for its self-referential, girl-power puffery. Women sit on couches, legs crossed, dangling their heels, with high-end recording gear and fancy PowerPoints and ear mics, recording conversations that signify literally nothing.

No one was more crestfallen by Ivanka's failure to bear the standard for women than those New York society peers who remained mystified by her wholesale conversion from progressive New York society woman to Number One supporter of a man universally reviled by some of those same society swells and progressives as the second coming of Hitler. That conversion—far more than the one she undertook becoming Jewish when she married Jared Kushner—was not, though, a wholesale shock to everyone, and in fact, was probably linked to the earlier switch.

"She struck me as a liberal New York Democrat and rather typical of her group," *Born Rich* producer Dirk Wittenborn said. "Mind you, the word 'Democrat' never came up, but the attitudes and opinions and philosophy she relayed in my presence was more Clintonian." But Wittenborn says he and others saw a change in her after her conversion to Judaism, and to being a mother, as she became more conservative.

She was in the process of updating her brand to another level— mommies who work—when her dad started running for office. This was Trump brand extension serendipity, appealing to the suburban white women he was going to need to steal away from Hillary. Ivanka soon cut an ad for her dad saying, "The most important job any woman can have is being a mother."

She did a Q and A with *Parenting* magazine, headlined "Ask Ivanka Trump." How does she motivate her kids? "I tell my kids Kushners love challenges!"

How did she maintain her focus with two kids and another on the way? "I caffeinate, meditate and exercise."

She said that "marriage made me a better person" and added that the lessons of motherhood applied to her business and political life. "Anyone who has tried to impose their will on a sleepy toddler knows that it just doesn't work well. And I think leadership is not very dissimilar. You really have to inspire people to come along for the ride as opposed to just jamming your ideas down their throat."

The image of Ivanka Trump, pretending to be a working mother, once the Trumps were in office, made progressives batshit. American feminists regard Ivanka's career with the same gimlet eye the French rabble aimed at Marie Antoinette deciding she might like to be a milkmaid at her faux farm in Versailles, the Hameau de la Reine.

"I am a real estate developer and an entrepreneur. More important, I'm a wife and a mother," Ivanka wrote in *Women Who Work*. "I design and build iconic properties all over the world; I have also created and am growing a business that seeks to inspire and empower women in all aspects of their lives. I'm busy teaching my children the value of hard work and the importance of family."

Oh, she was MAGA perfect, except that she wasn't.

◇◇◇◇

Ivanka likes power and she likes power chairs. And she's lucky because she has a daddy who likes to give both to her. One of his Russian friends took her to Moscow and arranged to let her sit in Putin's chair before she was thirty years old. At the White House, she sits in her own West Wing office, after much speculation that she'd be taking over the first lady's wing. At the G20 summit in Hamburg during the summer of 2017, foreign policy experts and journalists went crazy after Trump appointed her as his stand-in senior diplomat, sending her to sit in his chair while he was otherwise occupied. There she was, with Chancellor Angela Merkel presiding, sitting between Great Britain's Prime Minister Theresa May and President Xi Jinping of China.

Oddly, no one seemed to notice the precedent: a woman without a specific portfolio in the White House, with twenty-four-hour direct access to a president of the United States who has serious women problems, and whose own political inclinations seem to put her right in the middle.

She did not want an East Wing office. She wanted and would get a West Wing office, but only after she made sure Jared was securely established in his (walking the Orthodox Jewish patriarchal walk). And she had her own other agenda, and it was murkier and it did not involve single-handedly talking Daddy into saving Arctic ice. She was a White House power without portfolio, working behind the scenes on any number of issues on any given day, from foreign policy to trade. She was so sure of her own goodness that she was and is oblivious to ethics challenges. She even started her own foundation, and solicited foreign donors for it.

Almost everything about her political style was something Americans had seen before—very, very recently. Inside the White House, similarities to Hillary Clinton multiplied. Like Hillary, Ivanka provided cover for sexism; like Hillary, she promoted Davos-style globalist solutions; like Hillary, she held a vague and unlimited portfolio in the White House; and like the former first lady and secretary of state, her foes would see her as ethically challenged.

Finally, like their nemesis, Ivanka became a political and personal cipher whose real relationship with her father remains a deeply complicated mess of love and horror, and is fundamentally unknowable. When women contemplate Ivanka, as when they do the same with Hillary, they cannot do so without a sense of vicarious unease at best, distrust at worst. Women, of course, *know* just how angry Hillary is at her husband and just how appalled Ivanka—if she's normal—must at some fundamental level be by her father. Those presumed emotions, lurking just behind the masks, provoke chariness and suspicion.

Ivanka is not married to a serial philanderer: women don't have to snap on chastity belts before meeting Jared Kushner. But like Hillary with philandering Bill, Ivanka makes her own—to coin a euphemism—*feministically challenged* presidential relative more palatable to women. Both women provide a measure of cognitive dissonance, or a feministic warping, in the public perception of their men: while the men actually treat women like objects, reduce them to their sexual essence, they also seem to respect and even rely on one particularly smart woman who is not *a thing* at all.

In most White Houses, the spouse figures into the management flow chart somewhere, but not until Hillary came along did White House staff have to figure the powerful unelected relative's interests into every issue. Even with chief of staff General John Kelly deploying military rules of access, Ivanka gets face time with Daddy that no one else can. In the West Wing, Ivanka quickly became a White House power center. During the campaign, Trump said his daughter helps him with the woman stuff, but her portfolio actually has no limits, including advising her daddy to fire missiles at Syria, and to fire James Comey.

Her advocacy for female entrepreneurship is also straight out of the Hillary handbook. "The statistics and results prove that when you invest in women and girls, it benefits both developed and developing economies," she said in one interview. "Women are an enormous un-tapped resource, critical to the growth of all countries." Such talk is of course the cut-and-pasted, Davos-approved, market-based solution to gender inequality that was always the signature goal and achievement of Secretary of State Hillary Clinton.

Like Hillary, who promoted economic empowerment in lieu of actually using her podium to speak out against legalized, traditional misogyny in places like Saudi Arabia, Ivanka has yet to lend her weight to fighting the egregious sexism of Arabs in the Gulf, where she has advanced various Trump projects.

Like Hillary, Ivanka turned out to be a neocon hawk. The day after President Trump lobbed fifty-nine Tomahawks at a Syrian air base as revenge for chemical weapons attacks on civilians, Ivanka's brother Eric told a British newspaper that he was "sure" his sister had urged their father to attack. "Ivanka is a mother of three kids and she has influence. I'm sure she said: 'Listen, this is horrible stuff,'" he said. At a briefing, White House press secretary Sean Spicer said there was "no question" she weighed in.

Ivanka's ethical problems, starting with her brand, and including her continued relationship with her father's international, shrouded octopus of LLCs, her ties to Russians (earning her, among some Trump critics, the nickname Kremlin Barbie), and her and Jared's own hidden finances (Jared has had to revise his financial disclosure statement dozens of times because of the millions of dollars in assets he left out), all together appear to dwarf "Crooked Hillary's" alleged ethical lapses, from Whitewater to the Clinton Foundation.

Unraveling Hillary's financial entanglements was arguably financial forensic amateur hour compared with the ethical quagmire Ivanka finds herself in as a senior White House advisor. She has maintained a stake in Trump's Washington hotel, the five-star services of which are viewed by foreign dignitaries and their staffs as the ticket to win Trump's favor. It can be a criminal offense for a federal employee to participate substantially in matters in which he or she has financial interests, but Ivanka has, without seeming concerned about appearances or the ethical implications, sat in on meetings with Chinese and Japanese leaders while her company was arranging trademark and business deals in those countries.

As with Hillary, there is an element of secretiveness about Ivanka, a deeply protective crouch masked by the controlled domestic reveals of her Instagrammed kids. Both women are in the emotionally and logically contorted position of supporting men whose real behavior with women has been utterly reprehensible at best, illegal at worst.

Like Hillary, Ivanka is deeply guarded to the point of obsessive about her image, albeit more strategically capable of controlling it, possibly because she started young. Unlike Hillary, you won't find a bad hair day picture of Ivanka online—at least after the age of fifteen. She has written that she developed a hard shell after enduring the humiliation of her parents' divorce in paparazzi-infested, tabloid-crazed New York. In public, her face is a smooth, still mask.

And, much like Hillary, who relied on unctuous helpings of personal charm and public "listening" to balance out distrust with her self-protective stance, Ivanka uses an Instagram account loaded with shots of her engaged in the duties of mother and wife to divert attention from her role as an unelected player with unlimited portfolio at the top level of the executive branch.

Ivanka's Hillary-esque obsession with privacy might lead to her father's demise. Michael Wolff reported that to keep federal authorities away from the Kushner family's financial records, she and Jared urged Trump to fire FBI director Comey, setting in motion an investigation that ensured all those documents would be studied by legal financial sleuths.

Political professionals from Steve Bannon on down have called the sacking of Comey the greatest error a president has made in modern times.

"The daughter will bring down the father," Bannon predicted with Shakespearean gravitas, and no little amount of animus toward Ivanka and Jared, to Michael Wolff.

◇◇◇◇

In the White House, Ivanka started wearing more Zara, the affordable fashion brand. The switch was duly noted by fashion and gossip writers around the world who pore over the Trump women's outfits every day. While Melania continued to wear couture, including a coat that cost as much as a house in Akron, Ohio, Ivanka was taking her look down-market. She and Jared would file financials indicating they were worth as much as $700 million or more, but she would start dressing more like a Washington swamp rat—at least when she wasn't at Mar-a-Lago.

The fashion drawdown didn't reduce her queenly status, though.

Inside the White House, Jared and Ivanka worked on their own stuff, she on the woman stuff (minus the gender pay gap, sexual harassment, and reproductive rights issues) and he plotting Middle East peace by playing a decisive behind-the-scenes role in pushing the president to move the US Embassy to Jerusalem, cozying up with a Saudi princeling who would soon have his relatives arrested, and supposedly upgrading the federal bureaucracy's technological capabilities. When Reince Priebus asked Jared what he was working on, he brushed him off with "Reince, we aren't getting paid. What the fuck do you care?"

Staff who weren't inside the "Javanka" bubble took to calling Ivanka "Princess Royal" behind her back. All over the bureaucracy, she was treated that way too. A single email request from one of her minions could send an entire agency's upper-level staff into a weeks-long frenzy.

Take, for example, the man-hours of Department of Education staff working to prepare for Ivanka's presence for forty-five minutes at an Air and Space Museum event intended to promote STEM for girls during Women's History Month March 2017. Ivanka was not yet an official White House employee, but it required the mobilization of at least 21 government employees and 150 email exchanges to choreograph her appearance.

The event was attended by mostly local African-American school-children and featured a screening of the hit movie *Hidden Figures* plus short remarks from Secretary of Education Betsy DeVos, Ivanka Trump, and Kathryn (Kay) Hire, a NASA astronaut. The event was the brainchild of the office of DeVos, whom Ivanka had run into at a bill signing in the White House on February 28. On March 1, she emailed DeVos (using her private "Ivanka Kushner" email account) to inform her that she wanted their staffs "to continue [to] discuss . . . opportunities to collaborate on locational/workforce development and K-12 STEM education."

The next day, DeVos's chief of staff, Josh Venable, was sending emails around the White House, looking for "Julie in Ivanka's office." By that time, Ivanka already had space in the White House, and a staff including Julie Radford, the daughter of a Louisiana Republican, who would eventually be given the title of Ivanka's chief of staff.

According to another email from an Education Department staffer, DeVos had been searching for a way to connect "with Jared and Ivanka" since as early as February 7, the day on which she was barely confirmed to her post when Vice President Mike Pence, a fellow Evangelical, cast the tie-breaking Senate vote.

The emails highlight the careful attention paid to Ivanka's branding on social media—and Snapchat's involvement in that endeavor. On March 21, Radford emailed Venable that "Snapchat recently expressed interest in having Ivanka snapchat from events that engage with 'young people'—would your team be open to something like that?"

Ivanka's unofficial office left nothing to chance: staff vetted invitations to the event, studied seating and stage charts, requested floor maps, and inquired about DeVos's "social media language" and whether the event would be "open or closed press," which would determine Ivanka's arrival and departure times, presumably to control contact.

Panic ensued during the final days before the event, as Ivanka's staff was unable to give the DOE organizers a specific time for her arrival and departure, even as the participants were doing a walkthrough. "So sorry to bug," wrote DOE staffer Laura Riggs, one of several emails to the White House that tried to get a final time. "Any way we can nail down her arrival/departure today?" Radford replied that they had scheduled Ivanka for forty-five minutes (the organizers wanted an hour and a half) but were "working to move things around" to arrive a little earlier to comply with DOE's plan.

On March 28, the spectacle and photo op went off without a hitch. The *Washington Post* made Ivanka the lead item in its coverage: "At an event at the Smithsonian Air and Space Museum for local school kids 'Getting Excited About STEM' on Tuesday morning, Ivanka Trump needed no introduction."

A day later, she had a title: "assistant to the president."

◇◇◇◇

In May 2017, Ivanka Trump's second book, *Women Who Work: Rewriting the Rules for Success*, was published to nearly universal scorn. It was bad enough to have had her brand called "a mauve-colored Feminist Nightmare" (*Huffington Post*). Now Amazon reviewers relentlessly trolled her book. It was a morsel for book review editors to hand out to hungry female journalists looking to sink their snarky teeth into. And it tanked financially.

Whoever edited it had failed to vet it for things like her complaint that she was so busy during the campaign she couldn't get a massage. It was *Art of the Deal* "meets Gwyneth Paltrow's Goop," the *Boston Globe* wrote. She outraged Hillary people by pulling inspirational quotes from some of HRC's great supporters, including former State Department director Anne-Marie Slaughter, Oprah, and actress Mindy Kaling—all Trump-haters.

In the face of a wall of scorn, Ivanka skipped the book tour and said she'd donate the proceeds to charity. In June, she went on *Fox and Friends*. In one of her signature ice-skating dresses, a lavender blue, wearing the ubiquitous heels, and one leg crossed over and perched on the couch, she let down her guard a little and talked about how much it hurt.

"There's a level of viciousness that I was not expecting. I was not expecting the intensity of this experience," she said. "I think some of the distractions and some of the ferocity was—I was a little blindsided by on a personal level. I'm trying to keep my head down, not listen to the noise, and just work really hard to make a positive impact in the lives of many people," she said.

Social media went wild. *Viciousness.*

"So weird," tweeted Tom Tomorrow, the pen name of editorial cartoonist Dan Perkins. "Her father is such a pleasant and accommodating man, & his party so eager for common ground. who could have foreseen?"

Someone tweeted a picture of two Trumpers at the RNC convention wearing matching black T-shirts that read "Trump 2016. Fuck Your Feelings."

What the commenters failed to recognize was that it was perhaps quite possible that Ivanka Trump, chief deliverer of cognitive dissonance about Donald Trump, suffers from it herself. After all, the daddy she has known all her life provided her with access to celebrity, great schools, a fortune, a view over Manhattan, and the illusion that she was making it herself. So, yes, she'd been on the campaign trail, and heard the chanting about locking up Hillary. But that was just Daddy. He liked to poke and provoke. He was harmless.

And in the chute in which she traveled between gilded jet, back seat of limo, and Secret Service hustling her through the back doors of hotels, conference centers, and arenas, it was possible to believe that she hadn't noticed the skinheads and Nazis and the extreme resentment directed at everything that her friends in New York society held dear.

As her father's position juices her and her family's businesses, Ivanka joins an elite class of super-rich female scions in the developing world, made vastly richer after their dads turned their offices into family business dynasties. In her dual position at the White House, Ivanka now has more in common with glamorous daughters of legendary third world kleptocrats like Angola's Isabel dos Santos and Azerbaijan's Leyla Aliyeva than with Caroline Kennedy or Chelsea Clinton.

Angola's former president José Eduardo dos Santos disbanded the board of the massive state-owned oil company and made his daughter the chairwoman of the board. Isabel dos Santos is now Africa's richest woman. In Azerbaijan, Leyla—the thirty-three-year-old daughter of the notorious dictator President Ilham Aliyev—is in charge of the family brand. She also runs a fashion magazine on the side, while living large off the proceeds of a shell-company-shielded fortune that the Panama Papers revealed includes a gold mine and swathes of London real estate.

"When you are on the board of a state-owned entity, you are a government official and private business person, and you get this weird crossover position," said Alexandra Wrage. "Like the Aliyevs, the Trumps were in business, now they are in government. And one day they will move back to business. That is usually found in the strange muddied waters of developing countries. That is not usually the hallmark of a democracy."

Soon after he was elected president, Donald Trump set his daughter up to meet with world leaders. Before he was even inaugurated, she was famously seated next to the Japanese prime minister in a Trump Tower meeting inside the gilded triplex where she grew up. Japan had granted Ivanka three trademarks, bringing the total to fifteen, between June and December 2016.

A few months after she took an official position, Ivanka joined her father on his first trip to Saudi Arabia, Israel, and the Vatican. The Saudis put her in a women's roundtable and she came away from that trip with $100 million in donations for a women's empowerment project—a feat that shocked government watchdogs who pointed out that government employees are forbidden from fundraising.

In November, she was off to Hyderabad, India's fourth largest city. The country, hoping to attract American venture capitalists with fat wallets, spent millions to prepare—fixing streets, offering a bounty to get beggars out of public view, and scattering rose petals on the route taken by Ivanka, who was leading the US delegation. Other than delivering a speech in a widely noted Indian-inspired frock, Ivanka spent her time inside the palace with Prime Minister Narenda Modi, or touring the area. Meanwhile, attendees were shocked at how little the US delegation did at the gathering, throwing a relatively cheap outdoor party with a meal that consisted almost entirely of rice.

But she wasn't exactly there for America alone. The family brand was right behind her. A few weeks later, her brother Donald Jr.—titular head of the Trump Organization—flew to India after advertising that he would meet personally with buyers (those who had already forked over $40,000 condo down payments) in Trump-branded buildings. According to investigative journalist Anjali Kamat, who spent a year investigating Trump deals in India, permits for Don Jr.'s sales were "rushed through" right after Ivanka's visit.

"I think it was Donnie Jr. that said Ivanka did the princess thing really well and she does," said one of their New York pals. "I think she is an American princess. I think she's a credit to her parents, maybe their greatest gift to the world. She is well-spoken, she's poised, she's educated. And we know that she has a softer outlook on the climate and she wants Pre-K and she wants child care and she does want women's rights. And sure we can point out her products are made in China or Thailand but that's business. I think that her heart is in a good place."

Ivanka has faith that the disingenuous will inherit the world. "I try to stay out of politics," she told *Fox and Friends* in another June appearance. "I'm more interested in being for something than against something."

Cool and collected in public at all times, carefully deploying a few standard facial expressions, she hasn't quite got her feelings about Donald's woman problem under control. Representing America at the winter Olympics in Korea, clad in red, white, and blue, she sat for an interview with NBC. Expecting softballs about athletes, she released a nanosecond of steam when the interviewer asked her whether Trump's accusers should be believed. She appeared to compare herself to Chelsea Clinton, another daughter of another philandering POTUS, never asked to opine on Monica and the blue dress. She cloaks it better, but Ivanka has inherited Donald's Rodney "I don't get no respect" Dangerfield gene. Like him, she can't shake an abiding sense of being perpetually wronged—especially when compared to others. "I think it's a pretty inappropriate question to ask a daughter if she believes the accusers of her father when he's affirmatively stated that there's no truth to it," she replied icily. "I don't think that's a question you would ask many other daughters. I believe my father. I know my father. So, I think I have that right as a daughter to believe my father."

Another friend, one of the Manhattan social set Jared and Ivanka "exfoliated" for their public opposition to Trump, maintained that Ivanka is "actually a good person," which makes her failure to step up for women even worse. "She doesn't just want power. She cares about her hair and makeup, and she is always looking for the right light and good camera angle because they've all done this all their lives," said one exfoliated friend. "They are schooled in it. Half the base likes her because she's pretty and the other half—us—are like, Get to Work! Help Us!"

And when she failed to deliver that help, no single demographic was more furious than her own peers.

CHAPTER 26

◇◇◇◇◇◇

FLOTUS

There will absolutely be a room designated for hair,
makeup and wardrobe. Melania wants a room with
the most perfect lighting scenario, which will make our
job as a creative team that much more efficient, since
great lighting can make or break any look.

—NICOLE BRYL, STYLIST

Nothing in her life had really prepared Melania for anything but
to be a mannequin.

She had no causes besides beauty, which is not a traditional concern in the office of the First Lady of the United States. Of course she
wanted to put a "glam room" in the White House, for makeup, hair,
and other prep. So said stylist Bryl, who had worked with Melania
for ten years when she gave an interview to *Us* magazine right before the inauguration. Bryl also revealed that each makeup session
with Melania takes "about one hour and 15 minutes of uninterrupted
focus. If you want the look to be flawless and have it last [throughout
the day], you do have to take a little extra time to make that happen."

For the inauguration—six days away when the story was
published—Melania had her own "creative team" discussing looks for

each of the day's several events. Not that the team would be telling her what to do, Bryl said. "Melania will absolutely let us know what she envisions for herself, since she always has such a strong and secure idea of how she likes things. It makes it that much easier for the rest of us to team together and execute her vision."

That was the last anyone heard of Nicole Bryl or the glam room.

No one on Team Melania will admit that they installed such a room in the White House. But clearly, she has transformed the role of FLOTUS into her own image. "She has made it her own. She has a vision. And key to that vision is deciding what she will wear when she is in the public eye," said one of her advisors. The month her husband was inaugurated, she appeared on the cover of *Vanity Fair*, Mexico, twirling a string of diamonds on a fork, like pasta.

Her people occasionally talked a good game about rolling out signature projects. They always stress her personal involvement in those decisions and choices. "Everything that's going on is a rollout," said one of Melania's advisors, in September 2017, a few months after Melania moved to DC. "And I say this all the time, it's like a master chess game and every move matters to the nth degree. It's showing that she actually does genuinely want there to be a unified voice and that it's children that does bring everyone together. That's her cause. The umbrella will be children. And under that will be things that are important to the safety and well-being of children."

That fall, the *New York Times* published a story on promises of a FLOTUS schedule of charitable works "for the children." But headed into her second year in the White House it became clear that Melania's vision did not yet include any kind of standard first lady enterprise.

Only after Stormy Daniels erupted did she actually roll out her "Be Best" project with the vague and broad aim to help the "social, emotional and physical health" of children, by addressing their social media use and attacking opioid abuse. She announced her project in May 2018, just as journalists who covered the White House were scrambling to prove rumors that Melania was not even living at the White House anymore but bunking with her parents in Potomac, Maryland, near Barron's school. Within hours, political journalists were accusing her and her staff of plagiarizing—yet again—the Obamas. Her press secretary angrily denied that.

Meanwhile, it did not matter to the public whether she did anything at all. Her poll numbers soared compared to his, but other than making sure she photographs well beside her husband, she hadn't really done very much. Her beauty, like Ivanka's feminism, has always offered a dignified counterpoint to the president's boorishness. Melania may be beloved precisely because the Trump administration's ugliness accentuates her beauty and grace.

She stepped into that role during one of Trump's early presidential rallies in July, 2017. As she addressed a raucous rally at Youngstown, Ohio, wearing a dreamy Monique Lhuillier pink floral dress and pink Louboutins, Trump paced and hovered behind her, prompting a universal sense memory of his stalking Hillary across the stage in the second debate. "As president, my husband will continue to fight each and every day to ensure our security, defend our livelihoods, and rebuild the foundations of fortune that have made the United States the land of opportunity," Melania said. "Washington has fought him every step of the way, but I know my husband and he will never give up."

Trump nodded and clapped beside her, and she stood beside him at the podium as he unleashed his counterpoint. With a stage set of white people standing behind him, he talked about "liberating our citizens from this Obamacare nightmare" and "liberating" American cities from an immigration takeover. He also reminded the crowd that he was fulfilling campaign promises to build up the military and expand gun rights. "Yes, our Second Amendment is very, very sound again. That would've been gonzo, it would have been gone, but I never had a doubt," he said. The crowd roared.

The morning after Thanksgiving weekend 2017, as Americans

were still digesting the feast and rubbing sleep out of their eyes, the Trump administration carried out a brutal takeover of the post–2008 financial crash Consumer Financial Protection Bureau, installing at the helm a man who had publicly stated that it shouldn't exist. As the mini-putsch was under way, aimed not just to rip out Obama era rules that limited things like predatory lending, but demolish the agency that oversaw their implementation, television cameras and photographers recorded Melania unveiling her first White House Christmas decorations. Impeccably turned out in stilettos and a white dress, she stood as still as *Frozen's* Elsa on the White House stairs, supposedly surveying aisles of silvery twigs, among which darted ballerinas, performing *The Nutcracker Suite*. The theme, chosen by Trump herself, was "Time-Honored Traditions," in honor of past Christmases at the White House.

Media critics compared the decor to a surreal set in Tim Burton's *The Nightmare Before Christmas*.

More than a year into her White House role, Melania still speaks rarely, and when she does, it's so halting and grammatically incorrect that it is almost painful to watch, not just for her palpable unease, but because it makes clear that she spent her last twenty years with Trump exactly like Rapunzel, but with her Slovenian parents and sister to keep her company in the tower.

Her silence is preferred. Her looks have inspired thousands of online "galleries." Flick through them and sink into the astral pedicure chair, enjoy the fashion mag fantasy of beautiful women in beautiful clothes. There is the daily update on *Footwear News* and the *Daily Mail*'s haul of paparazzi photography, and shots from every White House appearance, inside and on the lawn, walking to Marine One.

Melania, who must look great in almost every sort of clothing, selects her outfits with great care. Hers is not a *go to the closet, today feels pink* situation. Choosing what to wear is the most serious decision she has to make on any given day. And to help her with it, she has in the White House French designer Hervé Pierre, a former creative director for the design house Carolina Herrera. Melania and Pierre have been collaborating on her looks since they worked together on her inauguration outfits, including the Jackie O suit and the cream off-the-shoulder number she wore during her memorably stilted first dance with her husband as president.

Together they have crafted the FLOTUS look, a melange of dramatic and subtle: wide sleeves, hot pinks and yellows, pencil skirts and tight tops, belted military attire. Hervé and Melania consider the culture of countries or visiting dignitaries: a blue, white, and red Dior dress for a Bastille Day dinner with the Macrons in Paris, a flowing print dress of bright India yellow for India's prime minister Narendra Modi, a wide-legged black palazzo pantsuit with gold belt for arriving on the Riyadh tarmac.

She rarely appears in the same outfit twice. She is a younger and more lithe Nancy Reagan, sharing "Fancy Nancy's" nonchalance about prices. Even on casual days, walking to Marine One or across the tarmac at Andrews for trips to Mar-a-Lago, she totes the crocodile Hermès Birkin bag, retailing for $50,000 or more. On moving day from the Tower to the White House, she donned wide-leg culottes from Bally and a Dolce & Gabbana shell. (Unlikely that she ate doughnuts like everyone else on moving day—she consumes seven pieces of fruit a day and no junk food.)

The fashion community revolted against the Trumps, including Melania, during the campaign, shunned the inauguration, and refused to dress her. But she still wears them, and by doing so, has won back some fickle hearts. Pierre anonymously shops for her clothes off the rack in New York, always first inquiring if anyone has worn them on a red carpet before. He has brought her coat dresses by Alice Roi and The Row; "militaristic suiting" by Altuzarra, Karl Lagerfeld, and Michael Kors; dons Delpozo, Jil Sander, Simone Rocha, Dolce &

Gabbana, Valentino, and many others. Pierre delivers the clothes to the residence, where Melania tries them on, accessorizing and studying the look, with Pierre, in the mirror.

There is a lot of beautiful and costly clothing in the world. Only a few women can afford it and look good in it too. Melania is one of them, and she is guiltless about wearing and looking good in opulent clothes. Unlike Ivanka, who has decided that the Trump political brand requires her to wear more affordable Zara, Melania remains in the role she has been training for since she left Slovenia for Milan and Paris, the role for which Trump selected and married her.

She *looks* expensive.

In September 2017, Melania's big help-the-children "rollout" started with a speech at a lunch she hosted at the US mission to the UN, for the wives of foreign leaders. She strode in in a $3,000 Delpozo hot pink dress with massive sleeves that gave the impression of her being encased in a large bright shell. She teetered to the podium, in a room filled with the scent of boudoir candles, an odd combination with the lunch, and gave a painstaking speech on cyberbullying and protecting the children of the world.

"No child should ever feel hungry, stalked, frightened, terrorized, bullied, isolated, or afraid, with nowhere to turn," she said in her speech. "We must teach each child the values of empathy and communication that are at the core of the kindness, mindfulness, integrity, and leadership which can only be taught by example. By our own example we must teach children to be good stewards of the world they will inherit."

She didn't offer any specifics. It was the thought that counted.

After that, whatever projects she had planned were swept away by hurricane relief duty. She famously approached her first trip to flooded Houston in her trademark stilettos. But by her second and third trips to hurricane-devastated regions, she was wearing boots, baseball cap, and bomber jacket.

At the end of her first year as FLOTUS, the absence of projects seemed to matter less than the delicious relief of the photo galleries to exhausted and angry Americans. Melania finished the Trump first year in office as the most likable figure in Trumplandia, with 48 percent viewing her favorably, according to a poll by *Economist/YouGov* conducted in early '18. Stepmother and stepdaughter had started the year equally well liked, but Melania's popularity rose, while Ivanka's dropped. She was even more popular than the president.

Looking good and doing nothing at all, it turned out, was what the people wanted.

◇◇◇◇

As the Trump clan rolled through the red state primaries, plastic surgeons in New York and Texas started noticing a mini-trend. Modern dermatology and surgery has made it possible for surgeons to offer faces the way salons offer haircuts. Women wanted The Look. Specifically "The Ivanka" or "The Melania."

By 2017, The Look was proliferating in certain enclaves in places like Houston and Manhattan, where women with disposable income cluster. The Look was copying and replicating itself, like a computer virus or like the screen in that iconic 1980s Fabergé shampoo ad, popular during Ivana's prime. "And then she'll tell a friend and then she'll tell a friend and then she'll tell a friend . . . ," and the face of the big-haired model doubles and then doubles again and again, multiplying in mathematical progression of idealized female beauty, until the television screen is filled with multitudes of the same gorgeous hair, symmetrical lips and eyes.

Plastic surgeons in New York and Texas reported that although they had seen women coming in looking to remake their faces into approximations of various movie stars, they never saw anyone who wanted to copy Ivanka's face before the Republican primaries. But by the summer of '16, they were coming in. One of the doctors, a Houston surgeon named Franklin Rose, reported that "Ivanka is sort of the new style icon for plastic surgery."

A combination of rhinoplasty, cheek fillers, and Botox costing around $40,000 could produce in a woman's face an approximation of The Ivanka: widened cheekbones, a slender nose, and large eyes.

Frank Lista, a Canadian plastic surgeon, credits Ivanka's "lowered brow" for her allure. "There are a few things about her face that are super-interesting. When you have someone who's extraordinarily beautiful, like a fashion model, they often fall outside the norms of measurement that dictate conventional beauty. But that anomaly makes the face beautiful and interesting. With Ivanka, her lowered brow makes her face look even more attractive to us," Lista says.

After the election, women were also paying for the "Melania makeover." One Texas mother, a forty-two-year-old named Claudia Sierra, had nine surgeries to get The Melania, including a Brazilian butt lift, liposuction, tummy tuck, nose job, eyelid lift, and something called "revision breast construction." She also got Botox and fillers.

Sierra told reporters she wanted to look more like the first lady she felt herself to be inside. "Melania for me illustrates power and strength; she is our First Lady and I am looking forward to more closely resembling her and becoming a better version of me and for it to show on the outside," she said.

CHAPTER 27

◇◇◇◇◇◇

Catfights in Trumplandia*

When women kiss it always reminds one of
prizefighters shaking hands.

—H. L. MENCKEN

There is something about a catfight—that most sexist of terms for women competing—that the media loves. Donald loves them too. As his alter-ego publicist John Miller once opined, winning Trump is "going to be very competitive" for females. "He loves beautiful women fighting over him," said one family member. "He really enjoyed the battle between Marla and Ivana." The Queens of Trumplandia are champion competitors who have never been reluctant to fight to the finish. They are the clawing, purring, fanged beauties straight out of *Dynasty, The Real Housewives of New York*, or *The Real Housewives of New Jersey*. With two ex-wives and favored daughter all vying against

---

* NOTE: The term *catfight* is, of course, a deeply misogynistic term, and the author does not personally see competition between females as the light and screechy entertainment that the phrase implies. However, the Trump presidency is so deeply—and usually, deliberately—linked to the reality-show format, in which the "catfight" is encouraged by producers and plays such a key, crowd-pleasing role, that, in this case, she has made an exception.

one another and countless other unnamed women for the pearl of great price, the permutations are endless.

Catfight #1: Ivana vs. Marla

In *Raising Trump,* Ivana writes of meeting Maples in Aspen: "This young blonde woman approached me out of the blue and said 'I'm Marla and I love your husband. Do you?'"

Ivana responded as a wife would: with shock and anger, and maybe some Czech profanity.

Ivana doesn't exactly deny those juicy details. "It was unladylike," she admitted in her book, "but I was in shock."

Decades after she divorced Trump, Ivana would still not accept Maples's apologies. In her 2017 book she made clear that she's never forgiven "The Showgirl" for stealing Donald and wrecking her home. She wouldn't even use her name.

She remained "The Showgirl."

During the divorce, Marla took Donald's side when asked, at one point implying that Ivana was gold-digging. But in 1999 she issued a formal apology. "I regret the harm I have caused Ivana and I've apologized to her. I know she lives in London now and, if she reads this, I want her to know again how sorry I am about everything. Donald was never the man I wanted to marry. He and his world were alien to me. . . . I'm so happy to be away from Donald and I'm just trying to move as far away as I can."

Ivana never accepted that apology. Marla "asked to apologize to me in the *Daily Mail* in London," Ivana said during the 2016 campaign. "They asked if I accepted the apology and I said no. Why should I? She broke my marriage!"

During the campaign she came out swinging too. After Marla appeared on *Dancing with the Stars,* Ivana got in touch with her old pals at Page Six, the *New York Post* gossip column, and unloaded.

First, she claimed she had originally been asked to do the show and declined.

"She broke my marriage and destroyed my family. And now she's nobody. Last year, during the presidential campaign, they asked me to do *Dancing with the Stars*. I could not do it because it would have been disrespectful to Donald. I was not going to be on the dance floor with my boobs hanging out, and my butt hanging out. But guess what? Marla Maples took it. She lasted one week. And when she lost I said, 'Hey, hey, hey, hey!' I was never happier in my life." (Ivana apparently had a change of heart, and, clad in a partially see-through red gown, appeared in Italy's version of *Dancing with the Stars, Ballando con le stelle,* in May 2018, to "thunderous applause," according to the *New York Post*.)

Marla, having spent years working herself into a love-infused inner peace higher plane of serenity, told that Ivana didn't forgive her, softly responded: "It makes me sad, because I wish her nothing but love. I love her kids, and if she's holding any kind of resentment toward me, I really hope, for her sake, that she can forgive me."

It doesn't matter how many sunny, champagne-sauced yachting hours on the Med have passed since that horrible day in Aspen. Marla's New Age Dixie molasses will forever stick to the jet-setting Czech.

Catfight #2: Ivana vs. Melania

While Ivana Trump was on a tour for her book *Raising Trump*, she threw some shade at Melania in a television interview on *Good Morning America*, where she called herself the "real first lady."

She claimed to speak to the president every two weeks or so. "I [don't] really want to call him there, because Melania is there," Ivana said. "And I don't want to cause any kind of jealousy or something like that, because I'm basically first Trump wife. OK? I'm first lady."

Ivana also added that Melania did not seem to enjoy her role or residence and that she—Ivana—could have performed the duties. "I think for her to be in Washington must be terrible. It's better her than me. I would hate Washington."

But: "Would I straighten up the White House in fourteen days? Absolutely. Can I give the speech for forty-five minutes without [a] teleprompter? Absolutely. Can I read a contract? Can I negotiate? Can I entertain? Absolutely. But I would not really like to be there. I like my freedom."

The first lady's office wasted no time in issuing a statement, straight from the White House, calling Ivana's remark "attention-seeking and self-serving noise" and pointing out how well Melania handled and loved her role.

"Mrs. Trump has made the White House a home for Barron and the President," a spokesperson for the first lady said in a statement. "She loves living in Washington, DC, and is honored by her role as First Lady of the United States. She plans to use her title and role to help children, not sell books."

The catfight, predictably, provoked deliriums of joy in some quarters.

"This is actually happening. All the wives are fighting. Even I AM SPEECHLESS," tweeted Andy Cohen, executive producer of Bravo's *Real Housewives* series. He offered to settle the dispute *Real Housewives* reunion-style.

They have yet to take him up on his offer.

Catfight #3: Ivanka vs. Melania

This catfight is the most complex, and the most subtle. It would be the mother of all catfights if the competitors were not so buttoned up. A stepmother, barely a decade older than the stepdaughter, the younger replacement wife with the same purring Slavic accent and cabbage-soup childhood as the scorned mother of the highbrow step-daughter.

The relationship between stepmother and daughter was always publicly cordial if cool. Ivanka went to their wedding (unlike the wedding to Marla). "I'm happy for him," Ivanka said to reporters at the gate in Palm Beach, adding, "I don't think my mom will be here."

But ten years later, two Trump-branded goddesses, feet curved into the required beauty pageant stiletto arch, to add four inches to their already long legs, flank the President of the United States. Both are deemed "hot" by Donald. Only one's an official advisor.

The other gets his ear at pillow-Fox-cheeseburger time.

What could possibly go wrong?

Before the election, the *New York Times* published what it called "election fiction"—a short story by novelist Chimamanda Ngozi Adichie, who imagined a day in the life of Melania, who could not stand her eldest stepdaughter.

"Melania breathed deeply. Even just thinking of Ivanka brought an exquisite, slow-burning irritation. . . . Melania had wanted to shout once at the girl, golden-haired and indulged by Donald, one summer when Ivanka joined them for breakfast in Palm Beach and did not once glance at Melania."

In real life, the relationship has been frosty. "They are grown up," Melania told Alex Kuczynski in 2016, of the Trump children. "I don't see myself as their mother. I am their friend, and I'm here when they need me."

Melania and Ivanka are engaged in a much more subtle battle, but it is the fiercest of all, involving Trump's idea of proper female roles, and their own attitudes toward power. There is no doubt that Trump abides in his daughter (a business mind, a colleague) what he will never again abide in a wife. And Melania never wanted anything more than to be the "traditional European wife" that Ivana claimed to be, but was not.

In the beginning, it looked like first daughter would be first lady in the Trump White House, a role switch that had happened in a few prior presidencies when bachelors or widowers were president. But that wasn't exactly what happened. Instead, Ivanka took a West Wing office while Melania dallied in New York City—not as rumored to stay away from the White House, but to keep Barron on target to finish the year at his school.

In Melania's absence, though, it became clear that Ivanka was happy to play replacement FLOTUS—of a type. DOPOTUS started showing up at important meetings with foreign dignitaries. She wasn't arm candy to be photographed next to the leader's wife. She was an active participant, on the couch, in the triplex, with Japanese prime minister Abe.

Then her husband—with a few years of being the young masthead real estate developer and a lifetime of having "my people" take care of legal, accounting, and other business matters—signed on as a senior advisor without a defined portfolio. She followed. Jared and Ivanka staked out their White House positions before Melania had even scoped out office space.

Rumors of "frosty" relations between stepmother and daughter sometimes leaked out. Two fashion industry sources shared this observation with *Vanity Fair*, to which FLOTUS's press secretary quickly responded. "Ivanka and Mrs. Trump have always shared a close relationship, and that continues today." A "source close to Ivanka" said that their relationship is "fine."

In fact, the competition between Melania and Ivanka is over access, influence, and the proper role of familial ties in public life. The first lady is not a big fan of Donald's public nepotism. Behind the scenes, she's fine with telling Donald what she thinks. And, as she told *DuJour* magazine, during the campaign the kids were calling her to get messages through to their dad. That remained true in the White House. "All of them go to her for advice," one friend said. "They all sit around and ask her for her advice. But you don't see it because she doesn't feel the need to explain herself."

But the Trump presidency is very much a family affair. In fact, its nepotism is historic, and unlike Bobby Kennedy and Hillary Clinton, the Trump children and son-in-law have absolutely no policy or government experience, or really any kind of life experience on which to rely when Big Daddy calls on them for advice about matters of dire global importance. The Trump nepotism is the highest level of Trump's nose-thumbing at expertise, his proud contempt for book-learned people. So the children are intimately involved in his decision making.

Only Melania doesn't think it looks good on them. "Look at who's taking a position and a role and what's going on and what's important to each of the people in his orbit," said one friend of Melania's. "Every time you look you'll see that one is never trying to be anywhere near taking a limelight. She couldn't care less about it."

Melania's influence is so discreet and Ivanka's is so public that for the first time since it was created in 2004, the 2017 *Forbes* 100 World's Most Powerful Women did not include the American president's wife. *Forbes* did, however, rank first daughter Ivanka at number 19.

If all that weren't enough, Melania and Ivanka are constantly paired off publicly in "Who Wore It Best?" contests, because they strangely sometimes wear the same or nearly the same outfits around the same time. In junior high–speak, this is called, snidely, *matchy-matchy*.

There was the "pussy bow," which Melania rocked first in a shade of pink when she went out to defend Donald for his "grab 'em by the pussy" remark. "Melania's £585 Gucci blouse was widely considered to be quite a statement, whether intentional or not," the British tab *Express* reported.

A half year later, Ivanka wore a dark burgundy version of the blouse. "Ivanka Trump arrived at an event for women's entrepreneurship channeling professionalism in a pink suit, with a dark burgundy blouse, as criticism rolls in over her father's Iran deal speech," reported one British tabloid. "Ivanka's feminine look flashed a peek of the 35-year-old mother-of-three's chest, and had a 'pussy bow' blouse tie around the neck."

In the fall of 2017, both women showed up within a few weeks rocking very slightly different versions of a plaid men's-suit. "It's hard to imagine 'twinning' with your stepmother, but Ivanka and Melania Trump have worn extremely similar plaid outfits in recent weeks," *Town & Country* observed. The difference: Melania's was a $3,280 Ralph Lauren from his 2018 spring collection, and Ivanka's was a "much more affordable version" from Zara. And Ivanka wore hers to a Capitol Hill press conference on child tax credits, while Melania modeled hers at the UN, where Donald was giving a speech.

Finally, and weirdest of all, they wore virtually identical dresses to Steve Mnuchin's June wedding to Louise Linton, his third marriage, presided over by Vice President Mike "I don't eat meals with a woman other than my wife" Pence. The two Trump women, who weren't photographed together at the event, wore pale pink gowns with drapey overlays on the top. Their dresses matched the color of the bridesmaids' dresses, but as they were not bridesmaids, it's unclear whether they planned to be *matchy-matchy* in honor of the bride's color scheme or their stylists just hit up the same source, each without knowing the other one had just been there.

The best catfight moment between first lady and first daughter played out before the world's eyes and was misunderstood by almost everyone. After weeks of outrage at the Trump administration policy of separating children from migrant parents, Trump caved into Ivanka's plea that it was bad optics and reversed course. The images of crying children behind chain-link fences and audio of their cries recorded inside a detention center had moved most of the world to horror, including apparently both the first lady and first daughter. But only one of them got credit.

One day later, Melania sported a jacket with the words "I really don't care, do u?" on her way to visit detained immigrant children at the Texas border. Her office tried to downplay the significance. Communications director Stephanie Grisham issued a statement: "It's a jacket. There was no hidden message. After today's important visit to Texas, I hope the media isn't going to choose to focus on her wardrobe."

Later in the afternoon, Trump himself Tweeted an explanation, blaming, of course, lying journalists: "I REALLY DON'T CARE, DO U?" written on the back of Melania's jacket, refers to the Fake News Media," he tweeted while his wife was still winging her way back north from the border. "Melania has learned how dishonest they are, and she truly no longer cares!"

After heaping helpings of post-Stormy wifely humiliation she might not "truly care." But someone else in the family very much still does.

To understand what the first lady was really up to, one must first understand that both her and Ivanka's competitive playing field is fashion. Optics is always the goal with the women, but Donald's occasional obeisance is the real prize. And while Ivanka can also sport the clothes while speaking fluidly from lecterns and on TV, and campaign for Congressional PACs, and plot strategy on the Hill, and possess an unlimited White House portfolio, and sit in presidential chairs on occasion, Melania is hamstrung. She might have his ear at pillow time (assuming they still spend any time in the same bedroom) her native reticence, difficulty with English and clear discomfort in her role as humiliated wife, and above all, Trump's preferred role for her as nonworking wife, presumably often limits her communication mode to fashion alone.

She would make two trips to the border, both without input from the West Wing. She was moved by the caged and crying children. And if she's still speaking to Donald, she clearly had mentioned it to him. But it took Ivanka to change Daddy's mind on this one.

So: what was the message behind the $39 Zara hooded olive drab jacket with the message scrawled on the back?

White jeans. Adidas. *I really don't care, do u?*

Clearly, Hervé Pierre had not previewed this particular outfit. Like the trip itself, Melania was flying this mission on her own.

Commentators and the internet took it as a flagrant insult, a pampered woman's message to anyone who cared about the kids, basically, the entire world beyond the alt-right. The *Washington Post*'s fashion editor, Robin Givhan, spoke for many in an article surveying all the frocks Melania had modeled in her various appearances on Trump's NATO-fuck-you trip, a few weeks after the Zara jacket incident. "Can there be fashion diplomacy after detonating the nuclear option?" she wrote. "After the crude fashion equivalent of throwing up the middle finger? That, after all, is what Mrs. Trump did in June when she flew off on a humanitarian mission to visit detained migrant children wearing a fast-fashion jacket inscribed with "I Really Don't Care. Do U?" Her disaffection was writ large as she walked across the tarmac in clear view of photographers. She didn't aim her disdain with the precision of a sniper. She sprayed everything within range with scorn."

In my view, her disdain and scorn were aimed quite precisely. She was only trolling Ivanka's optics. She might be on the world stage in her Balenciaga and Manolos and Dior every time she steps outside, but her real world remains as small and limited as it always was, in the tiny apartment in Sevnica or in the Trump Tower triplex. And always, she lives within range of the crawling paw of Trump, trying to hold her hand, for optics.

The jacket was just a cloistered and apolitical Slovenian wife's passive aggressive act of domestic rebellion.

CHAPTER 28

◇◇◇◇◇

Queens of the Realm

The White House without its extensions, including Mar-a-Lago and the Tower, is not big enough to contain Donald's pride of females. They need range, and he needs them to be out of his hair.

Instead, Melania is like an exotic animal, ready to bolt, prowling from Manhattan to Florida, literally disappearing for twenty-four days in May and June 2018. Ivana, the first first lady, is still hanging around. Helpfully promoting an Italian obesity diet aimed at fat Americans, the two mothers-in-law remain in close quarters. Marla lurks on the astral plane, the unwritten tell-all barely contained by daily Buddhist meditations.

And there's the adored daughter he can't say no to, trying so hard and attracting unfair media attacks, and he wishes she would just go home.

The lion in winter, Trump is a bit like the polygamous Mormon patriarch Mark Twain visited in the late nineteenth century, before famously concluding that *familiarity breeds contempt.*

What happens to the Queens after he's gone?

Brand deletion is not unusual at global corporations. General Motors deleted Hummer, Oldsmobile, Saturn, and Pontiac in the last fifteen years.

Unilever trimmed its brand portfolio from sixteen hundred to four hundred brands in the early 2000s.

Procter & Gamble has deleted more than half its brands.

"Companies can boost profits by deleting loss-making brands," according to advice in the *Harvard Business Review.* "What's more, even though revenues may fall in the process, brand deletion will provide a shot in the arm for an additional reason. Many corporations don't realize that when they slot several brands into the same category, they incur hidden costs because multi-brand strategies suffer from diseconomies of scale. Naturally, those hidden costs decline when companies reduce the number of brands they sell. In fact, some businesses have improved performance by deleting not just loss-making brands but also declining, weak, and marginally profitable brands."

Ivanka ditched her fashion brand once it became clear that it had outlived its purpose. As a brand, Ivanka Trump HQ had tested the outer-limits of cognitive dissonance, the day after porn star Stormy Daniels went on *60 Minutes* and told an audience of millions of people that she not only had sex with Donald, but that she didn't even like it. Twenty-two million people had watched a porn star talk about spanking Ivanka's father in his underwear, but it was just any other week for Ivanka Trump's brand elves.

"Bright Ideas," read the subject line for "Ivanka Trump HQ," on March 27. "It's time to shine."

The captions urged readers to "Complete Your Jewelry Box," and the delicious layout featured delicate earrings—"stone drop" and "geometric drop" and "classic stud." The cheap metal-and-paste facsimiles of the real gems Ivanka herself would wear were, in fact, bright, shiny, *and* affordable, all under $40 each. And, like Ivanka herself, hard not to enjoy looking at.

Everyone in Trumpworld, most of all she, but surely also her dad, believes Ivanka Trump as a woman is the future of the dynasty, and as a brand is the future of the brand. As a woman, she is certainly well schooled for politics. Forged in chaos and humiliation, tested in a living reality-show challenge, Ivanka Trump taught herself not to stumble or stagger. She also has an instinct for strategy—a talent she was born with, not something that can be taught at business school. Throughout the Trump campaign and presidency, she put her husband ahead of herself—classic Orthodox Judaism, but Jared is also a kind of buffer, through which she maintained access to power without having to take the fall, as Jared looks destined to do, should one come to the Jarvanka dyad. She kept her sights on the long game, positioned herself as a global brand ambassador, collecting useful contacts from India to China to the EU under the goal of "women's empowerment," while not advancing that goal within her father's presidency at all.

With the leaders of China and India and the EU in her pocket, with her dad dispatching her to sit next to Angela Merkel, or represent him with the leaders of all the South American nations while he took a military shot at Syria, what did it really matter if an American Mr. Big like Barry Diller, husband of American women's brand icon Diane Von Furstenberg (the DVF-wrap dress), throws shade at her? "I mean, we were friendly," Diller said in spring 2018 to Maureen Dowd of the *New York Times*. "I would sit next to her every once in a while at a dinner. And I, as everyone did, was like, 'Oh my God, how could this evil character have spawned such a polite, gracious person?' I don't think we feel that way now."

She believes, as does everyone around her, that she has a long career ahead of her. Once officially in the White House, Ivanka has had some real successes, albeit overlooked in the din and chaos of her father's presidency, or ignored amidst progressive rage at her complicity with the pussy grabber in chief. She worked both sides of the aisle in Congress and as of summer 2018, many Republicans were on board for a twelve-week paid parental leave, at 45 percent of salary—but limited to new parents and with funds taken from their Social Security. Not exactly Swedish or French in terms of mother-friendly, but a step in the right direction. She also won praise for initiating the Women Entrepreneurs Finance Initiative, nicknamed We-Fi and sometimes called the "Ivanka Fund." She discussed her goal of helping raise the number of women-owned or run businesses in the developing world, where women currently run just 30 percent of small- and medium-size businesses. She cooked up the idea for the fund with Canada's prime minister Justin Trudeau, and the president of the World Bank solicited funds for it from Saudi Arabia, among other nations (inviting criticism that she was setting up a kind of bribery scam, whereby countries felt obligated to donate in order to work with her father). Fourteen countries contributed $350 million. Then she handed off the whole thing to the World Bank, which has doled out funds to women in Mali and Sri Lanka, and the program is winning praise from policy experts on both sides of the political spectrum.

"There'll be more books, there'll be more brand work. And I don't think we've even begun to see what Ivanka can do. I don't think she'll be deterred by all the controversy and the chaos. I think she'll emerge from the storm. Hair will be perfect, dress will be perfect, makeup will be perfect."

Paolo Zampolli, whose career as a diplomat presumably took a boost from the Trump presidency, was, not surprisingly, effusive. The matchmaker turned first family courtier compared Ivanka to Lady Di—only better. "Lady Di, she had only the respect of the United Kingdom, but Ivanka will be loved even more. Listen, the family's gonna be there for forty years. That's how they see it, not eight years, he wants to be there eight years, but the family is gonna be there, because after eight years of him, Ivanka's gonna be ready. She's gonna conquer the women's vote, is what she's doing. She's gonna really get it done. She will really make a difference with Muslims. She wanted power, and she will change a lot of thinking, and she will engage the Muslim countries: Saudi Arabia will look like the fifty-second state of the United States."

Ivanka's centrality to the future of the Trump brand cannot be overstated. That's why Rudy Giuliani vowed to go full medieval if Mueller targeted Ivanka in the Russia investigation. "Ivanka Trump? I think I would get on my charger and go ride into their offices with a lance, if they go after Ivanka," Giuliani said to Sean Hannity in May 2018. "Now if they do do Ivanka, which I don't think they will, the whole country will turn on them. If they go after her, the whole country will turn on them. They're going after his daughter?" In the same interview he conceded that Jared was dispensable, but not Ivanka—and her gender was the reason why. "Jared is a fine man but men are . . . disposable," he said. For the Trump brand to survive in the #metoo era, Ivanka can't be lost.

Her father, Donald, sees all these wild possibilities—and more. Throughout his career, Donald has elevated certain women—his secretaries, his engineer, a few lawyers—above the common herd and into his confidence. He trusts some of them, the ones "he's not banging" as one of his friends put it. And that includes his daughter.

Among men, his mortal enemies in the zero-sum competition for wealth and respect, he is friendless. A small circle of New York billionaires took his evening calls from the White House residence, and listened to him rant, then shook their heads, laughed, and leaked as soon as he hung up. One man who used to golf with him in New York recalled him plaintively asking what he was doing later—and only then, with a shock, understood that the tycoon was friendless. "I realized he was the loneliest man I knew," he said.

◇◇◇◇

Inside that void, the women come and go. Grandmother and mother, long gone, left him their legacy of hygiene, propriety, and his mother's yearning for the royal.

That's all that's left of them.

He's had three wives. A number that belongs in a biblical parable. The first wife offered him the closest thing he ever had to a real partnership, and taught him that he wasn't up for it.

The second wife provided him with his first foray into the midlife experiment in branding a Trump woman. And then she cast it off.

In the last wife, Melania, he has molded the apotheosis of the brand—gilt, moisturized, spooling strands of diamonds and pearls on a fork like spaghetti, lolling nekkid in the gilded jet, and truly worthy of the outdated moniker *supermodel*, utterly capable of fulfilling the key requirement: to pique the envy of other men.

And then there is Ivanka.

Porn star Stormy Daniels and *Playboy* playmate Karen McDougal, two women he allegedly slept with while Melania was postpartum, both recalled that Trump brought up Ivanka during pillow talk, telling them that they reminded him of her. Their recollections provoked another round of prurient speculation about the true nature of his feelings about the daughter "I might be dating" if he wasn't her father.

But that's not it at all.

Ivanka is much, much more than that. She is the future of the brand. But she has a problem. It's a problem that professors of business understand.

At Wharton, where Ivanka got her economics degree, requirements include taking classes in how to sell stuff, starting with MKTG101 and going all the way up to more complex levels of branding like MKTG268, a class called "CONTAGIOUS." That course promises to teach students why some products fail, while others catch on "like wildfire," and explore how interactive media, word of mouth, and viral marketing are important for companies, brands, and organizations.

Ivanka Trump and her father—were they so inclined, which they are not—could teach such classes. Ivanka, the ultimate apprentice, has not only written a whole book advertising her father's marketing genius, but she has never *not* been a brand herself.

Now Ivanka confronts a challenge worthy of an MBA thesis. Unlike multinationals with diversified brands, the Trump brand—although diversified from water to steaks to towers and hotels and golf courses to Ivanka Trump's shoes and dresses—only has one logo—a confection of blond hair, a Mussolini jawline, a Taftian profile, and an increasingly negative perception among consumers.

The great challenge for the ultimate Trump Queen, the heiress to the brand Ivanka Inc., is going to be figuring out how to delete that logo and carry on.

If she pulls it off, it will be the marketing feat of the century, the truest test of everything she has ever learned by studying and emulating her father's marketing genius, and worthy of study at Wharton for a long, long time.

The Other Women: A Taxonomy

His Two Sisters, the Other Daughter,
the Employees, the "Hot Women," and the "Liars"

Donald's mother, grandmother, three wives, and daughter Ivanka were and are the primary women in his life. Each of them has played a role in the development of his attitudes toward women. But Elizabeth Christ Trump, Mary Trump, Ivana Trump, Marla Maples, Melania Trump, and Ivanka Trump are by no means the only women in Donald Trump's life. Beyond the inner circle, there is a constellation of other important females who have interacted with him. Many of them are far more famous than his own mother, and some stand to impact his presidency in ways still to be seen.

For better or worse, no story of the women in the life of the forty-fifth president is complete without the Other Women.

Because Trump is a man of fixed perceptions and long habit, the Other Women classification scheme here is fairly straightforward. There are his two mysterious sisters. There is, of course, the Other Daughter. There are the faithful employees. And then there is the long list of "Hot Women": all the bunnies, porn stars, models, and beauty queens. Finally, there are the "Liars": Donald's odious term for the women who have come forward to describe his unwanted groping and kissing.

This taxonomy could but will not include the miscellany of women with whom he has engaged in gutter-worthy public spats, from the late gossip columnist Liz Smith, to lifestyle brander Martha Stewart, to comedian Rosie O'Donnell, to all the women he has fat-shamed or otherwise insulted on the basis of their looks. Nor does it include the names of wives of friends, that unknown number of women Donald has, according to author Michael Wolff, connived to bed for the sheer joy of dominating their husbands, because it "made life worth living."

The Trump Sisters

If, since November 2016, you spent time around the environs of the Hamptons, Palm Beach, horsey New Jersey or Westchester, and kept your eyes peeled, you might have noticed two older and very discreet blond women, their ladylike dignity perfectly masking horror and embarrassment, keeping a low profile. Their dad was a patriarchal SOB, but he maintained certain standards of public display in the household in which they grew up, standards that little brother Donald has repeatedly transgressed on the world stage. Of course they owe him filial love, but they don't owe him their privacy and reputations. And so they dwell, for now, in the shadows.

Back in the Queens family home, Donald was preceded by two sisters, Maryanne Trump Barry, the eldest, nine years older, and Elizabeth Trump Grau, the third child, four years older than Donald. Both girls grew up to be blond, blue-eyed, delicate-featured women, like their mother and paternal grandmother, but otherwise very different from each other—and their brother. Maryanne went to law school while a young mother, worked as a federal prosecutor, and became a federal judge in Philadelphia. In a parallel universe—the one where

Donald had no chance of winning the presidency because the electorate was rational and educated—perhaps Judge Maryanne Trump Barry might have been a viable candidate, certainly in Hillary Clinton's league. A standout student from childhood, she graduated with honors from Mount Holyoke—one of the Seven Sisters colleges, elite institutions that produced Hillary Clinton (Wellesley) plus a generation of women leaders and liberal academics, members of America's intersectional feminist forward guard that put white, undereducated males on the defensive—a state of affairs that arguably got Trump elected president.

Judge Barry is not now, nor was she ever, a social justice warrior (although Ted Cruz did call her "a radical pro-abortion extremist" in the heat of the campaign). But she does have a strain of moderation, noblesse oblige, and civic-mindedness that her little brother lacks. Now eighty, and a millionaire many times over, she is a Republican who has donated $4 million to a Catholic college, Fairfield University in Connecticut, for a center on Ignatian spirituality. An early marriage produced one child, and ended in divorce, and a period of single motherhood, followed by law school and a second marriage to a fellow lawyer, in 1982, when she was the highest-ranking woman in the US Attorney's Office in Newark, as one of two women in an office of sixty-two people. A year later, Reagan appointed her judge— a nomination that might have been helped along by Republican lawyer and Trump fixer Roy Cohn.

Donald himself said he had nothing to do with her appointment. "I'm no different than any other brother that loves his sister," Mr. Trump said when asked about Cohn's influence on the Reagan administration's decision. "My sister got the appointment totally on her own merit." But Judge Barry gave him some credit in an interview with Trump historian Gwenda Blair. "There's no question Donald helped me get on the bench," she said. "I was good, but not that good."

As a young lawyer, she chain-smoked and drove a Jaguar, and tried to do it all. "I do the laundry, I do the shopping, I do the dishes," she told the *Chicago Sun-Times* in 1989 of her after-work hours. She has called her son, neuropsychologist and author David Desmond, her greatest success. For most of her career as a judge, her rulings were typical of a moderate New York feminist. On the appeals court in 2000, she struck down a New Jersey "late-term abortion" ban, and she has even written decisions siding with immigrants against a judge she accused of "bullying" in 2006.

Since the election, all Donald's three surviving siblings keep low profiles, but Judge Barry was photographed getting off the Trump jet for the inauguration.

Unlike her brother, she inherited a humility gene from somewhere in the family DNA bank. "Scared?" Trump Barry said at a commencement address at Fairfield University in Connecticut in 2011. "Every day of my life." She once described little brother Donald as P.T. Barnum, according to the 2005 book *Trump Nation*.

Trump's other sister, Elizabeth Trump Grau, is five years younger than Maryanne and four years older than her famous little brother. Her reticence makes Judge Barry's occasional appearances at commencements seem positively gregarious. Trump Grau graduated from what is now Southern Virginia University, and worked full-time in banking. At age 48, she married James Walter Grau, president of his own production company making documentaries and sports programs, and producing live events and concerts for TV. He once served as the director of entertainment for the Mar-a-Lago club. The Graus, who have no children, owned a house in Palm Beach near Mar-a-Lago, and are fixtures on the social circuit in the Hamptons, where they have also owned property.

Friends who know Elizabeth told the author she has been relatively cloistered since the 2016 election and doesn't approve of her brother's politics.

In his two big sisters, Donald saw smart and capable women. He took away from them the knowledge that some women might be almost as good as a man sometimes.

Almost, but of course, *not quite*.

The Other Daughter

The Trump brand aims to be "classy." Trump's daughter Tiffany—his fourth child, born out of wedlock—is the déclassé mirror image of her big sister Ivanka. She resembles her, but she was not to the Tower born. Through no fault of her own, Tiffany is associated in the Trump family legend with the most scandalous headline of its time . . . THE BEST SEX I EVER HAD.

Tiffany Ariana Trump—named after the iconic jewelry emporium that adjoins Trump Tower—was Donald's fourth child, born October 13, 1993. Donald was forty-seven. He had been with Tiffany's mother for at least five years, but hadn't got around to marrying his mistress, who was about to turn thirty.

Of Donald's brood, Tiffany is the only one, as far as is known, whose birth he actually witnessed in person, in a room at St. Mary's Medical Center in Palm Beach, an act so utterly out of character it bears repeating.

Her mom and dad married when Tiffany was three months old, and she was just three years old when they separated. She was never as close to Donald as his kids with first wife, Ivana. After Marla moved to California in 1999, Tiffany saw her father infrequently, possibly just a handful of times before she moved back east as an eighteen-year-old college freshman at the University of Pennsylvania. She has said she spent spring breaks at Mar-a-Lago, but for most of her life from age six to eighteen, she lived in Los Angeles with her single mother, who was trying to support them both on a reported $2 million settlement from Donald.

But by the time Tiffany was fifteen, big sister Ivanka was her conduit into the Trump universe. For Ivanka, welcoming Tiffany into the fold was both a token of filial love and a gift of forgiveness to their father for putting her through the Marla years. Before they started appearing together on campaign rally stages, Ivanka had not talked of Tiffany much publicly except in an odd anecdote in her first book, *The Trump Card*. In that book, Ivanka mentions the word *Tiffany* eighteen times—but mostly in reference to Tiffany the jeweler, including how she wished she could have grabbed its iconic shade of robin's-egg blue for her own brand. She only mentions half sister Tiffany in recounting a story about helping her get a credit card. As Ivanka recalled, when Tiffany was a teenager in California, she needed a little more money out of their shared father. She appealed to Ivanka for advice, explaining that she was embarrassed to ask him for it but wanted to be able to afford the lifestyle of her high school friends. "All she wanted really was a way to enjoy some of the privileges her friends got to enjoy, in the same way she would have enjoyed them if she lived under our father's roof," Ivanka wrote. She saved Tiffany the trouble of asking and talked their father into giving her a credit card with "a small monthly allowance on it" for Christmas. "Big Sis did an end-around to save Tiffany the trouble," Ivanka wrote. "Tiffany was thrilled and relieved. And so appreciative."

Also, she noted, Tiffany never knew about the favor—at least not until she read it in Big Sis's book.

After graduating from Penn—alma mater of Trump and three of his children—in 2016, Tiffany participated in the presidential campaign, occasionally appearing at rallies beside her older sister, both daughters in the beauty pageant heels Donald prefers to see on women. By now, Big Sis was giving Tiffany tips on how to appear in the public eye, to cross her legs in public, and what colors looked best on camera. Tiffany spoke on the second night of the Republican Convention in Cleveland (several days before the big moment of nomination night, a slot saved for Ivanka). In her speech, she recalled how her father would encourage her with "sweet notes" on kindergarten report cards—presumably long distance. She also praised his "desire for excellence. He possesses a unique skill in bringing that trait out in others."

Five months later, clad in a satiny pale blue minidress, a shinier version of the one on her older sister, and the teetering Trump standard stiletto pump, Tiffany followed Melania, Ivanka, Barron, Jared, and the Trump sisters-in-law onto the New York Hilton ballroom stage at 3 a.m., as her father claimed his election victory. Tiffany and her mom, Marla, then made small ripples of news as the nation settled into having the Trumps as first family. During the inauguration, there was the report of Marla and Tiffany requesting free hair and makeup in Washington in exchange for publicity. The paparazzi started following Tiffany and her then-beau, Ross Mechanic, out on the town.

Since the inauguration, Tiffany's visits to her father are just a short Secret Service van ride away from law school at Georgetown, which she's been attending since 2017. But she's not at the White House much. She showed up at the Easter Egg Roll, and at the Thanksgiving turkey pardoning ceremony, and spent part of Christmas at Mar-a-Lago. But despite her proximity to the White House, she reportedly rarely speaks to her father and may even disagree with his politics. She made headlines after she "liked" an Instagram shot from the March for Our Lives rally. One sign in the image said, "The next massacre will be the GOP in the midterm elections."

There's a chill in the father-daughter relationship now. "Since the inauguration, Tiffany and her father have sometimes gone for months without speaking and she went a very long time without seeing him," *People* magazine reported in April 2018. "The last time she was at a family function with him, it was awkward for her and she didn't feel totally welcome. They always had a strained relationship her whole life, and it got exacerbated by the presidency," the magazine said. "It's gotten much worse now."

The Employees

"It's funny. My own mother was a housewife all her life," Trump said in *The Art of the Deal*. "And yet it's turned out that I've hired a lot of women for top jobs, and they've been among my best people. Often in fact, they are far more effective than the men around them."

Trump described it as funny—in the sense of, presumably, *unusual*—that he hired a lot of women for top jobs. In the 1980s, women were unicorns in the C-suite for sure. But it was not that out of the ordinary for a businessman of his stature and era to have a few women in marketing and sales in the late 1980s, and a trusted executive assistant, a gal Friday, to mother him and organize his life. And Trump has had at least three of the latter in his business life.

Norma Foerderer

A matronly but stylish middle-aged divorcée, she came to Donald's side in his early forties, fluttering down like Mary Poppins after answering an ad that Ivana put in the *New York Times*. Norma was destined to become his trusty aide for decades to come, a loyal protectress during two divorces. More worldly than the average Trump Organization insider, Norma was fluent in French and had worked at the US Embassy in Tunisia. She would serve as Trump's surrogate mother, "special confidante," and spokesperson—when he wasn't pretending to be his own PR man.

She brought him his temperature-specific Diet Cokes. She told him what schools his kids went to, and reminded him when they needed to be praised or congratulated for events he'd missed. She issued edicts like making sure no one laughed about his relationship with Marla Maples. "We don't know how he really feels," she would say. But he "was entitled" to love now. Like all his enablers and "Mr. Trump" lackeys, she was devoted to him. And she felt pity and compassion (an emotion he was rare to show) for him, locked inside his unexamined life.

"Without Norma Foerderer, sweet Norma, running interference for me, I never could have gotten the time and access I needed," Trump wrote in *The Art of the Deal*. In a chapter about a typical day, she pops up repeatedly: "3 p.m.: I ask Norma Foerderer, my executive assistant and the person who keeps my life organized, to bring me lunch: a can of tomato juice."

In the same book, he said he liked her strength. He called Norma "sweet and charming and very classy, but she's steel underneath, and people who think she can be pushed around find out very quickly that they're mistaken."

Norma retired in 2006, after twenty-six years with Donald, and she died in 2013 in New Jersey. Trump marked her passing with a tweet: "I have just lost my beautiful & elegant long time exec. assistant Norma Foerderer. She passed away yesterday—a truly magnificent woman."

Rhona Graff

When Norma retired, Trump promoted a new executive assistant named Rhona Cheryl Graff, who had been working at the Trump Organization since the 1980s. She was six years younger than Donald and, like him, an outer borough native. She had a master's in psychology from Queens College and talked with a Queens accent. She took the job in Trump Tower after a career in sports marketing.

As Donald became a celebrity, Rhona became the gatekeeper, the woman whose phone number reporters and business associates needed in order to reach the man. "I like staying behind the scenes," she told the *New York Times* during the election, declining a *Times* request to shadow her for a day. "We're so intertwined when he's here," she said.

Graff was forced to come out of the shadows when she was swept up in the Trump Russia collusion investigation and called to testify on Capitol Hill. She is listed in the notorious Donald Trump Jr. email chain in which he agreed to meet at Trump Tower with Russians proposing to share dirt on Hillary.

Hope Hicks

Because she was attractive, young and a former model who had graced the cover of the first editions of the *Gossip Girl* novels' spinoff *The It Girl*, it was easy for rude people to assume that Hope Charlotte Hicks, who steamed candidate Trump's pants before rallies while he was inside them, among many other duties, was also servicing him sexually. And certainly Donald wasn't oblivious to her beauty. Steve Bannon wrote that Trump once told her he didn't understand why Corey Lewandowski, with whom she had an affair during the campaign, had broken up with her because she was "the best piece of tail he'd ever have."

Hope Hicks was not among the banged, but among the trusted *non-banged* women in Donald's life. Until she quit, she served him faithfully in a Norma/Rhona capacity. She was the youngest and prettiest of the calm, competent Girl Fridays. She was the one who happened to have the style, poise, and self-control on high heels to be both a classic Trump-branded female *and* a trusted gatekeeper/caretaker. Like Ivanka and Melania, stylish, soigné Hope in her pretty frocks and long brown hair, scooting around at a surly MAGA rally or tripping lightly down the stairs of *Air Force One*, provided—like

Ivanka and Melania—soothing feminine presence, especially when, for example, photographed beside disheveled King of Chaos Steve Bannon or hollow-eyed anti-immigration fanatic Stephen Miller.

Brought into the Trump Organization by Ivanka, Hope is a daughter of Greenwich elites, to the manor born. Precociously poised and armed with generations of taciturn Yankee blood in her veins, her rise and fall in Trumpworld happened before she had even turned thirty. After working with Ivanka, she worked for Donald. She had a calm equanimity dealing with reporters, and could always be reached during the campaign. Rumors of an affair with the married, head-busting hockey boy and sometime campaign manager Corey Lewandowski preceded him being tossed off the bus—not her.

She did jump off willingly in February 2018—resigning from her job as White House communications director still half a year shy of her thirtieth birthday. She quit a day after admitting to the House Intelligence Committee that she had told "white lies" to protect Trump. One perhaps related to a conference call with Trump and a White House lawyer, Mark Corallo, who said she promised that Donald Jr.'s emails about his Russian dirt-gathering meeting "will never get out." Her lawyer denied that she said that. But besides having admitted to white lies, she had been grilled by the Mueller investigators a few months prior, and, having endured enough, Hope quit. Donald has not replaced her.

Barbara Res and Louise Sunshine

Besides the Girl Fridays at his beck and call outside the office, Trump did put women in significant positions in the Trump Organization. At one time, lawyer Michael Cohen bragged that the Trump Organization had a higher percentage of female employees than other companies. Whether or not that's true—it's privately held, so the truth is impossible to ascertain—he has put women in top roles.

Among them are Louise Sunshine—a real estate saleswoman

Trump described in *The Art of the Deal* as being "as relentless a fighter as you'll ever meet"—and engineer Barbara Res. Both women have proclaimed that Trump mostly respected them on the job, and they credit him for hiring and promoting women. But neither woman escaped unscathed.

After she joined Donald Trump's real estate business, Sunshine, a harried mother of three, was fighting off weight gain. Donald—who never missed a flaw in a female figure—took to storing an unflattering photograph of her in his desk drawer. Sunshine, who worked with him for fifteen years starting in the 1970s, later called it a "fat picture." He would pull it out when she did something he didn't like. It was "a reminder that I wasn't perfect," Sunshine later told the *Washington Post*. "He just is that way."

Trump hired engineer Barbara Res to help him build Trump Tower. She eventually served as vice president of construction for the Tower from 1980 to 1984 and then as executive vice president in charge of development from 1987 to 1991, and later she was a consultant for the Trump Organization during the 1990s. Res calls Trump's hiring of her "daring" for the time, and she says the Trump she met in the late 1970s was deferential to women, and a completely different man. As his fame grew, she saw that he crafted a new sexist trademark for himself that became part of his brand.

"He's terribly sexist. He's a womanizer for sure," Res has said. "He hired me for a specific reason: Because I was really good. And he told me, and he believed this, that women had to work harder and be smarter and were willing to work harder than men, and that's what he wanted, and he had a couple of women working for him. . . . 'Men are better than women,' he said, 'but a good woman is better than ten men.' I think he thought I would take it as a compliment, and I think it was intended as a compliment."

Donald's sexist bullying of his female colleagues was of a piece with his bullying of all colleagues, male or female. The fact that they were female—or female and overweight—only gave him added ammunition in the quest for domination. And as one friend put it, he does trust some of the women he "isn't banging." And perhaps, sometimes, he trusts some of those women in a way that he doesn't trust men.

The "Hot Women"

The key to the successful Trump-trademarked female—plastic-looking and on heels—is that Donald has molded her, or she has molded herself, into the preferred image. He discovered his preference for the pleasure of molding a marketable female product while he was still married to Ivana, as she took control of the jobs he gave her, excelled at some of them, dragged him around the social circuit when he would rather be at home with a woman cooking his mother's meat loaf. His first marriage in its stable years was a temporary deviation from his legend-in-his-own-time self-image as a New York "model-izer," a keen judge of female flesh, and a ranker of hotness. While the marriage to Marla Maples didn't work out, Donald learned that what he truly wanted in bed with him was a woman with professional training in how to look and behave as close as possible to his *Playboy* magazine, airbrushed Madison Avenue ideal. For years, he satisfied his lust through unfettered access to models and beauty queens. The pageants were a personal pussy farm, where numerous young women have since reported that he ogled and hugged them, and asked them to meet him in a hotel room, manhandling them with a "a squeeze like a creepy uncle would," recalled one former Miss New Hampshire.

As pageant impresario, his dressing room entitlement and roaming were notorious and has been described previously in this book. Many of the girls would later say they were uncomfortable, but if he was aware of that, he didn't seem to care. In 2006, Miss North Carolina Samantha Holvey encountered Donald at the 2006 Miss USA pageant, and later said she was "disgusted" at the way he personally inspected her and the other contestants. "He would step in front of each girl and look you over from head to toe like we were just meat, we were just sexual objects, that we were not people." And she didn't like it. "You know when a gross guy at the bar is checking you out? It's that feeling."

But for every buzz-killing pretty girl like Holvey, who resisted him or found him disgusting, Donald could find others who succumbed to his charms, or let him believe they did. He spent his fifties and sixties ogling and bedding models and bunnies, refining his ranking act at the pageants and the modeling contests, like "Look of the Year," and screwing the occasional porn star.

Even after he had his own "supermodel," he remained in play—especially in the year after his supermodel gave birth to his last child. As has been discussed above, his revulsion for female biology made postpartum Melania taboo.

The full list of Trump's Other Women is probably never going to be public, given his practice of paying them for silence and the avalanche of contumely that awaits any woman who steps forward. Those who have come forward describe a similarly pedestrian wooing style—involving hotel suites, vague promises of television or modeling jobs, and often, mentions of his beautiful daughter Ivanka—if not a john-like explicit offer of money after sex.

Like many men of his ilk, born to money and surrounded by yes-men and sycophants, Donald reduces most human interactions to equations of domination and submission that involve dollars and emotional if not literal blackmail. In his worldview, there is nothing that can't be reduced to a transaction. Everyone has his or her price. Money *can* buy love.

His Other Women are of two types: Those Who Get It and Those Who Don't.

Those Who Get It are pretty much okay with being paid, or being reduced to Trump-branded products. They enter his orbit fully conscious that they are in a transactional space. They go in prepared to negotiate for what they want.

Those Who Don't are like the *Playboy* bunny who cried for days because Trump tried to hand her money after sex. They enter the hotel room or meet his fumbling hands behind a closed door at Mar-a-Lago, believing in the flattery oozing caramel from the Rat-Pack-at-the-Sands vocal cords.

They feel that maybe, they're "The One."

Melania was three months postpartum when adult film star and director Stephanie Clifford, aka Stormy Daniels, met Donald, beaming and sweaty in yellow polo shirt and red hat, at a golf course in Tahoe in July 2006. He was glad-handing among the regular-Joe chum, but celebrity golf tournaments apparently attract porn stars too. Stormy was on the premises hawking her porn tapes. A witty Louisianan who had long ago done her own math about what men want and what they will pay for it, she and Donald were a natural fit, philosophically if not sexually.

Invited inside his hotel room that night, Stormy knew she didn't really want to have sex with the guy, she would later say on *60 Minutes*. But once sitting on the bed with him, where he was watching "Shark Week," there was no wriggling out of it. They stayed in touch for a while afterward, with Donald casting out vague promises to get her on his show, until even that petered out. But ten years later, when he was running for president, Stormy had a valuable story to tell about that one encounter, which included such gems as him describing his fear of sharks and her spanking him on the butt (in his underwear) with a copy of *Forbes* with him on the cover, after which he told her she reminded him of his daughter Ivanka.

Weeks before the 2016 election, Stormy took $130,000 from Michael Cohen's Essential Consultants LLC to remain silent. She busted the agreement after the *Wall Street Journal* got hold of the contract in early 2018.

The news hit Trump-drunk America with the force of a marsh-mallow shooter.

More NDA-busting was to follow, also landing with a resounding "eh, who cares?" A month before his Stormy encounter, Donald had, it seems, met and commenced an actual affair with *Playboy* bunny Karen McDougal. In June 2006, Hugh Hefner, *Playboy*'s late pub-lisher, threw a pool party for *The Apprentice* contestants with dozens of current and former Playmates, including McDougal, voted runner-up for "Playmate of the '90s," behind Pamela Anderson. Trump "im-mediately took a liking to me, kept talking to me—telling me how beautiful I was, etc. It was so obvious that a Playmate Promotions exec said, 'Wow, he was all over you—I think you could be his next wife.'"

Not quite. After they allegedly had sex for the first time, Trump tried to hand her cash. "I looked at him and I said, 'That's not me. I'm not that kind of girl,'" McDougal later told Anderson Cooper. "And he said 'Oh,' and he said, 'You're really special.' And I was like, 'Thank you.'"

After Trump's bodyguard and former NYPD officer Keith Schiller took her home, McDougal said she "cried for a lot . . . I felt really ter-rible about myself." But she kept seeing Donald, and even showed up at events with Trump family members, including posing for a picture with Melania in the frame, and another time, at a party for Trump Vodka, with Eric Trump.

The *National Enquirer* paid her $150,000 and a promise to pro-mote her career as a fitness specialist in a "catch and kill" operation, burying her story in time for the election. After Stormy Daniels came forward, McDougal busted out of that agreement, calling the rela-tionship consensual and loving, and reporting, as had Stormy, that Donald compared her beauty and brains to Ivanka's.

As stated, it's impossible to list—because it's impossible to know—the names of all the hot women who have played significant roles in

Donald's life. Their number is legion, and he may also have forgotten them himself. Herewith a short list of the better known:

Kara Young

Trump dated the biracial model for two years from 2001. She told the *New York Times* that she "never heard him say a disparaging comment towards any race."

Kylie Bax

Trump dated this New Zealand model in 1995 and they have remained friendly. Bax, a slender, busty, tall blonde, defended him against claims of sexual harassment in an interview with the *New Zealand Herald* before the election.

Rowanne Brewer Lane

Trump spotted this model when she was twenty-six, at a pool party at Mar-a-Lago. She borrowed a swimsuit that belonged to his collection and, she told the *New York Times*, he commented: "That's a stunning Trump girl right there." After the *Times* included her account in the first major article about Trump's sketchy history with respect to women, in the summer of 2016, she came to his defense, saying: "He was a gentleman."

Gabriela Sabatini

Trump dated the stunning Argentine tennis player in 1989 while he and Marla Maples were broken up. After a month he returned to his Georgia peach.

Allison Giannini

Model Giannini was twenty-seven when she dated Trump in 1997 and has also defended him, calling him a "perfect, perfect gentleman." In 2016, she told *Inside Edition* that she was set up on a blind date with Trump in 1997 and that she believed he was still in love with Marla Maples.

Candice Bergen

Trump went on one date with Bergen when they were both eighteen and in college. He did not score. After Trump was elected, the actress told Bravo's *Watch What Happens Live*: "He was a good-looking guy and a douche."

Carla Bruni

Model, singer, and former first lady of France Carla Bruni has denied Trump's report—while impersonating his own PR man—that he dated her in the early 1990s. She has said she only tolerated him at a party with her friends at a suite in the Plaza Hotel, and has opined of his claims otherwise that "obviously he is a lunatic."

The "Liars"

After the Billy Bush tape aired, with Trump chortling about how women let him do anything because he was a star, including kiss them without consent and "grab 'em by the pussy," nineteen women publicly accused Trump of misbehavior ranging from groping to assault, over a period covering three decades. Several of them were beauty pageant contestants, mentioned above.

Trump has called them all "liars," as a candidate and from the White House. One of them is suing him for defamation, and a judge has ruled that Trump can be called to give a deposition. Three of the women have demanded a congressional inquiry. Unlike Harvey Weinstein, Bill Cosby, Charlie Rose and others, Trump has not joined the pantheon of men actually investigated and taken down by the #metoo movement. He and his staff, including females like Hope Hicks and Sarah Huckabee Sanders, have effectively used the bully pulpit of the White House to discredit the accusers. Trump the reality show star would have been erased by the accusations. The presidency shielded him from the wave that wiped out other men, accused of less.

After the first six women came forward with allegations of sexual misconduct, Trump stood behind a podium before a crowd of supporters in West Palm Beach, Florida. It was weeks before the election, and he blasted away at the women personally. "These vicious claims about me, of inappropriate conduct with women are totally and absolutely false. These claims are all fabulated. They are pure fiction and outright lies," he said, interrupted by cheers. "These people are horrible people. They're horrible, horrible liars."

Below is a selected sample of the accusers. Some of them have spoken to the author, others have not spoken to any media since the election. Some of them first stepped forward in May 2016—months before the Billy Bush tape—in a *New York Times* investigative piece titled "Crossing the Line: How Donald Trump Behaved with Women in Private." Others emerged in October 2016 and later.

Trump has denied all the accounts specifically or generally, usually in accusatory terms.

Kristin Anderson

Anderson, a former aspiring model, told the *Washington Post* in October 2016 that she was sitting beside Trump at a Manhattan club in the early 1990s when he ran his fingers up her skirt and touched her underwear. She has not spoken since the election. Three friends corroborated her account.

Lisa Boyne

Boyne, who was working at a think tank in 1996, was with the late notorious pedo model agent John Casablancas and Trump at a restaurant in Lower Manhattan. She told the *Huffington Post* in October 2016 that Casablancas had brought models, and seated at a circular booth, the women could only get out if they crossed the table. Trump ranked the women's underwear and genitals and asked Boyne which one he ought to have sex with. "He stuck his head right underneath their skirts," Boyne has said.

Rachel Crooks

In 2005, Crooks, working for a real estate investment company, encountered Trump in a Trump Tower elevator. Crooks told the *New York Times* in October 2016 that he shook her hand, wouldn't let go, and then pulled her in for a kiss on the cheeks and the mouth. "I was so upset that he thought I was so insignificant that he could do that," she said.

Jessica Leeds

Leeds also stepped forward in October 2016, and in the same *New York Times* article as Crooks, recalled that when she was a traveling saleswoman in the 1980s, she was seated beside Trump on a flight and he started encroaching on her space after the in-flight dinner was removed, eventually trying to embrace her and groping her breasts. She said that picking up the newspaper on the day after the 2016 election "was like a punch in the stomach."

Jessica Drake

Like Stormy Daniels, Jessica Drake, a porn star, met Trump at the 2006 Tahoe golf tournament. She told her story in October 2016, at a press conference called by Gloria Allred, a California attorney who has made a practice of representing victims of sexual abuse and harassment. Drake said Trump grabbed her "tightly in a hug" and kissed her without permission, before offering her $10,000 to go with him to dinner and a party.

Jill Harth

Jill Harth first met Trump in 1992 regarding a business proposal. She and her then-boyfriend, George Houraney, were pitching Trump to back their American Dream Festival, which featured a contest for a pinup girl calendar. Five years later, in 1997, she filed a lawsuit laying out a series of unwanted sexual advances, stating that Trump groped her under the table at their first meeting, and accusing him of attempted rape after he invited her to Mar-a-Lago to discuss their business deal and then cornered her in Ivanka's bedroom, where he kissed and groped her. Since the election, Harth, currently working as a makeup artist in New York, has continued to speak out about Trump, once tweeting, "My pain is every day with bastard Trump as President. No one gets it unless it happens to them. NO one!"

Cathy Heller

New Yorker Heller met Trump during a Mother's Day brunch held at Mar-a-Lago in 1997. She was the ninth woman to come forward after the Billy Bush tape. She told *People* magazine that as she listened to it, she said, "That's him, that's exactly how he acted, that happened to me." She recalled that when they were introduced, Trump forcibly kissed her on the mouth. "He took my hand, and grabbed me, and went for the lips," leaving her "angry and shaken."

Ninni Laaksonen

Laaksonen, a model and former Miss Finland, was the twelfth woman to come forward after the Billy Bush tape, telling a Finnish newspaper in late October 2016 that Trump groped her backstage at *The Late Show with David Letterman* in 2006. "Trump stood right next to me and suddenly he squeezed my butt. He really grabbed my butt. I don't think anybody saw it, but I flinched and thought, 'What is happening?'"

Melinda McGillivray

Photographer McGillivray was assisting another photographer at a Ray Charles concert at Mar-a-Lago in 2003. Trump clandestinely groped her after Charles's performance. McGillivray described it immediately afterward to the photographer she was with, telling him, "Donald just grabbed my ass." She recounted the incident to the *Palm Beach Post* in October 2016.

Natasha Stoynoff

In fall 2005, *People* magazine journalist and author Stoynoff was dispatched to Mar-a-Lago, to interview newlyweds Melania and Donald about their anniversary. With Melania in another part of the mansion, Trump gave Stoynoff a tour, eventually leading her to a room where he shut the door and began forcibly kissing her. "I turned around, and within seconds he was pushing me against the wall and forcing his tongue down my throat," she wrote in an article for *People* in October 2016. She reported that Trump did not relent until a butler arrived and informed him that Melania was on her way for their interview. Stoynoff carried on with the interview and reported the incident back in New York, where six people have corroborated her account.

Summer Zervos

Of all the accusers, former *Apprentice* contestant Summer Zervos is the only one to take Trump to court over his labeling her a liar. Zervos first met Trump in 2005 when she was a contestant on the fifth season of *The Apprentice*. In 2007, she went to meet him at a room in the Beverly Hills Hotel in Los Angeles to discuss job opportunities. Zervos has said he greeted her with an aggressive, openmouthed kiss at the door. "He then grabbed my shoulder and began kissing me again very aggressively and placed his hand on my breast," she told reporters at a press conference in 2016. "I pulled back and walked to another part of the room. He then walked up, grabbed my hand, and pulled me into the bedroom. I walked out."

Trump has denied the account, and his staff has said Zervos maintained contact with him and, as recently as 2016, invited him to visit her California restaurant. Zervos filed a defamation lawsuit against Trump in New York in January 2018. A judge ruled that she has the right to depose him before January 2019. Trump's sometime personal lawyer Marc Kasowitz has said he expects the case to go to the Supreme Court.

If Zervos's case goes forward, Trump could eventually find himself in a chair with some law books as backdrop and a video camera running, explaining his side of what happened at the Beverly Hills Hotel.

A Broad Coalition Of Women

Like Bill Clinton, who famously argued with lawyers over the definition of the word *is* in his 1998 deposition related to Monica Lewinsky and the semen-stained blue dress, Trump's Other Women—in and out of the shadows—posed such a significant potential threat to his political aspirations that during the 2016 campaign, his fixers bought many of their silence. Since his election, their stories have simply become part of the skein of scandal that makes him who he is. His foes keep hoping and waiting for the silver bullet, while revelations about hush money to porn stars and bunnies have lacked power to shock.

Yes, his dignified sisters are mortified. Of course they are. His other daughter is humiliated by proximity to him after years of physical and emotional distance from him and the family for what she represents. His former female colleagues are either still cheerleading for him or, having told their stories of bullying and abuse, gone silent. He always treated the Bunnies and Playmates and models like balls of fluff under the bed until a few of them turned out to be "killers" and needed the attentions of Michael Cohen. It's obvious Trump is still counting on his surrogates to trash them back into silence and his battalion of lawyers to run down the clock on lawsuits from "liars" or throw sand in the wheels of justice as they grind slowly toward answering the question of whether anyone broke election laws buying silence from women he had sex with.

Finally, there are the "Liars." The future of American womanhood does not depend on whether Trump's people ever believe them or not.

Their courage in stepping up during the campaign was the first assault on male abuse of power in the stage of the gender wars known as the #metoo movement. Their courage, and the outrage that Donald's treatment of his female opponent provoked among women, produced the Women's March, bigger by orders of magnitude than the inauguration, and that in turn encouraged the women who shared the stories that brought down Harvey Weinstein and others.

Every woman in America who has ever stepped foot outside her house has been, at one time or another and against her will, grabbed, poked, rubbed against, kissed, sexually harassed, or in some cases, much, much worse. These experiences start young.

Like "the talk" that parents must give black sons, mothers and fathers give their girls dire warnings from the day they can understand speech—about men very much like The Donald on the Billy Bush tape and The Donald described by the women at whom he punches down, "the Liars."

These experiences mold us into who we are. The strategies we employ to deal with them are different—from open resistance to humor to abject submission and everything in between. Our very movements, and our life choices, are shaped and restricted by such acts and how we respond to them.

It's entirely possible that Donald's presidency will survive the lone defamation lawsuit and that he, unlike Harvey and Roger and Bill and Charlie and Louis and Matt, and so many other men, will not be fired from the most powerful job in America, and will never disappear from the public stage until age or the law in some other matter catches up to him. But whether or not he's ever called to account, the pussy-grabber-in-chief, Great Leader of a regressive movement, hero to men who regard women as somewhat subhuman, has already left an inadvertent legacy: the empowerment of women, a true Broad Coalition.

ACKNOWLEDGMENTS

◇◇◇◇◇◇◇

I am grateful to my former *Newsweek* editor Jim Impoco, best mentor ever, and former executive editor Bob Roe, who initially green-lighted and edited the *Newsweek* cover story, "The Queens of Trumplandia," which was the seed for this book. Gratitude also to my unflappable, witty, and urbane agent, David Granger; my brilliant and kind editor, Mitchell Ivers; and super-smart Aimee Bell, who came in late but not least. The first section of this book is indebted to the work of journalist and author Gwenda Blair, who also generously gave me her time and thoughts. Thanks to my tireless assistant Corynne Cirilli for many months of research and organization. Also: Roberto Rabanne, Paula Froelich, Richard Johnson, and Laura Harris at the *New York Post*, and Rebecca Federman and other librarians at the New York Public Library and especially the Milstein Room. In Scotland, thanks to Councillor John M. MacIver. In the Czech Republic I was helped by Anna Mabettova, Hana Bellova, Jason Bell, and Oldřich Tůma. In Germany: Daniel Hildmann and Simone Wendel. In Slovenia: Adriana Gaspar and Maja Sodja. Also in Europe: my dear husband and traveling comrade, Erik Freeland, for driving in our mad dash around

Mitteleuropa, In the USA, besides the many people who talked to me on a confidential basis, and for whose time and recollections I am deeply grateful, I would like to thank: Hannah Smith Brown at Gallery; Barbara K. Maddux for fast and thorough fact-checking; Gary R. Scott, who donated his time and expertise in genealogy. I appreciate the time and insights of Barbara Res, Pamela Keogh, Vicki Tiel, Michael Gross, R. Couri Hay, Jack Bryan, Craig Unger, Janet Reitman, and Elisa Rivlin. Thanks to Rowan Hepps Keeney for transcribing. Thanks to my friends at *Newsweek* whose encouragement, forbearance, and mostly, great sense of humor, helped me on so many levels.

A special shout-out to Katherine Kay-Mouat, who, from her roost in Paris, did countless hours of photo research and turned up some gems that also helped me tell this story.

NOTE ON SOURCES

◇◇◇◇◇◇◇

This book grew out of a *Newsweek* cover story called "Queens of Trumplandia," published shortly after the inauguration in 2017. In it, I tried to assess the influence of the Trump wives and daughter Ivanka—in their poses, pageant shoes, modeling careers, brands, and side businesses—on The Donald, but more broadly, on American women. What did the fact that Americans had elected a man accused by multiple women of sexual assault, and who has celebrated trans-actional relationships with women, say about how the majority of Americans view the role of women?

Writing it, I started to think about his influence on his women and vice versa. We thought we were living in a post-feminist world, and yet, in it, Donald Trump had managed—as husband, father, and pageant and modeling impresario, as ranker of hotness with How-ard Stern—to not only advertise an archaic, Rat Pack meets *Mad Men* meets Hooters meets Hugh-Hefner-with-twin-Playmates-on-the-fur-rug ideal world—but to live in it himself. As rocker Joe Jackson sang, "Pretty women out walking with gorillas down my street. . . . There's something going wrong around here."

And I asked: What would possess women to enter this realm, conform themselves to it, and stay there? Was access to fame, jewels, yachts, jets, and purported billions enough? Was love involved?

A few months later, I published another, shorter article, about the Trump women's preferred shoe—the towering stiletto pump, the shoe of choice also for beauty pageant contestants and professional escorts the world over. That article netted me more personal hate tweets and email than I've received since I wrote about my ambivalence toward my kindergartner pledging allegiance to the flag every morning during the Iraq War.

Clearly, the shoe of choice, and the women whose feet were contorted into it, struck a strong, sensitive chord with millions of Americans.

Then I set off on this quest, for real.

Many of the primary sources in this book are people who know the Trumps but will not allow their names to be mentioned. They shared memories and observations, recounted anecdotes, and told me many, many things that I chose not to put in this book because I was unable to get photographic, documented, legal, or other confirmation.

Most of the research was done in New York City. With an assistant, I compiled a file of almost every word written by and about the women available online and in legal and academic document repositories—future historians, take note! The archives of the *New York Post* proved to be especially helpful, because of the wall of coverage they lavished on the family for three decades.

I spent three weeks traveling around Europe doing primary research in the hometowns of the four immigrants in Trump's life: Elizabeth Christ Trump's hometown of Kallstadt, Germany; Mary MacLeod's birthplace on the Isle of Lewis in Scotland; Ivana Trump's hometown, Zlin, Czech Republic (formerly Gottwaldov, Czechoslovakia); and Sevnica and Ljubljana, Slovenia, where Melania was born and raised. I also spent a few days in Prague, where Ivana went to university and where Cold War historians have created an archive of Czech Secret Police files at the Institute for the Study of Totalitarian Regimes.

The historical part of the book—the first section—owes an enormous debt to Gwenda Blair. She collected documents in Germany and talked to members of the Trump family years before he ran for office and before certain parts of the family shut down on the media. Her book contains some of the most important information known about the life of Elizabeth Christ Trump, Donald's German grandmother.

I also relied heavily on other books, including those written by members of the family themselves. Some of the books written by journalists before 2015 remain important sources for understanding the family and should have been in reprint and available at every airport kiosk in America during the campaign. The late journalist Wayne Barrett, who died the day after Trump was inaugurated, especially deserves to be more widely read.

Gwenda Blair. *The Trumps: Three Generations That Built an Empire.*

Wayne Barrett. *Trump: The Greatest Show on Earth: The Deals, the Downfall and the Reinvention.*

Michael D'Antonio. *The Truth About Trump.*

Harry Hurt III. *Lost Tycoon: The Many Lives of Donald J. Trump.*

Timothy O'Brien. *TrumpNation: The Art of Being The Donald.*

Bojan Požar and Igor Omerza. *Melania Trump: The Inside Story: The Potential First Lady.*

Donald J. Trump and Tony Schwartz. *The Art of the Deal.*

Ivana Trump. *Raising Trump.*

Ivanka Trump. *The Trump Card: Playing to Win in Work and Life.*

Michael Wolff. *Fire and Fury.*